Praise for *Mint Condition:*

"*Mint Condition* kept me spellbound and couch bound for two days. Its pages are redolent of basements, bubble gum, and bachelorhood. They teem with artists, innocents, and charlatans. Dave Jamieson fit a century-and-a-half of Americana on the back of a baseball card, a remarkable achievement."　　　　　　　　　　—Steve Rushin

"An absolute masterpiece."　　　　　　—Baseball-Reference.com

"By the early 1990s, baseball card manufacturers were printing 81 billion of the things a year, or 325 for every man, woman, and child in the United States . . . Of course it ended badly. How and why is the subject of Dave Jamieson's absorbing *Mint Condition.*"　　　—Bloomberg.com

"Engaging, informative, and full of unexpected pleasures, *Mint Condition* deserves a spot on any baseball fan's bookshelf. Dave Jamieson has hit it out of the park."
　　　　　　—Cait Murphy, author of *Crazy '08: How a Cast*
　　　　　　of Cranks, Rogues, Boneheads, and Magnates
　　　　　　Created the Greatest Year in Baseball History

"Dave Jamieson has written a definitive history of both a pastime and an industry. For those of us who grew up collectors—and still feel a sentimental attachment to those seventeen utterly worthless Dan Plesac rookie cards gathering mold in our basement—this is the book that explains everything"　　—Michael Weinreb, author of *The Kings of*
　　　　　　　　　　New York and *Bigger than the Game*

"Every time a rare baseball card brings a million-dollar price at auction, thousands of aging former collectors wistfully recall shoeboxes full of rookie cards and wonder if they lost a fortune when Mom cleaned out their rooms. The answer, according to Washington-based, award-winning journalist Jamieson is . . . probably not. . . . This is a fascinating history. . . . Superbly informative and entertaining."
　　　　　　　　　　—*Booklist* (starred review)

"Jamieson got interested in the history of baseball cards when he rediscovered his own adolescent stash only to find that its value had plummeted in the mid-1990s. His loss is our gain. . . . A fun read."
—*Publishers Weekly*

"The definitive treatment on the subject." —*Choice*

"A phenomenal primer in the pitfalls of personal investing and the dangers of believing something is valuable just because everyone says it is *(see: Tickle Me Elmo, Retired Beanie Babies)*." —*The Boston Herald*

"Fascinating . . . If this were just a business story, it would be compelling. We learn that business interests have always trumped baseball card collectors—and for a while even baseball players. We meet tough-talking auctioneers and see how card "graders" decide a card's value, and how card "doctors" inflate that value. But Jamieson does better than that. He tells the tales of the real players of the baseball card biz, the ones not in uniform." —*Star Tribune* (Minneapolis)

"Compelling . . . This very satisfying account of the development of baseball cards and our attitudes toward them is highly recommended even for those casually interested in sports or collectibles."
—*Library Journal*

"Jamieson chronicles the story of baseball cards with skill and bounce, from the earliest days of cards as inserts in tobacco products to the 1950s and '60s boom to the 1980s, when other companies broke the Topps monopoly. . . . Jamieson shows a welcome compassion for the obsessive hobbyists, from the collectors whose sets reside in museums to auctioneers whose morality varies with the market and their own conscience. It's a blast for collectors of all stripes."
—*Austin American Statesman*

"One of the more enjoyable books I've read this year . . . highly recommended." —*The Hardball Times*

"Jamieson elucidates with smooth prose and fascinating tidbits of historical trivia just how the production of baseball cards became a major industry. . . . Jamieson peppers his narrative with stories of the eccentric characters and colorful personalities. . . . The book is an essential read for the baseball fan or anyone who remembers ripping into a wax pack, hoping that their childhood heroes would be found inside."

—*New Jersey Monthly*

"Fascinating social history." —*The Midwest Book Review*

"Highly readable and entertaining."

—Kevin Kaduk, "Big League Stew," Yahoo! Sports

"A wonderful book." —T. S. O'Connell, *Sports Collector's Digest*

"The only history of baseball cards that matters." —DCist.com

"Jamieson's thorough research highlights the rise and fall of a tradition as American as the game of baseball itself." —Seamheads.com

"A fascinating history of a once-vital tradition."

—Robert Birnbaum, *The Morning News*

"A must-read for anyone who used to be able to tell between a Topps, Fleer, and Upper Deck card of the same player from across the room."

—*Uncrate*

"Fantastic . . . For those who consider baseball cards an arcane subject, always remember that a good writer can make you care about anything in dint of reporting and writing ability, both of which Jamieson has in abundance. . . . I defy anyone with the slightest bit of intellectual curiosity not to love this book." —Bibliobuffet.com

"Jamieson's take, that of a skeptical journalist on the trail of a long and funny story of need, greed, and irrational searches for simple pictures of ballplayers, makes the book a joy to read."

—*Niagara Gazette*

"Having spoken with collectors, retail dealers, auctioneers, museum curators, manufacturers, baseball players and their union representatives, Jamieson has put together an interesting examination of a fleeting hobby that turned into big business. . . . The value of the modern cards still remains a fraction of what it was, indicating that this once-lucrative corner of the sports-memorabilia industry may have been merely a house of cards."   —*American Way*

"Reading [*Mint Condition*] really does awaken a childhood passion."
—Ian Pickus, WAMC, Northeast Public Radio

"A skillfully written, thoroughly researched history of baseball cards and their place in the American experience."   —DingedCorners.com

"An interesting examination of a hobby that turned into big business and then fell back to earth."   —*Charlotte Observer*

"Jamieson explores the history of card collecting through an entertaining cast of characters—the visionaries and villains who turned a gimmick designed to boost tobacco sales into a billion-dollar industry. . . . The pictures in Jamieson's book are captivating, a veritable art gallery of the industry from its infancy in the 1800s to the slickly produced versions of today."   —Forbes.com

"A thoroughly compelling, entertaining, and sometimes tragic read, [*Mint Condition*] will provide even veteran collectors with new insight to the hobby they love."   —*Voice of the Collector*

"An elegant history . . . informative, fascinating, nostalgic."
—*Spitball: The Literary Baseball Magazine*

Mint Condition

Mint Condition

How Baseball Cards Became
an American Obsession

DAVE JAMIESON

Grove Press
New York

The author would like to thank The Topps Company, Inc., and The Upper Deck Company, LLC for permission to reproduce their card images.

Published simultaneously in Canada
Printed in the United States of America

ISBN: 978-0-8021-4532-1

Grove Press
an imprint of Grove/Atlantic, Inc.
841 Broadway
New York, NY 10003

Distributed by Publishers Group West

www.groveatlantic.com

11 12 13   10 9 8 7 6 5 4 3 2 1

In memory of Brian Fleury and Matthew Morahan

Contents

Introduction

In the summer of 2006, my parents sold my boyhood home in northern New Jersey. With the new owners eager to move in, I had about three weeks to get home and clear everything out of my old bedroom. This would be no small task. I'd gone through a few hard-core collecting phases in my younger days—Absolut vodka magazine advertisements, *Star Wars* toys—and I'd for years declined to dispose of any of my accumulated trinkets. Perhaps I was deluded enough to believe that my beat-up Millennium Falcon would bring in some money one day, but I suspect I clung to these knickknacks for reasons more nostalgic than financial. After all, they were mementos of my formative years. When I told my mother that I'd drive from Washington, D.C., to Jersey and back in a rental car, she worried that one particular boxful of memories might not be able to make the return trip. "You've gotta see this thing," she said. "It's *huge*."

The object in question sat impressively in the middle of my bedroom closet, so large it seemed as if the rest of the house had been built around it twenty-odd years ago. Strewn atop and behind it were other remnants of my childhood: three Notre Dame football jerseys, one of them autographed by wide receiver Raghib Ismail; a Darth Vader helmet and an Ewok village; assorted Don Mattingly posters; and a circa 1988 *Playboy* of unknown provenance. The box itself was so heavy that at first I thought it held my old Weider dumbbells from middle school, but then I noticed the block letters I'd markered on the side: BASEBALL CARDS.

This was my old stash: thousands, if not tens of thousands, of cards, most of them from the late 1980s, stuffed into shoe boxes. Kirby Puckett, Ryne Sandberg, and a presteroidal Barry Bonds all stared back at me with fresh young faces. I'd started collecting these cards simply because I loved the game and idolized its players. But like many kids of my generation, I gradually came to believe that there was money at stake in trading cards. A Rickey Henderson rookie card could fetch $80 back then, and for an eight-year-old that kind of sale was like adding an extra Christmas to the calendar. I remembered this when I found, amid the untold number of common cards in my closet, two small black boxes that contained the gems of my collection, rookie cards of the game's top players from two decades ago, all of them in fine condition and encased in plastic holders. *So long, old friends,* I thought. The time had come to cash in these long-held investments. After a few more moments of reverie, I decided to load every last card into my rental, haul them back to Washington, and put them up for sale.

There were so many cards that I couldn't fit them all into the trunk of the Civic; I had to load the spillover into the back seats. Once I got home, I realized that my modest studio apartment couldn't hold all of the cards, either. Rather than rent storage space, I decided to borrow a hand truck from the building's maintenance guy and wheel them to my newspaper office a few blocks away. As my trove teetered down the sidewalk, the topmost shoe box fell to the pavement and a mess of cards spilled into the view of passersby. Lest these strangers believe that a twenty-seven-year-old man still collected baseball cards, I fumbled to get them back into the box as quickly as possible and continued on my way. Once at the office, I filled every square inch of free space in my cubicle with the cards, stuffing most of them beneath my desk. As I made phone calls, my knees bumped against the likes of Mark McGwire and Ken Griffey Jr. The joke in the newsroom was that I'd brought in the cards just to be close to them.

Getting my collection to Washington turned out to be the easy part. Unloading the cards on someone else would prove nearly impossible.

I tried the phone numbers of card dealers I'd found online, but they all seemed to be disconnected. Not a good sign. Finally, I reached a human. "I've got a load of good cards I'm looking to get rid of—lots of nice rookies," I told the man confidently.

"When are they from?" he asked.

"The eighties, mostly," I said.

"Those cards aren't worth anything," he told me, declining to look at them.

I tried another shop that still seemed to be in business. I was told, "Maybe if you had, like, *twenty* McGwire rookie cards, that's something we might be interested in."

"Have you tried eBay?" asked the third dealer I got in touch with.

I duly checked the site, and I was shocked to see the going rates for my cards. On Craigslist the market looked even worse. The collectibles-for-sale board was littered with postings from clueless card holders like myself, who were pushing thirty and suddenly had to sell off a 1988 Fleer factory set. Under titles such as "tens of thousands of baseball cards for sale!" and "I am selling thousands and thousands of baseball cards," the lapsed collectors all but pleaded for buyers to haul the twenty-year-old cardboard out of their homes. "I need to make room," they implored.

Still, just about all of these postings ended with what I now knew was a hilariously untenable asking price. One guy wanted $1,500 for his ten thousand cards. He didn't understand: we *all* still had our ten thousand cards. I sent teaser e-mails to some of the sellers. I was accustomed to getting no response in Craigslist dealings, but I heard back immediately from just about all of the card sellers I reached out to, even if their postings had been putrefying on the board for nearly a week. *Yeah, man,* they'd reply. *Still got 'em. When do you wanna come by? I'm here all day* . . . Nobody wanted these things, and nobody could get rid of them, either. The baseball card market had apparently collapsed.

I headed to a nearby CVS to get a look at the latest card offerings, wondering if perhaps some deterioration in quality was to blame. I walked aisle after aisle in vain. "Where are your baseball cards?" I finally asked a young clerk.

She stared blankly at me. I might as well have asked where I could find the gun aisle. I couldn't believe it. When I was a kid, drugstores were synonymous with baseball cards. What had happened?

In search of answers, I headed to one of the few surviving baseball card shops in the Washington area, a small time capsule tucked in the back of a multivendor flea market in Manassas, Virginia. There, sixty-two-year-old Barry Sacks ran his eponymous Sacks Are Loaded Sports Card Shop. I sat with him for a good part of an afternoon, admiring the throwback feel of his store, where common cards were strewn among sports-magazine back issues and rookie cards sat in a display case with reasonable price tags. A friendly guy who'd been collecting cards most of his life, Sacks struck me as someone who didn't care much whether he made a lot of money. Good thing. Over the course of two hours at his shop, I didn't see a single customer stop by. I later wondered what Sacks would have been doing with that time if I hadn't been there talking him up.

"Now I don't really see any kids," Sacks said. "I'd say maybe ten percent of the customers are under eighteen. Kids got out for a bunch of reasons —the hobby got complicated, and I don't think it was well-advertised, either. There are very few shops now, and anyone opening a store wouldn't make it. If they tell you business is booming, they're lying. The future doesn't look good. You lose a generation, then you lose that generation's kids." Back in the day, Sacks used to have kids from the neighborhood sort vendor boxes of cards into ordered sets, then he'd reward each one with a set of his own. But he hasn't done anything like that in years. He assumes the kids are home messing with their PlayStations.

So began my return to the world of baseball cards. Over the next couple of years, as I tried to figure out where the cards came from and where they went, I stumbled across one obsessive card lover after another, some of them long dead and buried but each with his own story. The cards, of course, had been around long before I ever walked into a corner store looking for cardboard—but also long before my father did before me, or his father before him. The first boys to fall in love with baseball cards discovered them not in Topps wax packs but in cigarette boxes during the 1880s. America's tobacco moguls put them there in hopes of popularizing what was then an unconventional form of the product. Soon, baseball cards proved crucial in creating a new generation of smokers. In the 1930s some of the country's leading gum and candy makers discovered that baseball cards could help shoulder them through the darkest days of the Great Depression, with the card sets of the era keeping children attached to baseball even when their parents couldn't afford to take them to the ballpark. By the '50s, the cards had made their way into every neighborhood where baseball was to be found, thanks in large part to the foresight and aggressiveness of one Brooklyn candy company. In the end, Topps became an American icon, establishing the baseball card as an industry unto itself, which is how, some three decades later, I came to while away several years of my life playing with them.

I'd left the hobby at its peak, in my early teens, and never witnessed how it crashed. In 1994, baseball players walked off the job after months of wrangling with ownership over the possibility of a salary cap, sending the game's reputation among fans to new depths. During and after the 232-day work stoppage, children fled en masse to other dime-store diversions such as Pokémon and Yu-Gi-Oh! cards—not to mention video games. In truth, though, the industry had been heading south before the players and owners delivered the death blow. A lot of card dealers who didn't get out of the game early enough took a beating. "They all put product in their basement and thought it was gonna turn into gold," one survivor told me.

The dealers, the card companies, and the players' union had all helped to kill the golden goose, flooding the market with more than a hundred different card sets. Kids felt overwhelmed. The industry started to cater almost exclusively to what a *Beckett Baseball Card Monthly* employee described to me as "the hard-core collector," an "older male, twenty-five to fifty-four, with discretionary income." Manufacturers multiplied prices and tantalized buyers with limited, autographed, gold-foil-slathered cards. Baseball cards were no longer souvenirs of your favorite players—they were elaborate doubloons that happened to have ballplayers on them.

Of course, the great crash of '94 had been preceded by a boom period of wild speculation. On my street in a small town in northern New Jersey, cardboard served as the great equalizer among most boys between the ages of eight and twelve. Baseball card trading was our pastime and issues of *Beckett* were our stock tickers. I considered myself a major player on the neighborhood trading circuit. My favorite way to restart stalled negotiations was to sweeten the pot by throwing in an old Phil Rizzuto card that only I knew had once sat in a pool of orange juice. Even after a buddy somehow discovered that he'd been ripped off, he always got over it because there was always more trading to do. Aside from video games, our primary shared interest was in biking to the nearest convenience store, where we would each plunk down a buck or two for wax packs of Topps, Fleer, Donruss, and Upper Deck cards and then tear into them outside in the parking lot. Sometimes we dropped the accompanying gum on the ground as we shuffled through our new prizes. It always tasted pretty stale anyway.

If we were feeling ambitious, we rode another half mile to the nearest baseball card shop, which was tucked into a strip mall next to a couple of office parks. Back then, it seemed as if every town like ours had its own card shop, if not three of them. In the late '80s, a lot of grown men had come to believe that selling baseball cards was a lot like selling precious metals. The value of the product was intrinsic, the thinking went, destined only to go up. Unsurprisingly, many of their shops had a bank vault–like sterility. But I still treasured the time I was given in them, drooling over display cases filled with the game's greats, pining after vintage cards that I knew I would never own. I remember staring at the Topps 1984 Don Mattingly rookie card, encased in plastic and marked with a $32 price tag, wondering if it would be mine after the holidays.

By 1991, sales of baseball cards had reached $1.2 billion annually, meaning that cards were no longer just a supplement to help sell something else. The cards became the core component of an estimated $4-billion-per-year sports-memorabilia market, which was propped up by some 4 million serious collectors. A trade magazine called *American Printer*—as good a source as any, given that the card companies were wise enough never to release figures themselves—approximated that 81 billion baseball cards were being produced annually by the early 1990s. That's about 325 baseball cards for every man, woman, and child in the country each year, almost four times as many individual newspapers that were printed per capita. The 1991 National Sports Collectors Convention, held at the Anaheim Convention Center in California, attracted more than a hundred thousand attendees—a crowd so large that an additional thirty thousand had to be turned away by fire marshals. People waited for up to five hours to get inside, where the convention promptly turned into a near riot, with collectors making off with some $500,000 in stolen cardboard, sometimes wheeling entire display cases out of the venue on dollies. In retrospect, there couldn't have been a better sign of an impending crash.

But just as the manufacturers of new baseball cards were about to get drubbed, the market for vintage cards started to take off. The James C. Copeland auction of 1991 produced the first jaw-dropping sales numbers for old cards. In a then unique arrangement, Copeland, a wealthy California sporting-goods retailer, consigned his 873-lot baseball memorabilia collection to Sotheby's. Some eight hundred collectors came together to bid in the two-day auction, pushing many prices several times over their initial estimate by the time the final gavel dropped. Copeland netted about $5 million for his programs, ticket stubs, and baseball cards. The pièce de résistance was a 1910 Honus Wagner card issued by the American Tobacco Company—now known as the T206 Wagner, the most famous piece of cardboard in the hobby—which was purchased jointly by hockey legend Wayne Gretzky and Los Angeles Kings owner Bruce McNall for $451,000, more than $300,000 over the presale estimate. The Wagner card has roughly doubled in auction price every few years since McNall and Gretzky bought it, topping out in the fall of 2007 for $2.8 million. Long gone are the days when paying $1,000 for an early Mickey Mantle or Willie Mays card seemed preposterous.

The Copeland auction marked the ascendancy of a different kind of baseball card business, one that shunned gum-chewing kids and has spawned its own profitable subindustries. Over the past couple of years, I've seen a good deal of this world and the men who operate it. (No matter what else has changed, baseball card collecting remains an overwhelmingly male preserve.) There are now a dozen or so auction houses that specialize in baseball cards and sports memorabilia, each year putting together auction catalogs that eventually become collector's items themselves. It's estimated that these houses and non-specialty outlets such as eBay and, yes, Craigslist now churn up half a billion dollars in baseball card sales annually on the secondary market. And like any high-stakes and wholly unregulated industry, the vintage-card market is rife with allegations of corruption and malfeasance, from shill bidding to the fabrication of provenance and alteration of cards. As of this writing, it's been reported that at least one baseball card auction house is being investigated by the FBI.

So much money is at stake that a number of card-grading services have sprung up; the men at these firms devote themselves to determining the authenticity, condition, and ultimately the value of baseball cards submitted by collectors. There's really no choice for the serious collector these days but to have his cards professionally examined before selling them. In my visit to a grading house, I watched as a clutch of pasty-white graders hunched together in a dark room, examining card after card beneath black lights and magnifying glasses.

I also spent time with a multimillionaire whose card collection is so complete that he now commissions former Topps artists, to the tune of several thousand dollars a pop, to create unique cards of his own imagining. I came across another collector who couldn't bear to part with his cards, which were sitting in a chain of warehouses in Wisconsin and likely worth over $10 million, even as his health began to fail and death loomed. *It's just cardboard*, some like to say. But for these men it's much more than that. I sat with one auction-house president who's profited as much from the cardboard obsession as anyone else in the country, and even he couldn't understand the compulsion that drives his industry. "We auctioneers, I think we're more in the business of psychology than of collecting," he told me. "I don't relate to the mania the way I used to. When it was cheaper, it was a little more reasonable and it made sense to me. It doesn't make sense anymore."

It's tempting to suggest that the history of baseball cards parallels the history of baseball, which, according to conventional wisdom, has evolved from an innocent American pastime into a revenue-churning industry. But that arc is too tidy in either case. Baseball cards have always been serious business, and they've always been about making money. The very first cards became a significant weapon in the late-nineteenth-century advertising battles between America's major tobacco companies. In the 1930s, the controversial cards released by Gum, Inc., helped make J. Warren Bowman, the "Bubble Gum King," one of the wealthiest industrialists of post-Depression Philadelphia. A couple of decades later, Topps Chewing Gum, Inc. used its stranglehold on the baseball card market to drive other bubble gum firms out of business. Had Topps not then had to fight, sometimes ruthlessly, with the likes of Fleer and Donruss and Upper Deck for the hearts and wallets of sports-obsessed grade-schoolers, kids like me probably never would have turned baseball cards into a billion-dollar industry.

Cards aren't really a hallmark of childhood anymore; they're a way for collectors to return to it. In the end, I decided not to sell my own collection. I figured that my Wade Boggs rookie would be worth more to me as a keepsake of my card-shop days than as yet another online auction with a starting bid of ninety-nine cents. In that spirit, one day I did what card-collecting protocol had always advised against: I opened a handful of old wax packs that I'd stowed away in the late 1980s, sealed, as an investment. As I rifled through the cards hoping to score an All-Star, I felt a very particular twinge of excitement, one that I hadn't felt in about twenty years. I even tried the gum, which tasted no staler than it did when I was a child.

1

Please, Mister, Give Me the Picture!

Although an estimated five thousand Union soldiers would eventually die of starvation and disease inside its wooden stockades, the Confederate-run prison camp at Salisbury, North Carolina, was a great place for a ball game. Created seven months after the first shots were fired at Fort Sumter in 1861, Salisbury was one of the primary destinations for Yankee prisoners of war early in the Civil War. The only war prison in the state, the modest sixteen-acre compound included a cotton factory, a blacksmith's shop, and enough of an open field to accommodate a pair of baseball nines when weather and the warden permitted.

The first 120 Union detainees arrived at Salisbury shortly before Christmas 1861, and by the following spring there were a still manageable fourteen hundred prisoners sleeping in the camp's tenements. In these early days Salisbury, with its oak trees and water barrels and ample breathing room, was a rather pleasant place to suffer one's wartime capture. One Yank remarked that it was "more endurable than any other part of Rebeldom." As several prisoners' memoirs bear out, this agreeable atmosphere had a lot to do with baseball. According to the diary of imprisoned doctor Charles Carroll Gray, prisoners played ball nearly every day that rain or cold didn't prevent it. They even celebrated the

Fourth of July of 1862 by reading the Declaration of Independence aloud and playing a few innings on their makeshift diamond.

Baseball took hold at other encampments in both the South and the North, especially during the first half of the war. The game provided a respite from the wretchedness of battle and camp, with regimental soldiers routinely playing ball among themselves, their games sometimes broken off by the fire of cannons, muskets, and carbines. J.G.B. Adams, a member of the Nineteenth Regiment of Massachusetts, wrote that during his stay at Falmouth, Virginia, "baseball fever" broke out among both Yanks and Rebs, with Adams and his comrades close enough to their enemies across the river to cheer them on. "We would sit on the bank and watch their games, and the distance was so short we could understand every movement and would applaud good plays."

The war would temporarily cripple organized baseball as players in the North left their clubs to enlist, but it also helped to spread the game to new parts of America. As the *New York Clipper* noted in 1865, "When soldiers were off duty, base ball was naturalized in nearly every state in the Union." What had been a Northern gentleman's game closely associated with Brooklyn became a fixture in many cities in the South and West, with new clubs sprouting in pockets of the former Confederacy, such as Richmond, Virginia, and Galveston, Texas, where the best local team took the name of Robert E. Lee. After the war, the game began to blossom not only as a professional, revenue-churning entertainment but also as a fixture of blue-collar urban life. In his landmark 1911 book about early baseball, *America's National Game,* Albert G. Spalding, the pioneering pitcher and latter-day sporting-goods mogul, traced the sport's dawn to the war, arguing that the spirit of the game was inextricably linked to military conflict—and relief from it. The game, he wrote, "had its early evolution when soldiers, North and South, were striving to forget their foes by cultivating, through this grand game, fraternal friendships with comrades in arms. . . . And then, when true patriots of all sections were striving to forget that there had been a time of black and dismal war, it was a beacon, lighting their paths to a future of perpetual peace."

Among those Northern patriots returning from the war in 1865 was a baseball enthusiast named Andrew Peck. His parents having died when he was a baby, Peck was raised in a New York City orphanage and later sent upstate to work for a shopkeeper. After the start of the war, he enlisted with the Union army and was sent to the front with the federal Army of the Potomac, which included Major Abner Doubleday among its ranks and was renowned for its fondness for baseball. One soldier described the camp as "alive with ball-players, almost every street having its game." Once home, Peck started working as a street salesman in Manhattan, hawking baseball equipment, knickknacks, and games he created himself, some of which he managed to sell to the entrepreneur and showman P. T. Barnum. He also began manufacturing baseballs on the top floor of a building at 109 Nassau Street, where the following year he opened a sporting-goods store with his partner, W. Irvin Snyder.

Before being bought by competitor A. G. Spalding & Bros., the Peck & Snyder Base Ball and Sportsman's Emporium would have a profound impact on the leisure culture of nineteenth-century America. The company not only produced some of the very first baseball bats ("fine stock, clear of knots," a catalog proclaimed) and molded rubber baseballs ("which for finish, durability and superior workmanship are not surpassed"), it also put out the first modern canvas tennis shoe and helped make the magic lantern slide projector a fixture in American homes. And with its small series of cards depicting ball clubs, the sporting-goods company is believed by many to have given America its first baseball cards.

During the 1869 baseball season, Peck & Snyder produced a small advertising card, measuring just three-and-a-quarter inches by four-and-a-half inches and bearing a glue-mounted photograph depicting the ten members of the first explicitly professional baseball team—the Red Stocking Base Ball Club of Cincinnati, whose president was Union army veteran Alfred T. Goshorn and whose catcher, Doug Allison, had reportedly learned to play as a soldier in war encampments. On the back of the card is a cartoon showing a ballplayer with sagging eyes and a wispy beard, his back hunched as he hauls an armful of baseball bats, cleated shoes, and uniform belts. The cartoon is signed at the bottom: "Yours Respectfully, Andrew Peck." The ballplayers on the front of the card, lined up five to a row, were dour, hairy fellows with nearly all-white uniforms. Save for the knee-high socks, they looked like a group of convicts. Under the guidance of their British-born center fielder and team captain, Harry Wright, the Red Stockings recruited players from across the country, signed them to exclusive contracts, and instituted organized team practices at which the club developed innovations such as the relay throw. Traveling some twelve thousand miles by rail and boat to play before a couple of hundred thousand people, the Red Stockings logged a 57–0 record and a net profit of $1.39 on the season.

Peck & Snyder produced at least half a dozen baseball cards between 1865 and 1870, though they were hardly the first manufacturer to dole out free "trade cards" to promote its products. The advertising technique had originated in London and been growing for more than a century before hirsute American infielders started popping up on cards. Pushing household items such as Merchant's Gargling Oil Liniment and Lautz Bros. Soaps, trade cards featured either photographs or drawings of everything from actresses and war heroes to comic scenes and pastoral settings; either woven into the image or on the back of the card would be an advertisement for the company's wares. The earliest baseball-themed cartoon trade cards reflected the rough-and-tumble style of the post–Civil War game. Players are carried off the field battered and in bandages, as they were in real life. On some cards, umpires are shown being attacked by mobs of fans who hadn't liked their calls.

Baseball cards may well have been just one more piece of forgotten ephemera had it not been for another novel activity made popular by the war: cigarette smoking. Pioneering cigarette manufacturers would soon discover that coupling their smokes with the likenesses of ball-players was an exceptional way to move tobacco. The card-collecting hobby had no innocent beginnings. It was the by-product of a marketing technique used to establish the cigarette in the lives of Americans, particularly young boys. And within just a few years of first appearing in cigarette packages, baseball cards would help spur the creation of the greatest tobacco monopoly in American history.

Before the Civil War, Americans had been availing themselves of more tobacco per person than any other country in the world, thanks in large part to an agreeable climate for growing and a massive supply of slaves to work the fields. The tobacco capital of Richmond, Virginia, alone laid claim to some fifty factories devoted to its production. Yet the tobacco that many Americans enjoyed went either into their pipes or between their jaws as plug chew, for the cigarette was considered a bastardized form of the cigar suited only to the lower classes. That perception persisted until pipes and cigars proved too cumbersome for soldiers on the move. As the war progressed, more and more cigarettes made their way from factories in the Southern states to military encampments. Pre-rolled smokes continued to grow in popularity after the war, inspiring a good deal of hysteria among the guardians of public health. Weighing in on an 1884 proposal to criminalize the sale of cigarettes to minors, a *New York Times* editorial suggested a ban on selling them even to adults: "The decadence of Spain began when the Spaniards adopted cigarettes, and if this pernicious practice obtains among adult Americans the ruin of the Republic is close at hand."

Such pronouncements had no effect on James Buchanan "Buck" Duke, who recognized the massive sales potential of cigarettes better than anyone. His father, Washington Duke, had fought for the Confederacy and served time at a POW camp before walking 135 miles to his Durham, North Carolina, home after the war's climactic close at

Appomattox. The elder Duke sent young Buck to New York City in 1884 to help open an additional factory for the family tobacco company. Even then, Buck Duke's ambition was to make the cigarette America's go-to form of tobacco. Although he personally preferred a substantial plug to the dainty sticks, he viewed cigarettes as his family company's only chance to wrest American tobacco dominance from rival Bull Durham. Managing the Manhattan plant by day, he was known to spend nights walking the city streets picking up discarded cigarette packs of all brands, studying their packaging and trying to calculate what percentage of the market Duke Bros. had managed to secure. By all accounts he worked ungodly hours obsessing over advertising and marketing. "I hated to close my desk at night," he once said. "There ain't a thrill in the world to compare with building up a business and watching it grow before your eyes."

Duke soon came to understand the promotional power of celebrities, particularly buxom stage women. Duke Bros. salesman Edward Featherston Small, an advertising mastermind who is credited with inventing the cigar-store Indian, had obtained permission to use a lithograph of Madame Rhea, a curvy French actress on tour in the States in 1884, for advertising in Georgia. The company superimposed a pack of Duke smokes into her extended right hand, above the caption "Atlanta's Favorite," a ploy that helped Duke sell nearly a million cigarettes in what had previously been an impenetrable market for him. The front office was thrilled with Small's tactic, dashing off a letter to him: "We think you made a happy hit with Rhea. Give the Bull's tail another twist." Small procured many more comely ladies to promote Duke cigarettes, putting them on advertising posters and having them sell cigarettes on streets around the country. But the next big twist to Bull Durham's tail would come in the form of picture cards. Duke and Small wanted to put the likes of Madame Rhea *inside* their cigarette boxes, not just in their ads.

The idea was simple: give the buyer a collectible card to go with his pack of smokes, and he'll buy more cigarettes in hopes of completing the set. Duke and the other tobacco makers who followed him wisely numbered their collectible cards, usually twenty-five or fifty to an issue, which hadn't been done with earlier trade cards. It helped to create brand loyalty, and as a bonus, collector-smokers would be advertising the company to anyone they showed their cards to. It was one of the most ingenious marketing ploys of the nineteenth century. And advertising aside, the cardboard served a practical function by stiffening soft packs so that the cigarettes wouldn't be damaged while stuffed into a smoker's pocket.

To make sure that the country was blanketed with his cigarette packages and trading cards, Duke dispatched employees to New York's Castle Island immigration station, where they handed out free smokes to newly landed immigrants, who would then carry Duke's name off to all corners of America. Duke's competitors were quick to follow, and the cards they issued gave many Americans their first glimpses of exotic animals, far-off lands, and celebrities they'd read about in the newspaper, including ballplayers. They also helped the public equate tobacco with anything and everything American: state governors, heroes of the Civil War, river steamers, Indian chiefs, billiards stars, race horses, yacht clubs, and (in what must have been the dreariest of sets) newspaper editors. As one collector of such cards later recalled, "There were no newsreels, no roto sections, no picture newspapers. A good cigarette picture was no mere plaything for a boy. It was life. No wonder Mr. Munson, next door, would pore over my scrapbooks of a winter evening, using his reading glass under the parlor lamp." Still, some cards were of particular interest to kids, who pined after such sets as the Horatio Alger–esque Histories of Poor Boys Who Have Become Rich and the Terrors of America, which depicted all-American boys causing mischief.

Duke and his fellow card makers grasped the fact that children, then as now, have a say in where the household's discretionary income goes. Even though adults collected tobacco cards, the pursuit appealed primarily to kids. The children, Duke recognized, would beg their parents to buy whichever cigarette brand issued the card series they desired most. And with a foresight that would reshape popular advertising Duke determined that, of all potential tobacco-card images, two could unfailingly shill for a product that even then was known to kill people: scantily clad women and great athletes.

When it came to the former, simple headshots wouldn't suffice. The full-body photos on tobacco cards showed robust young women in elaborate yet meager tasseled dresses and calf-high boots. The models and actresses were thrown across chairs and sofas, fanning themselves, arms placed unnaturally behind their heads and cigarettes dangling from their mouths. The cards featuring these "cigarette beauties" inspired an 1888 ode in the *Chicago Tribune*: "Who are these beauties, fresh and fair with ebon locks and sun-kissed hair! Whose that brow of alabaster that makes the heart thump quick and faster! What their names! Where their abode!"

The sexual nature of the cards prompted the wrath of religious leaders and public-morality groups such as the Woman's Christian Temperance Union and the Society for the Suppression of Vice. A Methodist minister in Washington, D.C., decried them as "indescribably fiendish. To defile the body with tobacco is vile enough, but when all the processes of modern ingenuity in printing and picture-making are brought into use to stimulate and start the fires of unholy passion in innocent children, the crime becomes inhuman in its baseness."

Perpetrators of the card craze even earned a rebuke from the White House when a tobacco maker had the gall to print a card featuring the comely Frances Folsom Cleveland, wife of President Grover Cleveland and then the youngest first lady ever. Another inflammatory card was erroneously believed to depict Jeannette Halford, the daughter of E. W. Halford, the president's secretary. Cops raided the studios where cigarette beauties were shot and sometimes hauled photographers away to jail. When a reporter for the *New Orleans Daily Picayune* asked a young woman on the street if she'd ever allow her photo to be taken for a "cigarette picture," she bridled, "What a horrid suggestion! Only actresses, baseball players, and other dreadful people have such things taken."

To young card collectors, those dreadful ballplayers were every bit the prize as the pretty stage ladies, and the advertising war instigated by Duke would usher in the first golden era of baseball cards. The first tobacco company to put a baseball player on an insert card was probably Duke's competitor Allen & Ginter, a Richmond firm that had entered the cigarette market in 1875. (It's also possible that company president Lewis Ginter, a former Confederate army major known for his marketing savvy, had started putting trading cards inside cigarette boxes before Duke did.) Allen & Ginter packed their cigarettes tightly in paper wrappers swathed with brightly illustrated labels, and the firm's package designs were so ornate that they were featured in the 1876 Centennial Exhibition of the American Republic in Philadelphia. Allen & Ginter's 1888 Worlds Champions series included ten early baseball cards, along with another forty cards depicting boxers, billiards players, rowers, wrestlers, and gunslingers such as Annie Oakley and Buffalo Bill. The set could be housed inside an album that included more advertising for "the brightest, most delicately flavored" tobacco grown in Virginia. Duke answered with a set of baseball "cabinet cards": cardboard-mounted photographs large and attractive enough to be displayed behind glass in living room cabinets.

When it came to insert cards, Ginter tried to take the moral high ground, eschewing the actresses that Duke rolled out for what he considered more manly subjects such as athletes. But Ginter certainly did his best to split the difference with his Women Baseball Players series of 1887, which featured staged shots of curvy ladies in snug uniforms, one of whom managed to gaze seductively at the camera while sliding headfirst into second base. Around the same time, the genteel citizens of Atlanta flooded the mayor's office with complaints when a local tobacconist filled his window with images of the "luscious baseball nine," a group of bat-wielding women who injected the game with sex appeal. The scandalous cards and displays had originated from an unknown company in New York, where a local Christian group and several newspaper editorial boards, including the *New York Sun,* launched a crusade against them. The Atlanta dealer drew such a crowd with his "female baseballists" that police were called in to disperse the oglers. "When the pictures of the female baseball players were sent out every dealer in tobacco in the country was crazy to get them as show window attractions," the *Atlanta Constitution* reported. The story also noted that a college professor had threatened a group of students with expulsion when they decorated their walls with such cards; the students retaliated by putting a blind horse in the professor's apartment.

For baseball fans, the timing of the tobacco advertising battles couldn't have come at a better time. By the 1880s the sport had emerged as a far-reaching commercial force. Just a few years earlier amateur players and their fans were bemoaning all the money creeping into the game—the National Association of Base Ball Players, the first governing organization in the sport, had debated whether to declare professionalism "reprehensible" as recently as 1870. But the game's purists were fighting a losing battle, as more fans turned out for games and players demanded more compensation for their play. The professional National League (NL) formed in 1876, with the Philadelphia Athletics and Chicago White Stockings among its eight charter members. A rival American Association (AA) was founded in 1881 and included teams from Cincinnati and Louisville. Players and fans of the priggish NL sometimes sneered at the AA, whose games were renowned for low gate fees and copious amounts of booze, earning it the nickname the Beer and Whiskey League.

As star-powered clubs became increasingly profitable, team owners often poached top players from rosters in the other league. This practice stopped with the landmark Tripartite Agreement of 1883, in which the two leagues, along with the Northwestern League, agreed to honor one another's contracts. But the agreement also set the stage for a nearly century-long battle between players and owners by cementing the all-important "reserve clause" in baseball. The rule gave a team owner the right to "reserve" a player for another year at the end of each season, in effect binding the player to his squad in perpetuity. (The Tripartite Agreement also prevented teams from picking up players that had been blacklisted from other clubs, further limiting a player's movements.) The reserve clause was widely despised among players, even though salaries rose during the decade; by 1885 the minimum annual haul of a player was a working man's $1,000, with a cap of $2,000.

The agreement between the leagues may have been controversial, but it brought the sport the stability it needed to flourish. The May 31, 1886, game between the New York Giants and the Detroit Wolverines marked the first time a major-league game logged twenty thousand–plus fans in attendance; in October of that year the National League and American Association winners faced off in a world championship, a thrilling six-game series in which the AA's St. Louis Browns topped the Chicago White Stockings in the sixth and final game, winning on Curt Welch's "$15,000 slide" at home, so-called because of the cash prize it brought the St. Louis club. To mark the occasion, the Lone Jack cigarette company of Lynchburg, Virginia, put out a picture card for each of the thirteen St. Louis players.

In the months that followed, Goodwin and Co. Tobacco unveiled perhaps the most ambitious and fascinating set of baseball cards collectors would ever see. After a successful run of twelve cards featuring the hometown New York Giants, Goodwin began producing a series that would eventually number more than twenty-three hundred cards and depict more than five hundred players. Taken as a whole, the sprawling Old Judge set, named for a Goodwin tobacco brand, still stands as one of the great visual records of late-nineteenth-century baseball and the men who played it. The company's primary photographer, Joseph Hall, tried to take pictures of every ballplayer on the rosters of forty major- and minor-league teams. Although baseball scholars consider him one of the game's first great photographers, Hall probably spent more time shooting weddings and portraits than he did ballplayers. He was a chronicler of life in Brooklyn—one of his only surviving works aside from the baseball cards is a series of gorgeous photos he took of the borough's Green-Wood Cemetery. The imagination and sheer breadth of Hall's Old Judge photos, however, suggest that baseball was special to him.

Hall enjoyed plenty of artistic latitude in shooting the Old Judges. The cards were not mass-produced prints; they were sepia-toned photographs pasted onto heavy-stock cardboard. He shot some players in more than a dozen poses. In the photos, the mustachioed men wear dark, knee-high stirrups and collared jerseys buttoned to their Adam's apples. Most of the players stand in solemn, dignified poses, but the most intriguing cards depict staged action shots set up in Hall's Brooklyn studio—runners in frozen headfirst slides, infielders tagging out opponents as they look in the camera's eye. Balls hang from visible strings, bases lie on the studio floor, and painted background cloths show stadium walls and city skylines. As Hall probably knew well, not even a seven-year-old would have taken these for spontaneous photographs. But they convincingly evoke the showmanship of the sport, often with genuine artistry. Each of his full-body portraits is unique, as if Hall was trying to capture not the face but the personality, and some remain inscrutable today, like the one of future Hall of Fame outfielder Ed Delahanty, who cups his hands and looks to the sky as if in prayer.

The cards catalog what had become, by the 1880s, a thoroughly professional game, with players moving regularly from team to team and leagues morphing from season to season as established squads went under and new ones sprouted up. The Old Judges reflect the game's westward crawl, too, with players for such far-flung Western Association teams as Omaha, Nebraska, and Sioux City, Iowa, featured on cards in 1888. The final installment of Old Judges, from 1890, showed men from the newly formed Players League, a group that had splintered off from the National League because of labor issues, most notably the reserve clause. The Players League had no salary caps, but it folded after just one season.

It was clear that Goodwin's card makers followed the game closely, and the youngest baseball fans appreciated the attention to detail. In one of the earliest remembrances of card collecting, published in the *New Yorker* in 1929, Brooklyn native Arthur H. Folwell explained that, "To many a boy, back in the eighties, the pictures given with Old Judge cigarettes were the most fascinating. Birds, dudes, soldiers, flags of all nations were well enough, but miniature photographs of leading ball players in all the leagues, even the Western Association, were far and away the best. There has never been anything like the Old Judge ball players." The author went on to recount how stunned he was as a boy to learn that Goodwin and Co. managed to correct card issues after midseason trades between teams. On the card of celebrated outfielder and after-hours evangelist Billy Sunday, for instance, "The picture showed him, bat in hand, standing before a homeplate that looked suspiciously like a newspaper thrown on the studio floor." Sunday clearly wore the uniform of the Chicago White Sox, but he had the word "Pittsburgh" scrawled sloppily across his chest. "Old Judge watched over us," Folwell wrote, "and kept the record straight."

The basic premise of baseball card collecting has always been to obtain each card in a particular set. An avid collector could spend the better part of a lifetime trying to track down every Old Judge card, and even then, as the card historian and collector Lew Lipset noted in his *Encyclopedia of Baseball Cards*, "completion is hopeless." There are simply too many different cards for too many players; no one even knows for sure how many there are. Modern collectors tend to impose a discipline with Old Judges, such as pursuing all of the cards of a particular player or of a particular team. There are perhaps fewer than ten collectors in the world currently chasing the Old Judge set in its entirety. And those few must be prepared to spend an awful lot of money. In 2008, one pristine Old Judge card showing Hall of Famer John Ward sold for nearly $30,000 at auction. The set fascinates collectors in part because new cards that have never before been cataloged continue to surface in basements and attics around the country.

Conventional wisdom holds that the cigarette launched the baseball card. But one could just as easily argue that, in the United States, the baseball card launched the cigarette. News reports show that the popularity of baseball cards like the Old Judges helped win over not only smokers but tobacco salesmen as well. "I told him I wouldn't handle cigarettes under any circumstances," one New York tobacconist recalled telling Duke upon first meeting him. "[But] Duke began putting into each package a picture of a famous actress or athlete or the flags of all nations. That was a million-dollar idea, for the pictures came in numbered sets and the kids began pestering their dads for them. Soon collecting pictures became a craze and we had to order the cigarettes in quantity. I think this one stunt, more than any other, really put the cigarette over with the public."

In response to collector demand, Duke and Allen & Ginter printed loose-leaf, string-bound portfolios into which cards could be pasted. Throngs of children reportedly showed up outside cigarette factories in New York City on the weekends, vouchers in hand, demanding new albums for their cards. Every picture card had its market value among schoolboys, and hard-to-find cards could run as high as a quarter apiece, which was several times the cost of the cigarette pack itself. Boys badgered strangers on the street for the cards from their packs. "The life of the dude is made a burden when he appears on the public thoroughfares with the end of a cigarette gingerly clasped in his pearly teeth. He is besieged on all sides with requests of 'Please, mister, give me the picture!'" one news report explained. "Whenever a number of urchins can be found together, you can wager your last cent that they are comparing their treasures."

Though they didn't stir the unholy passions that actress cards did, baseball cards such as the Old Judges were believed to help hook children on smoking. The dangers of tobacco were a widely accepted fact in the nineteenth century, and cigarettes, due to their rapid consumption among kids, were considered a particularly treacherous form of the stuff. When a nineteen-year-old shoe-factory worker passed away in Camden, New Jersey, in 1892, the papers printed the habitual smoker's dying words: "Tell all my friends 'Duke's Best' have killed me, and beg of them never to smoke another." It wasn't unusual for a boy as young as ten to develop a cigarette habit. Excessive smoking was believed to damage the nerves and cause fits of madness, and concerned schoolchildren joined together in antismoking groups in the hope of saving their classmates. Laws prohibiting the sale of tobacco to minors sprouted up around the country but were generally ignored, allowing a child in 1887 to buy a pack of cigarettes just as easily as an adult in many towns.

News reports of the day suggested that tobacco makers were expressly targeting children with their cards. The cigarette "would lie down and die tomorrow" if it weren't for the high volume of sales to "small boys," one tobacco man told the *Chicago Daily Tribune* in 1888. Indeed, it was the fickleness of young consumers that made cigarettes among the most heavily and beautifully advertised products of the post–Civil War period. "Today he swears by the 'Troubadour Straight Cuts,' tomorrow he grows enthusiastic over the 'Old Judge,' and the next day calls loudly for the 'Perl's Pet,'" teased a reporter in 1889. Parents and teachers rummaged through their children's pants pockets and destroyed whatever cigarette cards they found, and even some tobacco salesmen grew convinced that the pictures were instrumental in turning a generation of city boys into cigarette "fiends" in the 1880s. One dealer told the *Tribune* that, "It would do away with half this boys' trade, I think, if there was a law prohibiting the giving away of pictures in packages of cigarettes."

Politicians in several cities around the country tried to put just such laws on the books. Charleston, South Carolina, effected an ordinance in 1887 prohibiting the sale of cigarettes with baseball cards, forcing tobacconists to strip their packs of the likes of Cap Anson and King Kelly. Duke had a pragmatic take on this new law, telling a Durham newspaper that he didn't begrudge the mayor one bit for it. In fact, he said he'd prefer to see a nationwide ban on tobacco cards: "We would give a chromo to the Mayor of Charlotte, and a nice per cent if he would stop the use of the pictures throughout the entire country, as it would save us $180,000 per year, or nearly $2,000,000 in the next ten years. Competition forced us to adopt this method of advertising."

Duke's competitors shared his frustration, because baseball and actress cards were brutally expensive to produce. Duke put the card costs for his own firm at about $500 per day, or about $62,000 per day in today's economy. The most attractive baseball cards could cost Duke as much as half a pack of cigarettes to make. One Manhattan plant alone was turning out seventy-five thousand cabinet cards daily, with hundreds of workers toiling around the clock to produce enough cards to meet demand.

Of course, if cards hadn't meant much to smokers, Duke and the other tobacco companies wouldn't have shrunk their profit margins rolling them off the presses. As the hobby of card collecting grew, the sale of cigarettes grew with it, and Duke proved as much a master of manufacturing as of marketing. When there were rumblings of a strike among cigarette rollers at Goodwin and Co. in New York, Duke managed to poach 125 of his rival's laborers by luring them to Durham with the promise of housing and generous wages. When smokers complained that they were mutilating their cigarettes as they pulled them from their soft packs, Duke developed a hard box that protected the smokes without prohibitively boosting their price. And to keep up with growing demand, Duke was determined to slash production costs by shifting from hand-rolled cigarettes to cheaper ones rolled by machine. For years, a mechanic from Virginia named James A. Bonsack had been tinkering with a contraption that, in theory, would be able to produce almost fifty times as many cigarettes per day as the average laborer could. After Duke bought the Bonsack roller in 1884, he and his team worked out the kinks and in their first year of using the machines rolled out 744 million smokes, which was more than the entire industry had been producing annually.

Duke then had the liberty to slash his prices, reducing a pack of ten smokes to a nickel, or about half the going rate. His competitors did what they could to stigmatize machine-made cigarettes as substandard—Allen & Ginter had foolishly taken a pass on an early version of the Bonsack roller, for fear that its customers would sneer at anything but hand-rolled cigarettes—but by the late 1880s, with Duke controlling almost 40 percent of the market, they had no choice but to adopt the same method. The massive production among just four or five tobacco companies created a handful of nationally recognized brands, nearly all of which felt compelled to give buyers more and more of the trading cards they craved.

Even so, card-collecting mania was helping to break Duke's rivals. The five highest-producing tobacco firms were splurging a combined $2 million per year on baseball and actress cards by 1890, a staggering expense for the time. The president of tobacco company F. S. Kinney, which offered Sweet Caporal cigarettes, believed that he was peddling cardboard as much as he was selling smokes, admitting that he was "most eager to get out of the advertising madhouse" and "the damned picture [card] business," both of which ate insatiably into his profits.

The card craze was also hurting Duke himself, who poured twenty cents of every dollar he made into advertising and marketing. He was coughing up nearly $1 million a year in advertising by 1889, much of it going to inserts and the larger cabinet cards. "Hit your competitors in the pocketbook," he once said. "Hit 'em hard. Then you either buy 'em out or take 'em with you."

That year, Duke decided it was high time to take his competitors with him. In typically ruthless fashion, he decided to spend even more money on marketing, forsaking his already slim profit margins just to bury the other companies beneath his advertising. His competitors realized that folding their companies into Duke's was the only choice; a trust would eliminate the need for expensive picture cards. Even Lewis Ginter, who despised Duke personally, proved willing to join in the budding monopoly. The heads of the five major tobacco firms met at a Fifth Avenue hotel in Manhattan in April 1889 and created the American Tobacco Company. "The great question that agitated them was how to stop this picture-giving business," the *Picayune* reported of the trust's firms. "For years the small boy has collected a valuable collection of Indians, painted in their most villainous dye, of sturdy athletes, baseball players and whatnot— enough to set up a Louvre gallery of art in Smallboytown. . . . As long as one [cigarette company] gave, the rest had to do it too, to keep in the tide of popularity."

In other words, the popularity of baseball cards helped to spur the formation of one of the most powerful monopolies in American history. The American Tobacco Company's new president, Buck Duke, managed to drop production costs to ten cents per thousand cigarettes and was well on his way to swallowing up some two hundred additional companies. The controlling parties divvied up their territories and kept out of one another's way. The tobacco trust had virtually no competition, and without competition there was no need for costly advertising —certainly not for elaborate insert cards, as much as the public adored them. Baseball and actress cards would all but vanish for the next twenty years.

The decency police deemed it a small victory. "They have probably concluded to kill the boys without corrupting their morals," a *Detroit Free Press* editorial said of the tobacco moguls, "and for this much the country should be thankful."

2

Anyone Can Get
the Cards

In 1909, Buck Duke's American Tobacco Company created the most hallowed card in all of collecting—the T206 Honus Wagner. Often referred to as the holy grail of the baseball card world, the finest Wagner specimen has fetched seven figures time and again at auction, bringing each successive owner a good deal of fame within the collecting world. Not surprisingly, the card has tended to attract wealthy cardboard fetishists with outsized personalities. Among them is Michael Gidwitz, a Chicago investment adviser who lives in an overstuffed apartment–slash–card museum overlooking Lake Michigan.

Gidwitz ranks among the most accomplished baseball card collectors in the world, yet he has come to hate almost everything about baseball card collecting. The evidence of a corrupted pastime is all around him, he believes. The hobby has been infected by greed, overrun with shady dealers, and distorted beyond recognition by prospectors who want to invest rather than collect. Gidwitz, the first person to sell a baseball card for $1 million, has certainly had a hand in bringing about these lamentable circumstances. But he sometimes wishes he hadn't. The monetary aspect of collecting has cost him friends and ruptured family relationships.

"People are so concerned with how valuable these cards are: *What are they worth?*" he fumed to me during a visit to his home. "They look for the rookies and throw out the others. Packs of cards have gotten so expensive. And now there are so many card companies. . . . It's impossible to get all the cards each year. When I was a kid, you could get all the Post cereal cards just by going to the store with your mother."

What Gidwitz hates perhaps most of all is professional card grading, a paid service in which an expert evaluates a card's authenticity and condition. A collector hoping to sell any card of significant value these days has no choice but to submit it to one of the grading companies that have sprung up since the practice began, in the early 1990s. The largest of these graders, Professional Sports Authenticators (PSA), requires a $99 annual membership. For each card graded, its fee can run anywhere from $10 to $250. PSA president Joe Orlando told me that the company first graded more than a million cards in a year in 1998 and has graded at least that many annually ever since.

Many collectors consider this a vital service, but Gidwitz sees it as a needless add-on that allows a cabal of self-proclaimed, self-interested experts to take a cut from the hobby. "In my opinion, I think that cards get graded [high] if they've been restored or if the cards were trimmed," he said, referring to the frowned-upon practices of touching up or cutting down worn cards to make them appear crisper. "It's just a way to make money. I've lost confidence in the process."

Gidwitz, a collector since childhood, has had only one card professionally graded in his life. He didn't pay for it or even request it—although some of his colleagues might suggest that he'd long been asking for it. For four years in the late '90s, Gidwitz owned the T206 Wagner. His $640,500 purchase of a near-perfect, celebrity-provenanced copy in 1996 made him, at age forty-six, a big name within the baseball card community. But baseball cards are just one of his many pop-culture obsessions. Another is impish *Mad* magazine figurehead Alfred E. Neuman. After Gidwitz's purchase of the Wagner, a friend put Neuman's face onto a baseball card in the style of the early-1900s

American Tobacco issues and gave it to Gidwitz as a gift. Aside from his freckles and menacing grin, the resulting character is a dead ringer for Wagner, right down to the old-fashioned Pittsburgh Pirates uniform.

Although few people could appreciate the inside joke, Gidwitz for years took the custom card around to card conventions and proudly showed it off, until finally the president of a card-grading service asked to borrow it for a minute. When Gidwitz got it back, his beloved Alfred E. Neuman card had been slabbed in plastic, free of charge, and assigned a grade that had never been used before on the company's condition scale of 1 to 10: zero. Gidwitz put the card up for auction as a gag. In April 2007, Robert Edward Auctions set the opening bid at $50, only because its policy wouldn't allow for anything lower. The card ended up selling for $1,293.

"There's a price for everything," Gidwitz said, shaking his head.

I'd come to Gidwitz's home on Lake Shore Drive to learn about the 1909 American Tobacco cards and the men who chase their rarest examples. But in spending a couple of days with Gidwitz, I ended up learning mostly about one man, and about how, for the most driven of collectors, even the rarest examples won't do. Frustrated with the prevalence of supposedly tough-to-find cards, Gidwitz has gone so far as to seek out unissued cards and the original art on which his favorite cards were based. To the tune of over $1,000 each, he's also commissioned cards of his own design, indulging his admittedly childish and bawdy tendencies.

Before I met with this eccentric, moneyed collector, Bill Mastro, an auctioneer who's done his own bit to make the secondary sale of baseball cards and memorabilia a sprawling industry, told me that Gidwitz is "like a cartoon character." As peculiar as Gidwitz might appear to some, he's also the jaded soul of card collecting. His life as a collector represents the hobby in microcosm—an evolution from the simple, inexpensive accumulation of the latest sets to a complicated, wallet-busting quest for ever more elusive vintage prizes. In childhood, card collecting provided Gidwitz with a common bond with his brother; in adulthood it's given him a way to return to his youth. But as money has infiltrated the hobby—some of it of course coming from his own pockets—he's become increasingly disgusted with his beloved pastime. In fact, he now repudiates baseball card collecting, and he's begun selling off his various treasures, even the ones he obtained as a child.

"They remind me of this bad, unfortunate thing," he said. "It's changed, and it's not fun in the way it used to be. Now it's all about money."

The 1909 Wagner that Gidwitz once owned has become to baseball card collecting what the erroneous 1918 Inverted Jenny stamp is to the philately world—a prize so uncommon, costly, and rich in backstory that only collectors with the very deepest of pockets can ever hope to have one. There are estimated to be just fifty to one hundred T206 Wagner cards in existence, a number disproportionate to this player's reputation. A former coal miner born into a large family of German immigrants, Wagner is widely regarded as one of the greatest shortstops in baseball history. Over two decades of major-league play, he earned a lifetime batting average of .327 and a then record-setting 3,415 hits. In 1909, in a disputatious meeting of two of the era's greatest hitters, Wagner's Pirates defeated Ty Cobb's Detroit Tigers in the World Series four games to three. Wagner cards from that year have trickled into the hobby over the years, but few, if any, are expected to turn up in the future.

Gidwitz possessed the finest Wagner card of them all, the one that had been rated 8 on a scale of 10 by PSA and was famously co-owned by hockey great Wayne Gretzky. At the time of Gidwitz's purchase of the card at auction, *Forbes* chided him for splurging. "Right now the greater-fool theory is being put to its greatest test," the magazine's reporter acidly suggested. "We wish Gidwitz lots of luck. For he may be the ultimate victim of the Honus Wagner myth." Years later, in 2000, Gidwitz escaped victimization by selling the card for an eye-popping $1.27 million, then the most money ever spent on a baseball card.

Gidwitz, who also collects fine art, pinpointed the Wagner card's appeal in a 1997 interview with *Vintage & Classic Baseball Collector* magazine: "I realized that if I went to the New York Metropolitan Museum of Art, or the Louvre, or Christie's, or Sotheby's and asked each expert they had, 'What's the best piece of art that's ever been painted?' they'd all have different opinions. Some might think it's the *Mona Lisa,* some might think it's *The Last Supper* or something completely different. But I also know if we went to the National [Sports Collectors Convention] and asked the sophisticated collectors and advanced dealers set up at the show, 'What's the best baseball collectible in the world?' they'd say it was the Honus Wagner card. And not just any Wagner card, but the Wagner card I had the chance to buy."

Gidwitz told me that he was careful never to consider the Wagner card an investment. "An investment is an equity, a stock, real estate, a bond. This here"—he gestured to some of his cards—"is all subject to whim. Maybe one day you get five thousand dollars for it, maybe another day you get five hundred. I don't care if my collection is the biggest, and I don't care if it's the best or if it's the most valuable. What it's about is having fun." It makes sense that a guy who's spent a career in finance would want his nearly lifelong hobby to be a more wholesome and pure activity than his day job. Yet Gidwitz seems incapable of entirely separating his competitive instincts from his card-collecting pursuits. As a fellow collector said, "This is a guy who is extremely shrewd. He manipulates the market, and he hates to sell anything for less than he can get. It kills him."

Gidwitz considers buying baseball cards a lot like gambling—if one isn't willing to lose the money altogether, then one shouldn't buy the cards. Gidwitz certainly had fun gambling with the Wagner card, but it was different from the kind of fun he had collecting as a child. The fun brought by a million-dollar baseball card comes in the form of attention: competitive collectors envy you, newspapers run profiles of you, noncollectors speculate on your sanity. "I had one of the best collections, but no one knew I existed except the guys I had been buying cards from," he said. "The Wagner card gave me a pedigree." In other words, his grand purchase was less about making money than getting attention.

I asked Gidwitz if he regretted selling the card so quickly, in light of the fact that it's been sold twice since he unloaded it, once for $2.35 million and again for $2.8 million.

"No," he answered immediately. "Because it had to go to a million dollars before it could go for two million. And things go in stages. Maybe if I hadn't sold it, it would've sold for a little more than I'd gotten for it, but it probably wouldn't have sold for two-point-three million dollars. I think I sold it at the right time. You don't want to keep it forever." Though naysayers such as those at *Forbes* believed that the mythology behind the Wagner card had inflated its price well beyond its value, Gidwitz had the keener insight into the nature of collecting. He recognized that an absurd sum merely adds to the card's legend. And with the Wagner, the legend largely is the value.

American Tobacco released the Wagner and the rest of the so-called T206 set just as the company was losing hold of its monopoly. Between 1890 and 1907 it had devoured an estimated 250 independent companies in the tobacco industry, not necessarily because they were competitive but because they controlled coveted brand names. Duke immediately shut down many of the cigarette factories he acquired, understanding that branding is the key to success with cigarettes, not the quality of the tobacco or the manufacturing. After the turn of the century, American Tobacco accounted for more than half of all U.S. tobacco sales, marketing cigarettes under a hundred different brand names. Such consolidation obviated the need for intensive advertising, especially through pricey trading cards, but Duke revived the baseball card tradition in 1909 when he inserted into his slide-shell boxes colorful portraits of ballplayers that advertised at least fifteen of the company's cigarette trade names.

Exactly why Duke's people did this in 1909 is hard to say. The government had launched antitrust action against Duke's Standard Oil–like monolith almost as soon as it was formed, and the previous year a circuit court had ruled that American Tobacco had violated the Sherman Antitrust Act and ordered that the alliance be broken. The case was appealed and kicked up to the Supreme Court, where it wouldn't be decided for another couple of years. Perhaps Duke saw the monopoly's eventual breakup as inevitable and hoped to get a head start on an advertising onslaught against his future competitors. If so, he was right. In 1911 the High Court handed down a trust-busting decision analogous to its oil-biz ruling of the same year.

The T206 set, issued by American between 1909 and 1911, is also known among collectors as "the Monster." At least 524 professional players are featured on the cards, but what makes the set so expansive is the fact that any given card can bear one of twenty-odd back types, each emblazoned with the name of an exotic-sounding cigarette brand such as Hindu, Tolstoi, or El Principe de Gales. This means that several thousand distinct cards might still be in existence. As with Old Judges, the nearly boundless nature of the set demands that a collector apply a certain discipline. Some collectors try to obtain as many of the different players as possible, while others seek out specimens bearing the same back. Gidwitz's method was uncomplicated and austere: he cared only for the Wagner card. "I bought the Wagner because I figured I had this great collection," he said. "I loved collecting as a kid, and I felt this was the best card in the world. I don't have any kids, I'm not married, and I have the money to do what I want."

Whether the Wagner card is the best in the world is a matter of opinion. What's indisputable is that it's the most sought after. Not because of its rarity—card historian David Cycleback has identified at least seven vintage cards that are scarcer—but because of its lore. By 1909 American Tobacco had started asking players for permission to reproduce their images. The vast majority of them agreed but, for unknown reasons,

Wagner declined. According to a story that appeared in a 1912 edition of the *Sporting News*, a local sportswriter had asked for permission on behalf of the tobacco company and been told that Wagner "did not care to have his picture in a package of cigarettes." For years, Wagner was considered a moral visionary for objecting to the sale of cigarettes in conjunction with kid-friendly premiums. His granddaughter Leslie Blair has bolstered that version of events a number of times, once explaining that, although Wagner himself chewed tobacco, "his concern was he didn't want children to have to buy tobacco in order to get his card."

Another possible scenario is that Wagner believed he wouldn't be appropriately compensated for the use of his image. If so, he would have been a visionary of a different sort, given that professional athletes of his era generally had no inkling of their true publicity value. As many card collectors have pointed out, Wagner apparently had no reservations about his image being reproduced on cigar bands, which seems to belie the argument that he objected to shilling tobacco products.

Whatever the grounds, the Wagner card was pulled from production after an extremely short print run, and the uncertainty surrounding its story has served it well over the years. Even among the earliest of collectors it was known to be a rare and special object, capable of fetching thousands of dollars in the 1960s. The card's mystery intensified in the '70s, when an American Tobacco "proof strip"—a band of five uncut T206 cards, including the Wagner—was discovered in a pocket in Wagner's own circa 1938 coaching uniform after his Pennsylvania home was sold. Many wondered where the Hall of Famer had obtained the strip and why he had held on to it for so many years. Some believe that the American Tobacco Company mailed the strip to Wagner so he could see his picture alongside such revered players as Cy Young and Mordecai "Three Finger" Brown and reevaluate his decision not to sanction the card.

Gidwitz enjoyed the reputation given him by his purchase, but the card itself was another matter. Indeed, owning it was a lot like dealing with a $1 million bill. In his postauction rapture, he posed for a few giddy photos with the two-and-a-half-by-one-and-a-half-inch piece of cardboard, but then he had to figure out what to do with it. The card is almost too small to be displayed safely. Several times in the past, guests and friends had walked out of the Gidwitz abode with more modest fortunes stuffed in their pockets. After someone stole the Babe Ruth cards from his 1933 Goudey bubble gum card collection, Gidwitz had to sell the set for about $60,000 less than he could have had it been complete. Besides, the grading house had long ago slabbed the Wagner in plastic stamped with the company's logo, a grade, and a serial number, thereby robbing a good deal of the card's charm.

For Gidwitz, who buys baseball cards and other pieces of popular art largely for their visual impact, the irony of the Wagner card was that its value precluded it from being flaunted. He put it in a safety-deposit box, where it sat for nearly four years, until the time felt right and he sold it. Anyway, there were greater rarities to be found than the Wagner.

Since childhood, Gidwitz had dreamed of having one of the world's great baseball card collections. He can say with a degree of certainty that he started collecting cards as a seven-year-old, for somewhere in his closet is a 1957 Topps card with his name scrawled in pencil on the back. Gidwitz was born into a well-off family and grew up in a large apartment on the same block as the famous Drake Hotel, across the street from the Lake Shore Drive waterfront. His grandfather had established a successful company that manufactured paper boxes, and his uncle became one of the cofounders of Helene Curtis Industries, the beauty-and-cosmetics giant. Gidwitz's affinity for collecting must have seemed predestined. His mother's assemblage of nineteenth-century British silver and furniture was so valuable that auction houses started courting the family even before she passed away. And Gidwitz might have inherited some of his eccentricity from his father, an amateur painter who loved his 1967 Bentley so much that he threw a bar mitzvah party on the car's thirteenth birthday. Though his father died years ago Gidwitz still has the car garaged.

During the summers, his family would escape their home downtown for a rented house in the Chicago suburbs, where Gidwitz usually spent his dime's allowance on baseball cards, having been schooled in the art of collecting by his brother Jimmy, six and a half years his senior. Gidwitz abandoned cards during high school and college and the early years of his financial career, but in 1974 he ordered a complete Topps set from the back of the *Sporting News* as a nostalgic birthday gift for his sibling. For weeks after receiving the gift, Jimmy would call up Gidwitz and ask him a trivia question from the back of one of the cards: *Q: Who was the only player ever to pinch hit for Ted Williams? A: Carroll Hardy.* Gidwitz reconnected with his inner card-loving child. A young professional then in his midtwenties, he started buying wax packs from a grocery store near his house.

"Then one day I saw a little ad in the paper," he recalled. "There was a card show at the Hillside Holiday Inn. I went and walked around. There were twenty-four tables. I called my brother and said, 'Come on out here. You won't believe it. Our cards are probably worth five thousand dollars.' There were cards we were missing, like the 1966 high numbers, and I thought it would be fun [to try to find them]. We decided we would collect. The cards were pretty cheap. I spent a couple hundred bucks on them. I think I bought my first [uncut] sheet at one of those shows. I traded a guy a Kaline rookie and a Harvey Kuenn for the sheet, and I bought another for ten dollars. That's really what got me started. I made lists of the cards I needed to fill in the sets, because I never knew how to get the cards you were missing when I was a kid."

Gidwitz's mother had thrown out Jimmy's cards. Michael's childhood collection, however, remained intact. And he now had more than enough money to fill in the holes. Having bounced from Rothschild Securities to various brokerage firms, he increased his assets to the tune of several million dollars operating on a simple principle: "Spend less than you make and invest the difference." As his collecting passion grew, Gidwitz put a good chunk of that difference into baseball cards. He ran small advertisements in the classified sections of the local alternative newspaper—"Don't let your mom throw your cards out. Call me!"—and pinned index cards to supermarket bulletin boards. He replaced his imperfect cards with finer examples and cast off his doubles and triples for cards he didn't have at all. "I just wanted them. I didn't think of the money," he said. Soon he found himself spending several hundred dollars at shows, which was a lot to drop on cards in the 1970s. If someone walked through the door with a boxful of rarities, Gidwitz wanted to leave with it.

Yet even the most seasoned card collector has to recognize that he has no unique items, baseball cards being the mass-produced prints that they are. Knowing there are at least a few copies of every card imaginable, including the venerated Wagner, Gidwitz found it harder and harder to care about them. After a while, he wanted to obtain only objects from the baseball card world that no one else could have. "Anyone can get the cards," Gidwitz said. "I don't give a shit about the cards."

Gidwitz owns two apartments near the top of his building. He bought the second one because his cards and collectibles outgrew the first. He described this ancillary dwelling, next door, as "a museum that every once in a while I cook something in." In this museum are a large number of art gallery–style flat files, each holding the one baseball card collectible that has held Gidwitz's attention ever since he attended those first shows: the uncut sheet.

Uncut sheets are pages full of cards that were printed but never divided into individual pieces of cardboard. Depending on the printing method used, an uncut sheet may hold anywhere from five cards, as in the one 1909 American Tobacco sheet that survives, to several dozen. For a long time, uncut sheets were considered a bastard form of baseball cards, sought only by folks like Gidwitz who wanted to frame them and hang them on their office walls. He handed out his phone number at shows and told anyone willing to listen that he wanted all the sheets they could find. For years, he felt as if he was the only one pursuing them. Finally, collectors started to tune in to the sheets' eye appeal and scarcity, and the most exceptional examples became worth hundreds of dollars, then thousands of dollars, and eventually tens of thousands of dollars apiece. By that point Gidwitz had gotten his hands on some of the finest available.

Uncut sheets represent the process of card making—or, to be more exact, a break in that process. Cards in sheet form never saw the light of day in a candy store, and because they were never meant to have survived they have an aura of privacy, even secrecy. (In the early '90s, officials at Upper Deck threatened to sue dealers who were trading in uncut sheets that were never supposed to have turned up on the open market.) Therefore, said baseball card auctioneer Rob Lifson, collectors now tend to look upon them with "a sense of wonderment." Many of the card sheets that survive today are one of a kind, or nearly so, which is, of course, what attracted Gidwitz to them. He has one of the only surviving uncut sheets from American Tobacco's 1909 "silks," soft baseball cards made of fabric rather than cardboard. He has perhaps the only complete set of 1933 Goudey bubble gum baseball cards in uncut form, in a series of sheets that he wouldn't sell for under $1 million. In his second apartment he has reams of early uncut sheets from the Topps and Bowman companies, each worth several thousand dollars, rolled up in the closet. He bought most of his sheets because they look beautiful matted and framed, but he has the space to display only about twenty-five of his several hundred at a time.

"He was way ahead of the curve on this," said Lifson, a friend of Gidwitz's. "He gravitated toward uncut sheets when they were unpopular, and he started collecting them before other people. He noticed that the uncut sheets were really special and that they didn't get the attention they deserve."

Eventually, Gidwitz started seeking baseball card items that were rarer even than uncut sheets. He wanted the original artworks that inspired his favorite cards, thereby guaranteeing that he would own something unique. As we strolled through the apartment where Gidwitz sleeps, he opened a cabinet in his living room to show me the one-of-a-kind baseball cards that have become the focus of his collecting: the original painting for the 1962 Gaylord Perry rookie card, the original painting for the 1960 Willie McCovey All-Star Rookie card, and the original painting for the 1960 Frank Howard rookie card. Each of these pieces is paired under glass with the card that it inspired.

"My collection is not just baseball cards—it's art," said Gidwitz. It's hard to say what these drawings by Topps artists would fetch on the open market, because there's no reliable barometer for past sales. Gidwitz scooped up much of the original Topps card art at the Topps Guernsey auction of 1989, when the company sold some twenty-five thousand items from its archives for nearly $2 million. But the astonishing growth in demand for such items in the past two decades has rendered those sales figures meaningless.

Even more incalculable is the value of the Topps-style artwork hanging in Gidwitz's kitchen. In the late 1960s, the Topps Company released a set of die-cut trading cards lampooning consumer products. The products were common enough and the humor infantile enough for children to get most of the jokes. Among the inaugural issue of Wacky Packages were Crust Toothpaste ("brush teeth twice a month"), Weakies cereal ("breakfast of chumps"), and Kook-Aid ("2 quarts will drive you kooky"). The gags might have been corny, but the mildly subversive cards spawned a fad that survived more than fifteen series printings. Wacky Packages, which were created by such celebrated Topps artists as *Zippy the Pinhead* creator Bill Griffith and future *Maus* auteur Art Spiegelman, arrived too late for Gidwitz to experience as a child, but he grew fascinated with them as an adult. In the early and mid-1990s he swallowed up whatever original art to these cards he could find.

"Gidwitz was the guy who drove the price from $1,000 to $10,000 apiece [for Wacky art]," said Greg Grant, one of about half a dozen hard-core collectors in this niche. "He's the guy who bought all this stuff when everyone else thought he was a fool. He had a lot of fore-sight, he was in the right place at right time, and he sold at what seemed like an incredible price. He's probably made more money on Wacky Packs to this day than anybody."

Though he's best known for clearing some $600,000 in his deac-cession of the Wagner card, Gidwitz has probably reaped even more money trading in Wacky Packages. In 2001 he sold a trove of roughly eighty pieces of original Wacky art to Eric Roberts, son of billionaire leveraged-buyout maven George Roberts, for a rumored half a million dollars. As stunning as the figure seems, it could have been bigger had Gidwitz just waited. A couple of years after the sale, Topps rereleased Wacky Packages in six series, garnering media attention that helped send the market for the original art into the stratosphere. The cache that Gidwitz unloaded is probably worth $2 million today.

As he was buying and selling much of the series' original artwork, Gidwitz was also commissioning former Topps artists to render the Wacky Packages that he couldn't get out of his head. He put it this way: "What if I had the freedom to be art director, and I didn't have to worry about whether they were too racy or too spicy for kids?" Among Gidwitz's unique creations are Porn Flakes, Pizza Slut, Star-fucks Coffee, Prosti-tooties, Cap'n Crotch, S&M Candies, and the McDumbell's Crappy Meal. The artwork for these cards that never were hangs in Gidwitz's kitchen, for any guest to see. Although the appeal of something like Gay's Potato Chips, a hate-crime-themed homage to the Lay's potato chip bag showing an overheated goon stomping a feeble-looking man wearing a pink sweater (slogan: "Can't stop beatin' 'em!"), might seem minimal, Gidwitz claims that "there are guys who collect Wackys who like mine better than the originals. I've had guys offer me real serious money for these."

"It doesn't matter if you're someone's biggest customer," Gidwitz said of the artists he hires. "What matters is that you're their favorite customer. These guys love working with me. They can go over the edge and they're not restricted. It's almost as if they're a horse and you're riding them, and when you're Topps, you're reining the guys in. But if it's me, we're going full speed ahead. If there's a line, I want to cross it. And I don't just want to cross it—I want to cross it bare-ass naked."

Like Wacky Packages, Alfred E. Neuman is something that Gidwitz has become interested in only in adulthood. He never even read *Mad* as a child. He bought his first piece of original cover art for the magazine in the early 1990s, then acquired more examples at auction as he built a collection of about two hundred *Mad* covers. All the while, he was forging friendships with their artists and hiring them to do *Mad*-themed work of his own imagining. "He was ahead of the curve on how important *Mad* art was," said artist James Warhola, a longtime member of *Mad*'s "Usual Gang of Idiots" and the nephew of Andy Warhol. "Mike's a real character. He always wanted to meet the artists and strike up a correspondence and commission them. I think by collecting it, he's giving it the importance it deserves."

Word of Gidwitz's personal commissions eventually reached the *Mad* offices, and he received a call from the magazine's counsel regarding copyright infringement. Gidwitz's lawyer told both his client and the magazine that so long as Gidwitz didn't try to put Neuman's image on merchandise, he could do whatever he wanted with his *Mad*-inspired art. *Mad* backed down. "So I took Alfred and I put Alfred on the most famous baseball cards, comic-book covers, movie posters, and record albums," said Gidwitz.

His home became a mishmash of kiddie culture from the 1950s and '60s, typified by one of the "baseball cards" on the wall of his apartment, a portrait-size rendering of a 1956 Mickey Mantle Topps card that, instead of Mantle's all-American smile, bears Alfred E. Neuman's gap-toothed grin. As on the Mantle card, the background action shot shows Neuman leaping with his glove over the outfield wall, trying to nab a home run shot before it falls into the crowd. It's the very picture of sporting heroism—except Neuman's pants are around his ankles and his genitals exposed. Gidwitz paid an undisclosed sum to Brazilian artist Rogerio W.S. to have the artwork done. Such oddball commissions have led auctioneer Mastro, an estranged friend, to assert that Gidwitz is "attached to shit."

"I look at all of them together as one art project," countered Lifson. "It's a body of artwork. Whether it will be economically rewarding for him, I don't know. Historically, things that Mike does because he enjoys them turn out pretty well for him. But I think their value as a collection is greater than their value piecemeal. I'm not sure whether it's about *Mad* magazine or popular culture or the process of putting a collection together, or whether it's just about Mike Gidwitz. But all together it's something special. We're not talking about Malcolm Forbes with $8 billion, forcing the world to pay attention to him. It's just Mike with an unusual sense of humor. Even if it's worth zero dollars, it doesn't change the significance for Mike."

Gidwitz doesn't care whether his custom-made objects mean anything to other collectors. He's been commissioning original works of art in part because he's soured on the cardboard that others trade in, and not simply because it offers little opportunity for unique ownership. Despite his own role in raising the price of the Wagner card, Gidwitz believes that the rapid escalation of baseball card values over the past two decades has irreversibly damaged what was once an enjoyable hobby. He claims that he's been burned so often by unscrupulous dealers that any financial gains from the Wagner's doubling in price under his ownership have long since been erased. "I was sold cards from dealers that were trimmed, and I was sold cards that were restored," he said. "And what happened was . . . I would find out it was trimmed. I believe a lot of the [dealers] took advantage of people. And that still goes on. . . . I think there are a lot of problems with baseball cards, with auction houses. If you've got a sheet that's a one of a kind, at least you know it hasn't been altered or damaged in some way."

Another reason for his bleak assessment of the hobby is more personal. The value of Gidwitz's collection has become a source of conflict between him and his brother. Although they both got back into collecting in the 1970s, Gidwitz was the only one to move his cardboard around with the prescience of a money manager. Because their collections had commingled at certain points over the years, his brother eventually began asserting a right to roughly half of Gidwitz's cards, a claim almost certainly worth millions. The hobby that had been a bond between the brothers quickly became a wedge.

"He came over here several times," Gidwitz recalled. "'That's my Hank Aaron rookie, that's my Ernie Banks rookie.' He took two or three different Ernie Banks rookies, and I'd go buy new ones. He'd say, 'This one is better than the one you gave me.' I got tired of that. It's not what it was. He's jealous of me and the collection, and he doesn't have his cards anymore."

Recently, Gidwitz has made plans to sell off much of his baseball card collection. He's consigned to a dealer all of the individual Topps and Bowman cards he has from the 1950s and '60s—the very cards that got him into collecting as a kid. Gidwitz is fond of saying that prolific collectors have four reasons to sell off their cards: death, debt, divorce, or a sudden lack of enjoyment in their acquisitions. Save for a few uncut sheets and some of his unique artwork, Gidwitz's collectibles no longer give him much pleasure, he said. A hobby that had served him for many years as a return to childhood now evokes the problems of adulthood.

Besides, anyone can get the cards.

3

People Chew Harder When They Are Sad

Even the most well-heeled card enthusiasts started their multimillion-dollar collection with just a few cents at the corner store. The cards that boys like Michael Gidwitz pulled from penny and nickel packs were so beloved that it's hard to believe they were never intended to be the main attraction. But in fact the cards were at first merely an incentive to buy something sweeter and less permanent: bubble gum. Had it not been for the invention of that kid-friendly gum, baseball cards may have had no reason to exist after the end of the tobacco wars.

The start of the second golden age of baseball cards can be traced to an August day in 1928 when a twenty-three-year-old accountant at a Philadelphia candy firm decided to try his hand at experimenting with gum formulas. The Fleer Corporation was already producing a successful lineup of gums and sweets that reached well beyond Pennsylvania, and the accountant, Walter Diemer, had no background in chemistry and no expertise in gum making whatsoever. But tinkering with sugars and resins and sampling candy and chewing gum, as the firm's chemists did each day, must have struck Diemer as a worthy enough diversion to pull him away from crunching numbers for a few hours.

The gum that Diemer created that day was unlike any that he'd chewed before. It was flexible enough that it could be blown full of air but not so sticky that it clamped onto his chin when it burst. The gum snapped back, ready to produce more bubbles. "Everybody tried some," Diemer recalled before his death in 1998. "We were blowing bubbles all over the office." The fun was short-lived, however. The very same batch failed to produce bubbles the next day, a disappointment that Diemer attributed to temperature fluctuation. But more experimentation over the next four months led to a successful three-hundred-pound batch that Diemer mixed for company executives and factory workers. With the recipe finalized, all Diemer needed was a color. "Pink food coloring was the only one I had at hand," he remembered.

Diemer's employer had been hawking candy, gum, and novelties to children for decades, but Fleer got its start before the Civil War manufacturing food flavorings. In 1897 Frank H. Fleer created the firm's first big hit in the gum market by adding cola flavoring to his chicle-based chew. He later introduced a primitive incarnation of bubble gum he called Blibber Blubber, but the formula proved too brittle for bubble blowing and didn't last long on store shelves. More successful was the gum inspired by the Jordan almonds found on store counters at the turn of the century. Fleer gave its pieces a hard sugar coating and called them Chiclets, a trade name that would become one of the most durable in American candies. But none of these products changed the gum market quite like Diemer's elastic creation did.

The day after Christmas 1928, wrapped chunks of Fleer bubble gum went on sale in a neighborhood candy store in Philadelphia. Christened Dubble Bubble, the new gum sold out quickly, and soon it became Fleer's most popular product. Surprisingly, Diemer and Fleer never bothered to patent the formula, figuring that such a public record would only help copycats to hit the market sooner. More than a dozen pink-hued imitations quickly followed Dubble Bubble into stores. A national bubble gum fad had begun.

With the first successfully marketed bubble gum, Fleer managed to carve a niche in a rapidly growing industry controlled largely by William Wrigley Jr.'s eponymous Chicago-based colossus. Until Dubble Bubble came along, gum had been chewed for any number of reasons, including the relief of all kinds of everyday ailments, from nervousness to heartburn. During the Panic of 1907, when runs on banks across the country contributed to a nearly 50 percent drop in the stock market, gum was apparently valued for its therapeutic effect. As with "vice" items such as cigarettes, liquor, and candy, it continued to sell as other nonessentials languished on store shelves. "People chew harder when they are sad," Wrigley remarked.

As Fleer was surely trying to suggest with its silly-sounding product name, however, gum consumption could also be fun. Dubble Bubble was food meant to be played with, and at a penny per piece it was cheap enough that any child could buy it without his mother by his side. Fleer was attempting to create an industry directed expressly at preteens. And because this demographic shows little brand loyalty, it soon became necessary to entice children with oddball humor, imaginative graphics, and fun premiums—so much so that the line between product and packaging would become blurred.

In 1930 Fleer first swaddled a piece of Dubble Bubble with a comic strip featuring its Bubble Twins, Dub and Bub, launching a dime-store culture that would eventually birth not only Topps baseball cards but also Mars Attacks cards, the Garbage Pail Kids, and other candy and toy novelties that would fascinate children for generations. As they faced the country's worst economic downturn in history, Fleer and its competitors realized that these throwaway marketing schemes were essential to their survival. Company suits may have seen bubble gum cards as ephemeral premiums to go with an ephemeral product, but kids recognized them as something far more vital and lasting. The Civil War spawned the baseball card, and two generations later the Great Depression gave it an enduring place in American boyhood.

* * *

Fleer's first big rival in the kiddie-gum market was the Goudey Gum Company, whose Nova Scotian founder, Enos Goudey, was never able to prove his long-held claim that his firm had invented the first marketable bubble gum. To steer children away from Fleer's comic-wrapped gum, Goudey started packing his product with trading cards depicting Native American leaders. Based on portraits obtained from the Smithsonian, Goudey cards showed chiefs such as Tecumseh, Powhatan, and Sitting Bull regally posed with headdresses and passive faces, with tepees, rivers, and full moons in the background. Indian Chewing Gum sold wildly among school kids in 1932 and 1933.

Although Fleer had been including baseball cards with its five-cent candy packages, their cards were cheaply designed and hopelessly ugly. Indian Gum cards, by contrast, captured children's imaginations with museum-worthy artwork that evoked another culture and time. Weeks after the product's launch, Goudey was rolling out gum twenty-four hours a day to keep up with demand. The company followed Indian Chewing Gum with Big League Chewing Gum, a richly illustrated 240-card issue. With superstars such as Babe Ruth and Lou Gehrig appearing multiple times in different poses, some based on the work of celebrated baseball photographer Charles M. Conlon, the Goudey Big Leagues remain among the most artfully designed and collectible baseball cards ever produced.

It was an odd time for Goudey to have sunk a precious $50,000 into a batch of cardboard. After all, just as the company was sending its first baseball cards off to the printer, the United States was experiencing the worst of the Great Depression. In 1933 the nation's financial system was heading toward collapse, leading President Franklin D. Roosevelt on March 6 to declare a four-day bank holiday that left most Americans without access to cash.

Professional baseball would endure its most financially challenging season in years. As the New York Yankees toured Florida during spring training, *New York Herald-Tribune* sportswriter Rud Rennie wrote, "We came home . . . through Southern cities which looked as tho they had been ravaged by an invisible enemy. People seemed to be hiding. They even would not come to see Babe Ruth and Lou Gehrig. They simply did not have the money to waste on baseball games or amusements." During the 1933 season, "All over the major-league baseball circuits one saw stores for rent, silent shops, idle factories, half-empty hotels, and slim crowds in the ball-parks, night-clubs, and places of amusement." That year, player salaries were trimmed, teams shrank their coaching staffs, and the pennant-winning New York Giants and Washington Nationals failed to sell out a single World Series game. As all this was happening, Goudey's one-cent gum-and-baseball-card packs provided a link to the game at a time when a trip to the ballpark was too great an expense for many.

Under such conditions, Goudey not only survived, it thrived. Enos Goudey bought himself a $125,000 mansion in Newton, Massachusetts, the same year that the stock market crashed. He sold Goudey in 1932 but stayed on as a consultant as the company's sales continued to grow. His gum and cards were so successful among young buyers that William Wrigley came to call Goudey the "Penny Gum King." The effect of the introduction of Big League cards was staggering. Goudey's total sales were a modest $335,000 in 1932; they soared to a whopping $1.47 million in 1933, perhaps the most cash-strapped year in American history. When competitor American Chicle filed for bankruptcy in 1937, Goudey would be there to scoop up its assets, including the company's baseball card brand. The Goudey Depression-era juggernaut was built on promotions—and the best promotions, it turned out, involved cardboard heroes.

When it came to devising methods for teasing pennies from children during hard times, the firm was innovative and relentless. Like the album-offering tobacco companies of the 1880s, Goudey coaxed young buyers with the promise of fun premiums. If a boy mailed in fifty gum wrappers, for instance, he received a large portrait of either Babe Ruth, the World Series–winning New York Giants, or the American or National League All-Star team. As the Depression dug deeper into

American pockets and stamps became too precious a commodity to be wasted on gum wrappers, Goudey changed its tactics and started offering its premiums in-store, which might have been an even better arrangement for the gum maker because it brought kids back to the register. "Your store keeper will give you a postcard size photographic reproduction of a well known ball player, *for only 2* Big League Gum wrappers," packaging promised. "Start your collection now." When these enticements ran their course, Goudey created others. It introduced flip-book cards called Thum Movies, which let kids see the likes of Mel Ott and Paul Derringer in animated action. It issued a series that let children assemble puzzles from multiple baseball cards, encouraging numerous buys per child. The company even reduced the price of its flagship Oh Boy Gum by 50 percent, offering two sticks for one cent, a discount that, promotional materials assured, "in no way affected it's superior quality and excellent flavor."

Had Goudey's cards cost five cents, or even three, the series probably wouldn't have been tenable. Collector Norm Brauer, who grew up in rural Dalton, Pennsylvania, during the Depression, used to walk two miles into town to buy a single pack of Goudeys. "Pennies were rare suckers, so purchases rarely went beyond one or two one-cent packs, and it was virtually unheard of for a kid to have a nickel for five packs," Brauer wrote in *Vintage & Classic Baseball Collector*. "The wrappers, as I recall, offered membership in the Knot Hole Club and various prizes, none of which appealed to us because saving the minimum number of wrappers *plus* ten cents was quite a hurdle. . . . Cards were carefully placed in our jacket pockets, never to be bent, nor soiled, but kept clean and neat. One thing the Depression taught us was to be frugal and to appreciate what we had. No flipping cards or placing them in bicycle spokes, if you were lucky enough to have a bike."

It was wise to treat Goudeys with care. Despite their celebrated aesthetic qualities, the cards were issued on thin cardboard, and children found that they often came apart when played with. But a much greater frustration was card #106. The trouble was, no one could find it.

Though the back of each Goudey card identified it as one of a set of 240, kids searched in vain for the card that, according to checklists, was supposed to depict retired second baseman and longtime Ty Cobb rival Napoleon "Nap" Lajoie. The card was apparently never printed in 1933, and it has since become hobby lore that Goudey excluded the Lajoie card knowing that the average boy would buy pack after pack of gum in a futile attempt to find it. Card-issuing companies understood that kids collect in part because they love the thrill of the chase. Collecting has never really been about the transitory enjoyment of a penny piece of bubble gum; it's always been about the desire to find something elusive. To all appearances, Goudey exploited the child's quest for completion as well as anyone could have.

Ruses like the Lajoie appear to have been a pattern with the company. The same year that Big League Chewing Gum appeared, the company put out a set of pirate-themed picture cards called Sea Raiders, which it advertised on wrappers as a series of 240, despite the fact that even the most avid collectors would discover a bounty of no more than forty-eight unique cards. Similarly, under its Canadian imprint, World Wide Gum, Goudey released a series of animal picture cards called Jungle Gum ("Start a Zoo as You Chew") in which the latter half of the purported forty-eight-card offering was skip-numbered, meaning that kids searched in vain for certain nonexistent even numbers. Either the company had to cut short its intended print runs unexpectedly or it went to diabolical lengths to get youngsters to part with their pennies.

In a 1977 letter to card collector Bruce Dorskind, former Goudey executive George C. Thompson offered his own version of the Lajoie story: "I believe that someone suggested that we include some of the real old timers. As the sale of bubble gum at that time was mainly limited to children six to fourteen, Lajoie did not mean a thing to them. They only wanted to collect the players who they could associate with and therefore I feel that a majority of the Lajoie cards were discarded."

Unfortunately, Thompson's story raises more questions than it answers. If either the company or the kids really did throw out most of the Lajoie cards solely because he was an old-timer, then why didn't they destroy the 1933 Big League cards of Eddie Collins, who'd been retired for three years, or the 1933 Goudey Sport Kings cards of Ty Cobb, whose heyday had come two decades earlier? Uncut sheets from the '33 set have surfaced over the years, and they appear to contradict Thompson's version of events. Lajoie doesn't appear on the sheets at all; where card #106 should be, one instead finds a Babe Ruth card listed #144, which was apparently double printed on the sheets.

Indeed, if Goudey had produced the Lajoie card in 1933, as Thompson maintained, then why do all of the Lajoie cards that have surfaced bear the design of the 1934 set? Most collectors are convinced that Goudey printed the card only after the mothers of aggravated children perceived foul play and sent letters of protest to the company's offices. Goudey never quite admitted to any wrongdoing, but in hopes of restoring goodwill in 1934 it mailed a #106 Lajoie card to all of the collectors who'd formally complained. Those few corrective Lajoie cards are believed to be the only ones ever released to the public, with only six hundred or so estimated to have been printed and about one hundred having survived to the present. Because of the Lajoie card's scarcity and unique history, examples have sold at auction for more than $100,000. Only the T206 Wagner has a greater legend.

Many Goudey cards are believed to be scarcer even than their circa-1910 counterparts—a fact attributed to the paper drives of the 1940s, which likely swallowed up many a boy's baseball card collection. The company itself didn't do much to preserve its cardboard. When Goudey was foundering during the winter of 1961 to 1962, Thompson, then president, directed that the company's back stock of '30s-era trading cards be thrown into the furnace to help heat the building. It was the last winter that Goudey workers would have to endure. The insolvent company shut its doors permanently that January.

* * *

After Goudey's sales skyrocketed in 1933, other gum makers such as National Chicle and DeLong began producing baseball cards, too, giving kids a variety of penny packs to choose from at the register. But to a Philadelphian named J. Warren Bowman there appeared to be plenty more room in the market. One of the most colorful figures of American entrepreneurship to rise out of the Great Depression, the hulking Bowman had a reputation as a swashbuckling, somewhat menacing risk taker. Over the course of two decades he would do more perhaps than anyone to put bubble gum into nearly every preteen mouth in America.

Long before he earned the handles "Bubbleman Bowman," "King Bub," and the "Clown Prince of Bubble Gum," however, Bowman tried his hand at every wild enterprise that happened to present itself to him. Born in Pennsylvania Dutch country and raised on a ranch in New Mexico, Bowman lit out for Los Angeles when he turned eighteen, launching a used-car business that would go under upon the start of World War I. In his later years he would joke that, by his twenty-first birthday, he was "married, divorced, and bankrupt"—milestones that he would revisit many times over in his lifetime. After abandoning auto sales the six-foot-three, two-hundred-pounder worked briefly as an LA cop, but he was fired when a superior caught him in a squad car filled with young women.

After stints running a limousine service and hauling fruit by truck, Bowman headed south to Tampico, Mexico, having heard a rumor that the city was in dire need of a laundry service. Instead of cleaning oil workers' clothes, Bowman wound up transporting mahogany logs by boat on the Panuco River. But his stay in Tampico gave him a revolutionary idea. Stunned by the volume of coffee imbibed by locals, Bowman became fixated on creating a candy or lozenge that would give the caffeinated buzz of a cup of joe. He sold his log-hauling boat and returned to the States, tinkering with the concept at the Mellon Institute of Industrial Research in Pittsburgh to no avail.

Though his coffee gumdrop never came to fruition, Bowman still hoped to break into the confectionery industry. Taking a boat one night from Cleveland to Detroit, he met a salesman who said that he pulled down some $60 a day hawking chewing gum. Bowman started selling the stuff to grocery and corner stores, giving out butcher knives and blankets as premiums to retailers. During a visit to Chicago, he stood in awe outside the floodlit Wrigley Building, built just a few years earlier by the nation's leading gum mogul and modeled on the cathedral in Seville, Spain. To grow rich, Bowman figured, he needed to manufacture gum, not simply peddle it.

After marketing his own lines of standard chewing gum unsuccessfully in Michigan, Bowman took his last $25 and returned to Philadelphia, where he borrowed a friend's gum-making machinery and started to manufacture bubble gum. He figured that Wrigley had already cornered the chewing-gum market and that the company's brand recognition was insurmountable. The healthy profits of the upstart Fleer Co., however, demonstrated that there was room for a novel gum marketed specifically to children. Bowman opened his own plant in Philly under the name Gum, Inc., and in 1929 he unveiled his flagship bubble gum called Blony, a name that the *Saturday Evening Post* described as "vaguely revolting."

Bowman's gum-mogul inspiration, William Wrigley, once remarked that "anybody can make gum—selling it is the problem." What made Wrigley one of the ten wealthiest Americans by the early 1930s was his marketing savvy. He employed beautiful young women as street vendors, paid to have his gum stocked near cash registers, slathered trains and subways with gigantic advertisements, and doled out millions of free samples to telephone-service subscribers, all in an effort to make chewing gum a part of everyday life. Gum was so cheap, Wrigley's reasoning went, that it could give Americans "something for nothing" during hard times. First, though, they had to want it.

Bowman and Fleer applied the same logic to children, whose pennies were clearly worth fighting for. Bowman marketed Blony as the largest piece of penny gum in the world and claimed that it could produce bubbles twice as large as its competitors'. The wrapping on a 210-gram piece of Blony promised, "Three Big BITES for a penny," and a photo from that *Saturday Evening Post* article shows the suit-and-tied King Bub himself blowing a bubble larger than his head. Even though its moniker suggested processed meat, Blony sold briskly, and the gum quickly supplanted Fleer's Dubble Bubble as the best-selling bubble gum in America, claiming about 60 percent of the market.

During the early and mid-'30s Bowman followed Goudey's lead and inserted cards depicting Indians and gun-slinging cowboys into his gum packs to entice young buyers. In 1936 he released the now cult-classic G-Men and the Heroes of Law Enforcement card set, which glamorized both cops and criminals. A few years later he put out three seasons' worth of Play Ball baseball cards. To supplement these kiddie products Bowman created a series of pinup-girl cards that he marketed to adults, sans gum, as American Beauties. With titles like "A Perfect Pair," "Peek a View," and "Thar She Blows," the cards featured the upskirt artwork of some of the finest pinup illustrators of the day, including Gil Elvgren and Zoe Mozert. Bowman didn't mind using copyrighted art, either, as he did on cards showing stars W. C. Fields and Mae West, as long as the name Gum, Inc., was kept off the backs of the cards. Like Wrigley, Bowman grew outrageously rich even as much of the rest of the country fell into squalor. In 1932 he spread his gum empire overseas, flying to Japan and opening that country's first bubble gum factories.

A story in *Time* magazine described the "burly, brown-eyed" Bowman as "one of the lustiest characters in Philadelphia," and an ugly divorce from his second wife, who claimed a verbal agreement to half of Bowman's company holdings, became fodder for high-society gossips. His flamboyant personality and aggressive business tactics also had a way of landing him in court. In 1930 Bowman had agreed to give half of his corporation's stock to a New York manufacturer in exchange for a gum base to be used in Blony. But Bowman tried to wiggle out of the contract just two years later, when he heard that a cheaper and better base had been created. During the ensuing litigation he lost his seat as president of Gum, Inc. But the court found in Bowman's favor after his lawyer, a state senator, arranged to have the judge sample the two gum bases; the judge came around to Bowman's point of view when the older gum clung to his dentures. Bowman won the right to use the newer base and was reinstated as president. As it turned out, during his leave of absence, Bowman had secretly recorded meetings of the company's board of directors and took care of those who supported him once he returned.

Bowman had watched as the popularity of Goudey's baseball cards gave his competitor a substantial chunk of the bubble gum market. He wanted to make sure that the next big craze among schoolkids carried his name. One evening in 1937 he dreamed up what he believed was the perfect concept as he listened to a radio broadcast detailing atrocities carried out by the Japanese in the second Sino-Japanese war. His idea was to release a set of trading cards that espoused pacifism—or at least purported to espouse pacifism. Collaborating with the Philadelphia advertising man George Moll, Bowman devised a set of some 288 cards that bear disturbingly violent scenes from three contemporary conflicts: the Second Sino-Japanese War, the Italo-Ethiopian War, and the Spanish Civil War. Bowman gave the series the wonderfully pulpy name the Horrors of War and congratulated himself in the product's publicity material: "Gum, Inc. has created these cards in belief that through them could be directed a favorable attitude toward peace. The whole idea was the inspiration of J. Warren Bowman, President of Gum, Inc." Perhaps to ameliorate the inevitable backlash from parents, the reverse of each card bore the line "To know the HORRORS OF WAR is to want PEACE."

So-called war cards were nothing new—the tradition stretched back to the earliest cigarette cards of the nineteenth century, some of which feature images of American Civil War generals and naval commanders. But those old tobacco issues are generally staid affairs. What set the Horrors series apart from previous war cards is that they depicted ongoing, politically sensitive skirmishes in the goriest manner possible. As a *Life* feature on the set explained at the time, "Gum Inc. gets its wars hot off the battlefield. . . . The course of the war in China may be confusing to adult Americans, but it is becoming very clear to myriad American youngsters who are bubble gum chewers." For a penny, a child received one piece of gum and one piece of cardboard filled with a war scene. To help launch the issue, Bowman was said to have sent Horrors of War cards into the sky over Philadelphia by balloon.

The Horrors of War set was unlike anything American children had ever traded before. It shows bayonets being plunged through torsos, close combat in which men strangle each other, and women and children being slaughtered. Atop the back of each card is a title such as "Suicide Squad of Japs Is Blasted at Woonsung," "Japanese Bomb Orphanage," or "Big Shells Kill Madrid Children at Play." In their promotional materials, Gum, Inc., claimed that "many peace organizations" had sanctioned the cards. Nonetheless, no endorsement was forthcoming from parents. An irritated father in Chicago wrote a letter of protest to his local newspaper: "A few years back I used to collect bubble gum cards with baseball players' pictures, but what warlike element is now being allowed to implant itself in the minds of our children?"

The cards' political insinuations were just as potentially inflammatory as their imagery. The Chinese were portrayed as heroic martyrs, the Japanese as pitiless brutes. Bowman's siding against the Japanese is something of a surprise, given that he still had extensive business interests in the empire. "War has always been a cruel butcher of men, a relentless destroyer of civilization," one card pontificates. "Japan's undeclared war against China is even more horrible because it has caused the wholesale destruction of innocent families, defenseless women and children. . . . What is to become of the World . . . if War is not outlawed!" The *Life* piece on the cards noted half jokingly that if a war were someday to erupt between the United States and Japan, future historians might attribute it to the fact that the youth of America in the late 1930s had been indoctrinated with "anti-Japanese prejudices."

George Moll, Bowman's chief collaborator, was a devout Baptist and Sunday school teacher with reportedly antiwar sentiments. Less clear are Bowman's own motivations for creating the set. He would later release a profitable card set lionizing the American armed forces, and at times the Horrors of War cards seemed to critique the isolationist zeitgeist of the days before Pearl Harbor, with one card proclaiming, "America's noble dislike of War is largely based on ignorance of what modern War really is. Even pictures cannot show War in all its horror and ugliness. They may paint some of the carnage, some of the destruction, but they leave unrecorded the utter heartbreak of a whole people." Regardless of one's politics, this was heady stuff for an elementary schooler.

The Japanese, at least, failed to appreciate Gum, Inc.'s attempts at education. When a shipment of the cards arrived in Japan they were confiscated by police. Bowman insisted that Chinese merchants in Honolulu and Manila must have sent the boatload of cardboard as propaganda, though it was rumored that Bowman himself sent it as a snarky gift. The set touched off an international controversy, much of it stemming from cards that detailed Japanese atrocities in Manchuria as well as those that depicted the December 12, 1937, Japanese bombing of the U.S.S. *Panay* while it was anchored in the Yangtze River. "American flags, prominently displayed, gave warning of its status," the back reads. "Imagine the bitter surprise of its crew when at 1.39 P.M. Japanese planes appeared overhead and began dropping bombs on its deck!" The Japanese embassy in Washington complained to the State Department that the cards were a gross misrepresentation; the U.S. government declined to address the issue with Bowman. In 1937 King Bub was formally denounced by

Japan and banned forever from the empire, and Gum, Inc., was ordered to cease production there immediately.

Ultimately, the company ran through a printing of 100 million Horrors of War cards. Given that there were about 5.3 million American boys between the ages of six and nine at the time, that figure allows about nineteen cards for each. One of those kids was the noted war historian and Korean War vet Stanley Weintraub, who told me that he believes the Horrors series set him on a path to writing about war. Weintraub was an eight-year-old Philadelphian and avid baseball card collector when, in 1938, he set about accumulating the Horrors of War set, which he kept in a wooden Breakstone's cream-cheese box. Telephones weren't common in households then, so Weintraub would wait for someone to ring the community phone at the corner store, then relay the call to one of his neighbors for a nickel. He put all of his change toward the cards and learned about wars that were esoteric even to adults.

"The narratives were propagandistic, always exaggerated, and the images on the cards themselves were just as melodramatic," Weintraub told me. "They were gaudy and bright and poster-like, which in many ways was not what war was at all. I was just learning how to read. This was all very exotic—we'd never heard of countries like that before." The cards were so popular among kids like Weintraub that Bowman began preparing a set called Z Gum, which was to chronicle British war efforts through the eyes of a hero named the Briton. The set was to include renderings of Germany's recent blitzing of London, but Bowman spiked the issue after the Japanese bombed Pearl Harbor and the United States entered the war. American children wanted cards showing American soldiers in action. So Bowman gave them War Gum, a toned-down version of the Horrors of War series that focused on Allied heroics instead of the massacre of foreign innocents.

This remarkable demand for war cards, as opposed to baseball cards, may be explained partly by the flagging popularity of baseball during the war. Sensing that American involvement in the war would severely disrupt the sport, baseball commissioner Kenesaw Mountain Landis asked FDR shortly after Pearl Harbor whether he should even schedule games. The president urged that baseball continue normal play: the nation's few hundred major-league players provided an important "recreational asset" to some "20,000,000 of their fellow citizens," the president wrote. But pro ballplayers were no more exempt from the draft than common laborers, and soon the leagues suffered a talent drain unlike anything experienced during the Civil War or even World War I.

As more veteran players enlisted, managers were forced to fill their deteriorated rosters with unseasoned youngsters and those who were ineligible for war service, most notably the St. Louis Browns' one-armed outfielder, Pete Gray. In 1944 the Yankees opened the season having lost every starter who'd been in their lineup at the beginning of the war. The league's weakened play was on full display that year, when Yankees first baseman Nick Etten took home the American League batting crown with an unexceptional .309 average. Facing a nationwide rubber shortage, baseball manufacturers were forced to replace the traditionally rubber portions of their products with a latex known as balata. Used at least during the 1943 season, the so-called balata ball, which also included an inferior-grade cork, was believed to have less pop than a traditional Spalding, possibly contributing to the weak hitting during wartime.

Philip K. Wrigley, owner of the Chicago Cubs and heir to his father's gum fortune, was so concerned the major leagues might fold that he established the All-American Girls Professional Baseball League, which debuted in 1943. Their earliest games looked more like modern softball, but the women played according to the livelier base-running rules of baseball and eventually adopted overhand pitching. And though the women learned the art of femininity at cosmetics mogul Helena Rubenstein's Chicago "charm school" during spring training, a *Saturday Evening Post* writer claimed the players had all the gritty hallmarks of their big-league male counterparts—save for the "cud of tobacco."

Still, Wrigley couldn't find a home for the women in major-league parks, and the teams were relegated to smaller venues in such midwestern cities as South Bend, Indiana, and Rockford, Illinois.

With the men's game in a woeful state, stadium attendance plummeted during the war years to an average of fewer than 7,500 fans per major-league game, a fraction of the number seen during healthy seasons. As stars such as Hank Greenberg and Ted Williams went on active duty, kids' imaginations drifted away from baseball and toward war, a development that greatly benefited Bowman. In spite of the lost business with Japan, Bowman's war cards raked in gobs of money for Gum, Inc. Bowman claimed to be pulling down some $40,000 per week for himself when the Horrors of War cards peaked in popularity —a princely sum in the days before World War II. One might even call Bowman a war profiteer. He had a Philadelphia mansion and another in Pass-a-Grille, Florida, as well as a fleet of cars, a speedboat, and a personal schooner, which he used to ferry discounted sugar from Cuba to the States. His business grew so large that he had a Washington lobbyist on retainer. According to one reporter's account, inside his Philadelphia plant Bowman presided over a Dr. No–like office, in which the walls were covered with mirrors and he used an electronic switch to buzz in visitors. He would throw another switch to open a hidden door to his conference room, where there was a cocktail lounge and bar. Bowman's home life was equally playboyish. He went through five wives, the fifth of whom was twenty-eight years his junior and had collected Horrors of War cards as a fourteen-year-old.

For bubble gum and card makers like Bowman, World War II proved to be a mixed blessing. Gum production was eventually crippled. The price of chicle, the main ingredient in natural gum, shot up in the 1940s, and Siamese jelutong, a tree-borne latex that could substitute for chicle, had become scarce on the international market. American bubble gum makers had to reduce or altogether halt production.

Bowman temporarily shut down, and Fleer gave its supply of jelutong to the Rubber Reserve Corporation, which President Roosevelt had created to boost U.S. rubber holdings during the war.

"The wartime chewing-gum shortage has dealt Americans a cruel blow," the *New York Times* declared on Christmas Eve 1944. "The reasons for the shortage are clear. The demand has increased mightily—people are more jittery than they were—and the supply has been cut. . . . There has been no wartime substitute at all for bubble gum. Latex has been completely turned over to our war machine. This shortage has crushed the portion of our population under the 13-year-old level, who can no longer purchase Blony and Dubble Bubble."

Just as the supply of bubble gum tanked, demand for it skyrocketed, in part because of the treat's inclusion in U.S. Army rations. Commonly believed to reduce mental stress and muscle tension, it also helped boost morale and keep tired soldiers awake. In one survey, a majority of American soldiers declared gum one of just three "musts" in any ration, along with cigarettes and candy. A study of Britain's Eighth Air Force found that providing pilots with gum before bombing missions drastically reduced the number of crash landings due to fatigue. Wrigley stopped producing gum for domestic consumption and sent all of its product overseas to American servicemen and -women.

During the war, home-front grocers boosted the price of whatever back stock of bubble gum they had, and children lined up at stores willing to pay several times the normal rate for a chunk of the stuff. They even put chewed gum into glasses of water at night to preserve it for future use. When an Indianapolis café owner told his young customers that they couldn't buy bubble gum unless they first purchased a yo-yo, a throng of preteens picketed against the maneuver with signs that read "We can't chew Yo-Yos" and "No bounty for bubble gum."

Sales exploded after the war ended and synthetic gum bases became readily available. By the late '40s, there were 2.5 billion pieces of bubble gum flowing into stores annually, roughly double prewar production levels. The stuff had become so widespread that a 1947 outbreak of sore throats and vomiting among American children spurred a special investigation into bubble gum by the Food and Drug Administration. The federal agency procured four thousand bubble gum samples and fed them to seventy-five human guinea pigs, twenty-five of them children, who chewed as many as six pieces at once for up to eight hours at a time. Doctors also fed the gum to monkeys and implanted it in the skins of rodents. No hidden dangers were discovered.

Fortunately for the card collectors, the growing popularity of bubble gum happened to coincide with two other postwar phenomena: the baby boom and the glory days of professional baseball. In the years following Bobby Thomson's 1951 "Shot Heard 'Round the World," more children than ever before would be willing to queue up at the candy store to buy gum cards of their heroes. If a manufacturer could find a way to dominate the market, there appeared to be a highly profitable future in baseball cards.

4

Cartophilia

As a curator at the Metropolitan Museum of Art in New York, A. Hyatt Mayor was accustomed to dealing with members of high society. Presiding over one of the finest prints departments in the world, Mayor often found himself looking to the collections of wealthy art patrons in Europe and America for new acquisitions. So he must have been a bit surprised by the potential benefactor who showed up at his door one day in 1947, when Mayor was a year into his post at the museum: a haggard-looking stranger who claimed to have devoted his life to collecting old cigarette and candy cards. At first glance, this unusual endeavor appeared to have taken quite a toll. The man, who wore round-rimmed glasses and cocked his head slightly to the side, looked gaunt and weathered well beyond his forty-seven years. As Mayor would later recall, "On first meeting, one felt sorry for this racked, frail man, with black-lashed eyes of a haunting gray violet."

Jefferson Burdick had traveled from upstate New York by train with the express purpose of introducing himself to Mayor and checking out the Met's print collection. He suffered from rheumatoid arthritis, a chronic, systemic, and degenerative form of the disease, and he wanted to find a home for the massive and as yet unorganized collection of trading cards that was crowding him out of his modest boarding room in downtown Syracuse before his illness progressed much more. He had no exact count, but the cards numbered in the thousands, and they included everything from 1880s tobacco sets right up to the latest issues. Even though by then a small hobby had sprouted up in which like-minded collectors bought or swapped such cards with one another, Burdick said that he wanted nothing in the way of money for his collection. Instead, he hoped only to pass away knowing that his cards would be well preserved and available to the public.

Mayor showed Burdick the cards that the museum already had in its collection, which were few, and urged him to visit other institutions, such as the New York Public Library and the Museum of Fine Arts, in Boston, that could care just as well for his collection. Mayor wasn't exactly brushing Burdick off, but he wasn't taking the man and his cards all that seriously, either. "I did not know then how large it was, I must say," Mayor later said of Burdick's cache, "or I would not have been so cavalier about it." Burdick took the curator's advice and spent a few days on the road sizing up other museums in the East.

He was back at Mayor's door within a week. He said he liked how the Met took care of things, which was his way of saying that he wanted his baseball and trading cards—then considered by most people to be worthless ephemera —kept in the country's preeminent art museum, in the same department as prints by Albrecht Dürer and Edgar Degas. Mayor accepted the donation on the condition that the benefactor organize the collection himself—an unusual arrangement for a museum bequest.

"Mayor didn't have the curatorial staff to do it himself," Elliot Bostwick Davis, a former Met curator, told me. "It was a huge job, and I think he saw that Burdick was willing to do it. It was a life's project."

Burdick returned to Syracuse and set to work. That December Mayor received the first shipment of Burdick's cards, all of them neatly tied up and labeled according to their sets. Each year from then on for more than a decade anywhere from two to six cartons holding several thousand unique cards would arrive from Syracuse as Burdick ordered his collection according to a system of his own devising. What had been an after-hours avocation became a full-time obsession. As his health deteriorated, Burdick gave up his day job at a manufacturing plant and moved to Manhattan in hopes of transferring his entire collection to the Met before an almost certain early death.

Now a cult hero among hard-core hobbyists, Burdick was the first truly monomaniacal card hunter, and many people credit him with establishing an organized hobby that now includes thousands of collectors. A reasonably well educated recluse who spent most of his days performing manual labor, Burdick threw all of his spare time and money into trading cards long before it was believed that such items could hold serious value, whether monetary or cultural. The tobacco and gum industries had yielded enough cards by midcentury to make Burdick's project a colossal one: he wanted to identify and order every American trading card ever made. The pioneering research he did on baseball cards starting in the 1930s provided the foundation for today's thriving secondary market.

In spite of his poverty he also assembled what remains one of the most impressive card collections in the world. Containing hundreds of thousands of rare vintage cards, some ten thousand of which are from early baseball issues, the trove at the Met is unlikely to be bested by any present-day collection, including those assembled by the wealthiest of baby boomer nostalgia nuts. That's not simply because Burdick was a pioneer. He was also one of the most passionate lovers of cardboard images the hobby has ever known. Indeed, as Burdick toiled frantically at the museum in the years leading up to his death, his few friends would come to believe that the cards were the only thing keeping him alive.

Little is known about Burdick's personal life. He never married or had any children; he had no confidants as far as surviving acquaintances can tell; and during his lifetime few people considered his collecting pursuits worth writing about. His 1963 death went unnoticed by his hometown newspaper, and his anonymity was such that his ashes lay in an unmarked grave between his parents' for more than thirty years. By 1997, after his name had become legendary among collectors, a casual friend who'd once worked alongside Burdick sprang for a tombstone: "Jefferson Burdick—One of the greatest card collectors of all times."

Nearly all that can be said of Burdick's early existence is that he grew up on a dairy farm run by his parents in Central Square, New York, and that he harbored a peculiar love for trading cards, every set of which he would one day call "a glorious picture window of the past." For what might be the only newspaper story written about him while he was alive, Burdick told a reporter from the *Syracuse Herald-American* in 1955 that the very first cards he collected were the cigarette issues of his youth. In Burdick's preteen years, most of those would have come from the American Tobacco Company's myriad products. "Practically every small boy saved these kinds of cards. We made our dads use certain brands whether they liked them or not," he explained. "Some ask how anyone becomes interested in cards. You don't become interested—collectors are born that way. Card collecting is primarily an inherited love of pictures."

As a boy fascinated with paper and images, Burdick was fortunate that his childhood happened to coincide with what some collectors consider the second heyday of card production, the period running from roughly 1909 to 1915. Having seen how baseball cards worked marketing wonders for Buck Duke and American Tobacco, companies from the candy, dairy, bread, and publishing industries began releasing their own sets of kid-oriented trading cards in the years leading up to the Great War. Like their forerunners of the 1880s, these cards depicted anything and everything American, but the ones most treasured by children bore the faces of ballplayers. Companies such as American Caramel and the *Sporting News* all helped provide kids with portraits of a generation of future Hall of Famers that included Walter Johnson and Christy Mathewson. "Perhaps the cards held in closest affection are those given away with candy and gums about 1910," Burdick wrote in a 1950 *Hobbies* magazine article. "Many a collector remembers putting those precious pennies on the candy counter and pointing to the caramels with the cards."

Some of the finest baseball cards of this era were those stuffed into boxes of Cracker Jack as part of the company's new "A Prize in Every Box" initiative. In 1914 alone, the candy maker produced twenty-five million baseball cards on thin paper stock, with artfully illustrated portraits superimposed over soft red backgrounds. Among Cracker Jack's cards' many admirers was a young Burdick, who went to great lengths to secure cards that hadn't been stained by the greasy caramel-covered popcorn and peanuts with which they had shared a box.

As Burdick carried his inherited love of pictures into adulthood, he grew serious about obtaining and identifying all of the cigarette and most of the candy and bubble gum cards that had ever been issued. "If anyone has the idea that a complete collection of cigarette cards is a small affair easily gotten together, he is in for a big surprise," he wrote in *Hobbies* in 1936. "No one, probably, has ever had a complete collection or even a nearly complete one. I know of no records or data regarding the number of sets issued and even the number of cards in some sets is unknown." Resolving such mysteries would become Burdick's life's work. Collectible cards being an unexplored field, he started from scratch: "I must rely mostly on data gleaned from the cards themselves. No doubt much of it will be proved inaccurate and I'm sure most of it will be incomplete. But things have to start in some way." The first sets Burdick cataloged were from Duke, Goodwin, and Allen & Ginter.

Burdick found that the best way to complete his sets was to keep in touch with a network of other devoted collectors through the mail. One of his better connections in this cardboard community was a baseball card fanatic from Illinois named Lionel Carter. Not long before he died in 2008 at age ninety, Carter invited me to his home in Evanston to talk about Burdick and the early days of the baseball card hobby. Shortly before my visit, the retired bank manager and World War II veteran had earned his fifteen minutes of wire-story fame when he sold off the massive and unusually pristine card collection he'd been accruing since 1933. All told, his auction lots netted more than $1 million.

Nothing inside Carter's modest rambler betrayed his recent financial windfall, and nothing in his demeanor did, either. It didn't seem possible for a recently minted millionaire to have looked more sullen while explaining how he'd come into his money. "I feel terrible, just awful," Carter said of parting with his collection. "I'll never recover from it."

The auction of his cards had been spurred by a robbery at Carter's home, after which the Evanston police told him that he shouldn't leave his collection sitting unlocked in a cabinet like second-rate silverware. Because the cards would have been no fun in a safe-deposit box, he decided to unload them. He'd never collected with the intention of selling his cards, and he seemed to resent the exorbitant values his cards had attained. Like Gidwitz, he told me that high prices had "ruined the hobby," even though he, too, benefited from them.

To understand just how debased the card market has become, Carter told me, I would have to understand collecting as it was when it sprouted up around Burdick in the 1930s and '40s.

In 1937, Burdick launched a crude but comprehensive newsletter called *Card Collectors Bulletin,* in which he editorialized a bit on collecting and, more important, listed the individual cards and sets that other collectors were willing to put up for sale. (Burdick himself didn't sell cards—he wanted only to obtain them.) Although it landed in a mere handful of mailboxes every few weeks, the newsletter served as the first means of discussion among a band of adults who were hooked on a child's pastime and perhaps felt a bit sheepish about it. It surely gave some collectors a sense of relief when they recognized like-minded souls in its pages.

As Bill Mastro, the auctioneer who sold Carter's collection, explained to me, "There really wasn't a hobby back then. There were no conventions. It was really—and when I say this, I don't mean it as a lack of respect—it was a hobby full of old men who were closet collectors. Even in the 1960s, if you said you were into baseball cards, people looked at you like you were a fag. *Oh, isn't that nice?* That's what you got. You didn't talk about it because you were an outcast."

The cards advertised in the *Bulletin* typically went for little more than a penny apiece. In fact, values were so secondary that when Carter submitted an advertisement reading "I WILL PAY TEN CENTS A CARD FOR ANY CARD I NEED," Burdick dashed off a testy note in which he scolded his colleague for boosting prices. "He said, 'You'll ruin the hobby. You're going to start inflation,'" Carter recalled. "You'd never find a card in there priced at more than two or three cents apiece. And that's when it was fun." He said that he once had the opportunity to buy the T206 Honus Wagner for $125 but that he took a pass, even though his wife urged him to make the purchase. Carter firmly believed that he made the right move and insisted that $125 is an outrageous price to pay for a baseball card.

Burdick was of a similar mind, knowing that the more prices climbed, the more difficult it would be to obtain the cards he wanted. In this regard, he was the archetypal purist collector, believing that money could only degrade his hobby. It was Burdick's love for the cards themselves, independent of their values, that prompted Carter to pen a tribute to him after his death: "Jeff Burdick lifted card collecting from an almost forgotten and unorganized level to the high plateau it now occupies. In the years before Burdick, there were no dealers, no catalogs, no publications dedicated to card collecting. Yet he stood not to gain from his efforts, and did not. . . . There will never be an equal to J. R. Burdick in our hobby."

By the time he and Carter began trading letters, Burdick had started assembling a catalog in which he hoped to document every set of cards issued from the nineteenth century on. This would have been an incredibly challenging pursuit, given the difficulties collectors had communicating —long-distance calls were too expensive for average Americans to place regularly in those days—and the fact that some cards were issued only in certain regions of the country. His work in progress was called *The American Card Catalog,* and he eventually put out three editions that are now considered the foundation of the baseball card hobby. Creating and updating his catalog appears to have been a constant source of stress for Burdick, who had to square the importance he saw in such work with the fact that he probably wouldn't break even on it after publishing expenses. "A book is just a pound of waste paper unless you can sell it," he lamented to Carter in a letter.

In his catalog, Burdick assigns each card set a number as well as a letter to note which industry it came from—T for "20th-century tobacco," E for "early candy and gum," R for "recent candy," and so on. This is how the American Tobacco Wagner received its famous T206 designation. Indeed, all of the designations that Burdick created, first published in 1937, are still in use today. "Burdick was like a vacuum cleaner when it came to rare cards," card auctioneer Rob Lifson told me. "And one of the great things that his system did, it allowed people to easily refer to a certain set. It also gave people some organization to collecting—and all of collecting is in part about organizing. He understood the landscape of what existed in cards more than anyone before him, and he came up with a way to order it. I think it's an intelligent way, a way that allowed collectors to communicate about cards. He created order out of chaos, and everything is built around that."

As difficult as it was to find rare card issues, Burdick took no shortcuts in his cataloging. When Carter informed Burdick of some baseball sets he hadn't been aware of, he was surprised to hear that Burdick wouldn't put the issues in his catalog until he verified their existence in person.

"He would never put anything in his catalog unless he saw it himself," Carter recalled. "So he came all the way from Syracuse just to see those cards. He was badly crippled up, I mean terribly. I don't know how he even traveled. . . . Anyway, we chatted, and I had a two-bedroom apartment, so I offered that he spend the night with me. He wouldn't do it. I don't think he accepted anything from anybody. He had a show he wanted to go to in Evanston where they had some tents set up, selling everything imaginable: Christmas cards, greeting cards, even personal cards—he collected all that stuff. He bought a little something from every table, and he said, 'You want to do that, because someday the guy you bought from might have something you really want, and he'll know who you are.' None of it interested me but baseball cards. But he was into everything imaginable. He went right back to Syracuse that night."

Pen pals like Carter were often aghast when they finally met Burdick in person. His arthritis knotted his hands and twisted his neck and back, contorting him so badly that an acquaintance once remarked that an act as simple as putting on his hat required of Burdick "a good minute's engineering."

He might have been crippled by his day job. He worked as a parts assembler at the Crouse-Hinds Electric Company in downtown Syracuse, putting together electric switches for mines and flour mills. It was exacting work done with the hands, and though Burdick's acquaintances marveled at how he did such labor, the even greater mystery is why. Although Burdick never completed an undergraduate degree, he did receive a certificate in business administration from Syracuse University in 1922. Surely he could have found administrative work that was less taxing on his body. Perhaps he simply enjoyed working with his hands, just as he enjoyed handling small cards and pasting them into albums. "He was just a quiet guy," said Milton Juengel, a ninety-one-year-old from Liverpool, New York, who worked in the same room as Burdick at Crouse-Hinds. "Every once in a while, I'd help him get his cards together at his apartment. Very nice guy, but a loner."

Burdick traveled far in search of rarities, and though such time on the road and rails was spent alone, he seemed happy when on the hunt.

During one trip to Florida, he wrote a letter to Carter: "Tuesday I'm going to Lakeland to buy an album from a school teacher . . . a lot of T206s and over 100 Contentneas and I'll have to pay about catalog [price]. Friday I'll go over to Augustine to see their antique show and hope to find some cards, but probably not. The South isn't good 'card country,' although I once did get a big cigar box full of dandy old cards from South Carolina. You never can tell when they'll turn up."

His job at the Crouse-Hinds plant afforded Burdick just enough money to rent a room downtown and keep up with his cards. As his physical condition deteriorated, he moved into an apartment directly across the street from his workplace. He never owned a house and, as a bachelor, never really needed one. Met curator Mayor surmised that it was Burdick's arthritis that kept him from finding a wife. "Illness probably prevented him from marrying," he wrote in the introduction to a museum publication on Burdick's collection. "The energy that he may have put into making a home and bringing up a family, he poured instead into studying insert cards, into editing the *Card Collectors Bulletin*, until he had made himself into an expert whose opinion carried authority far and wide."

Or perhaps it was collecting that kept Burdick from having a romantic relationship. To judge from Juengel's description of Burdick's apartment, the man had no room for anything in his life aside from cards. Even fellow cardboard accumulator Carter, who probably heard as much from Burdick as anyone, seemed utterly stumped when asked what the father of baseball card collecting was really like. If Burdick was never understood by his collector compatriots, who shared his one driving passion, then it comes as no great surprise that he never let a woman into his life. It didn't help that his favorite pastime put him in touch almost exclusively with men. In an article entitled "Cards for the Ladies," which Burdick wrote as part of a series on trading cards in *Hobbies* magazine, he bemoaned the lack of women interested in the hobby. "One would think the many beautiful designs would have a stronger attraction," he noted wistfully.

Perhaps the one collector who hunted tobacco cards as aggressively as Burdick did was his correspondent and British counterpart Edward Wharton-Tigar. Like Burdick, Wharton-Tigar was a general-interest collector obsessed with cardboard images; he once told an interviewer, "I would like to have an example of every card ever issued. It's a form of megalomania of course. But not, I think, a bad form." Unlike Burdick, Wharton-Tigar had a rich and adventurous life outside of cardboard, having been a decorated spy for the Allies during World War II and later a powerful executive in the diamond industry. Though he would go on to accumulate more than a million cards and donate them all to London's British Museum, Wharton-Tigar didn't consider collecting his life. Rather, it was a distraction from it. As he wrote in his autobiography, "I fully recognise that there are those who think, and will always think, that people must be very odd to devote time, effort and money to the collection of such things as stamps, matchbox labels and cigarette cards. For me, my collection has not only afforded countless hours of pleasure, but in a busy business career it provided a diversion and relaxation in times of stress. . . . If to collect cigarette cards is a sign of eccentricity, how then will posterity judge one who amassed the biggest collection in the world? Frankly, I care not."

Mayor, who died in 1980, was just as impassioned a collector as Wharton-Tigar or Burdick. Born a year after Burdick, in 1901, he was the nephew of a sculptor and wealthy art patron, and he studied art history at Princeton, continuing his education at Oxford as a Rhodes scholar. After he assumed the curator's position in the Met's print department, he made his mark in the art world by acquiring much of the collection belonging to the Prince of Liechtenstein. While most interested parties wrangled for the Rembrandts, Mayor sought out the less expensive and more underappreciated of the prince's possessions, including engraved copies of works by Raphael.

Because of acquisitions like that, Mayor is remembered in the museum world as a visionary. A *New York Times* art critic once called Mayor "one of the most remarkable men ever to hold a curatorial post," explaining that his brilliance was in how he scooped up rarities that few museums appreciated: "The print department at the Met, as it was eventually reshaped by Hyatt Mayor, has the peculiarity that it includes material of almost every imaginable kind. It has the masterpieces that people expect to see in a great museum—the prints by Goya and Goltzius are good examples—but it also has areas in which Hyatt Mayor did the work of a pioneer." Many of the unconvential pieces of ephemera that he acquired, such as sheet music covers and antique commercial catalogs, "are rarer than Rembrandt, yet Hyatt Mayor was able to buy them for almost nothing," the critic explained.

Indeed, Mayor knew how to acquire pieces at knockdown prices. According to some of Mayor's old colleagues, one dealer offered Mayor his private collection at an outrageous price, knowing full well how badly the curator wanted it. Mayor demurred, waiting ten years for the dealer to pass away so he could buy the works on the cheap. "Undertaking," he quipped, "is a big part of this job." He had a special love for the kinds of prints and cards that he believed were "meant to be seen by people who did not mean to see them"—wine labels, film posters, and other everyday ephemera. As his colleagues note in an introduction to a memorial volume of his writings, "Hyatt not only went out of his way to be helpful, but also took pains never to take the edge off someone else's special enthusiasm, no matter how peculiar it might appear in the academic world. An intelligent report on beautifully designed and printed tissue wrappers for oranges could entertain him a great deal more than a student's rapture in repeating in English everything about Dürer learned from German texts. And besides, he had nothing but laughter for the pompous and pretentious."

It's no wonder that Mayor took a chance on the rheumatic switch assembler from Syracuse and his card collection. By 1959 the maverick academic was even sharing his work space with the inspired amateur.

Severely ill, Burdick had left his job at the factory and headed to Manhattan, where he settled in a room at a hotel near Twenty-sixth Street and Madison Avenue. He took a small oak desk to the Met, placed it in the corner of the print department, and began working as if against a clock. According to Mayor, Burdick's nook in the museum "at once became the American headquarters of cartophiles from everywhere."

Although Burdick was only fifty-nine, in his letters from this period he writes dispassionately about the imminent death he saw for himself. He seems concerned not so much with dying as with the prospect of leaving his grand undertaking incomplete. He explained his decision to quit work in a letter to Carter.

I do think that every collector should arrange for some disposition of his collection when he passes on and if he can foresee the date of passing, it might be OK to dispose of them himself shortly ahead of such date, but you aren't in that category, yet. [When] I made arrangements for my cards . . . I was getting rather poor physically and I didn't know how long [I had]. . . . I still say the trick is to retire early enough. As time goes on, I see ever so many waiting until they literally have one foot in the grave before they quit. Then the retirement period is too short, as it probably will be for me. Nobody can figure accurately how many years are left for them.

Burdick's first challenge after the Met decided to accept his donation was figuring out how to mount his cards for public viewing without damaging them irreparably. Baseball card lovers who now visit Burdick's collection invariably comment on how foolish he was to glue his cards into albums, wondering if perhaps he didn't realize that the adhesive could ruin the cards. But Burdick knew the dangers well. In his catalog, he told readers to use art corners and a cellophane covering to hold cards in place. "Never stick cards down with paste," he stated flatly. So why did Burdick ignore his own advice and risk damaging the massive collection he had spent his life assembling? Perhaps he didn't mind diminishing his cards' monetary value so long as their research value remained intact. After all, he considered his cards visual records of America's past. What did it matter if they couldn't be pulled from their albums without skinning their backs?

The card mounting was a tremendous undertaking. Burdick had completed a mere thirty-four albums when he headed to Manhattan in 1959, leaving an additional three hundred yet to do. He had accrued well over three hundred thousand cards, all of which had to be glued down in the order that he had laid out in *The American Card Catalog*. Even unnumbered sets of baseball cards were arranged in a Burdick-determined sequence, team by team. Given Burdick's declining health, his daily progress must have been infinitesimal. "My health is definitely on the down trend," he wrote in a letter to Carter from New York. "A few years ago a doctor examined me and pronounced me a 'Medical Museum.' Today I have at least two or three additional ailments—rather bad ones. I hope to hold together long enough to complete the card-mounting job here, but there's no guarantee. . . . I'm getting pretty badly bent and twisted out of shape and my clothes, for example, just don't drape around me gracefully any more. Some might say I looked like something the cat dragged in."

One winter morning, I headed to the Met to see the albums as Burdick had assembled them. The Jefferson R. Burdick Collection has been a major attraction for the museum ever since it started putting selected cards on public view in the American Wing, in 1993. Though it's the most expansive and valuable gathering of cards in any American museum, the Burdick collection isn't exactly a consensus favorite among Met staffers. One doesn't typically pursue a doctorate in art history with the idea of someday handling 1939 Play Ball cards. "I thought baseball cards were put in bike spokes, not museums," one curatorial assistant in the print department complained to the *New Yorker* in

1990. "I love Old Masters prints, but most people who make an appointment to visit our collection have no interest in seeing them."

All they want to see is Burdick's baseball cards. And so museum officials hoping to boost foot traffic began using the cards as a draw for a new generation of easily bored children. As Davis, the former Met curator, wrote in a 1994 article, "The decision to place baseball cards on permanent exhibition at the finest museum in this country was strategically calculated to attract a younger audience to the museum." Burdick's cards have become a blessing and a burden, requiring an allotment of resources that some museum staffers might believe could be better used elsewhere—although Davis, for one, has become a great admirer of the collection. "They tell a history of popular printmaking in the United States," she said. "They documented a way of approaching sports figures and portraiture itself. I began to really love the Play Ball Hall of Fame set of '41. They did a lot with shadows."

When I visited the Burdick Collection, Catherine Jenkins, an assistant curator in the prints department, asked that I request to see only a few of the albums containing baseball cards. The albums with Old Judges and T206s and Cracker Jacks, she explained, had been pulled for visitors so frequently over the previous twenty years that they'd grown worn and fragile. I'd had to submit a special request to the curator just to get in the door. "If we let everyone see all the baseball cards they wanted, then that's all this space would be used for," Jenkins said of the study room. I gave her a meager list of seven albums, which was all the card viewing that one day will allow me, and she returned and placed the first one on a foam cradle in front of me.

When I opened it, the first thing that struck me was the handwriting on the title page. The words "U.S. Advertising Cards" had been sketched in a shaky hand, then written and rewritten over, as if by a child trying to get it just right. Apparently, scrawling even just a few words was an ordeal for Burdick in the last years of his life. Turning the pages, I discovered Burdick's collection was more wide-ranging than I'd been led to believe, containing not only cards but matchbook covers, cigar bands, gum wrappers, and lapel buttons—all stuff that was meant to be seen by people who did not mean to see it. A social history of the late nineteenth century was told by the earliest cards, some of them charming in their pastoral simplicity, others disturbing in their racist caricature of African Americans. Knowing that Burdick was a lifelong bachelor who lived alone makes it impossible to view the many cards showing beautiful Victorian women and cherubic children without feeling a little melancholy. As sentimental as he was, the collector would have been moved by such romantic images, as he suggests in the introduction to the 1953 edition of *The American Card Catalog.*

People were saving all these cards—to look at again and again during long evenings when snow piled high outside the windows. Thus our love of picture cards is an inherited one from many generations back. Today we have highly illustrated books, magazines and papers, plus movies and television, but many of us still enjoy drifting back to the days of our forefathers and reliving the scenes and customs of those bygone times. Even the old scrapbooks bring back a picture of loving fingers clipping and pasting to make the cards more presentable, and incidentally preserving them for our enjoyment long years afterward.

Rather than organize his cards by time period, Burdick grouped them according to the industries that created them, under headings such as "bread, flour, pastry" and "starch, yeast, sodas." In Album 246, which is filled with tobacco issues, Burdick pasted eighteen pages' worth of the famous T206 cards, numbering around five hundred specimens, including five different Ty Cobbs; three examples of the scarce Eddie Plank, which is probably the third most valuable baseball card known; and, of course, the celebrated Wagner card, which was removed in 1993 and put on display in the American Wing. Burdick knew the story behind the Wagner and had apparently struggled to obtain one for himself. Even as he tried to keep card prices down, he acknowledged the Wagner's scarcity and value, pricing it in his 1960 catalog at a whopping $50—the highest of any card—compared to just ten cents for most other T206s.

In a testament to the genial nature of the early network of card collectors, hobby legend holds that an acquaintance of Burdick's who had a double of the Wagner card gave him one for free. Burdick also managed to obtain a handful of the controversial 1934 Goudey Napoleon Lajoie cards after sending the gum company a letter asking why the card had never turned up in packs. He gave away most of the cards that the company sent him, including one that he presented to Carter and was sold for more than $31,000 at auction. Some modern collectors credit Burdick for disseminating a good portion of the few Lajoies that are still in existence.

I found some of Burdick's most valuable and visually arresting cards in Album 315, which is loaded with inserts put out by candy companies. Here he pasted nine pages of Cracker Jack cards, amounting to two complete sets in fine condition, one from 1914 and the other from 1915, either of which could fetch hundreds of thousands of dollars today. Looking at the Cracker Jacks in particular, I was surprised by how fastidious Burdick had been with his mounting: all of the cards seemed to be in perfectly straight rows.

Such careful work would have been impossible if not for the early 1950s advent of the wonder drug cortisone, which Burdick credited with keeping his fingers functional enough to build electric switches at work and to handle cards at the museum. Mayor recalled how feverishly Burdick worked under intense pain: "We bought him more and more scrapbook binders, more and more pure rag pages, and more and more pots of paste. As he labored, his stiffening arthritis obliged him to take an amount of cortisone that made him feel still worse. He was boxed in the choice between dying of the disease or dying of the remedy. The mounting pile of full scrapbooks drove him to work at an ever more desperate pace. From time to time he would say quite impersonally, as though he were talking about a race horse: 'I may not make it.'"

Even to some of his fellow collectors, Burdick's monomaniacal project must have appeared a poor use of his ever dwindling time. He seemed never to return home to Syracuse, and even fairly close acquaintances weren't sure whether Burdick had anything close to a family beyond his band of cartophiles. Preston Orem, who assembled a legendary collection of baseball cards himself, assisted Burdick in editing *The American Card Catalog,* along with Woody Gelman, who at the time was leading the design team for Topps baseball cards. Orem looked upon Burdick's mission at the Met with a degree of pity. In a letter to another collector he wrote, "Jeff Burdick is a prince, an astonishing one-track mind on nothing but cards. . . . [But] no museum for me, shudder to think of pasting the cards down with library paste as they are doing. . . . Actually, cards are a stepchild at the museum, but Burdick does not realize it." Orem, of all people, should have sympathized with his friend's frantic and financially compromising labor. At the time, he was traveling the country assembling an extensive anthology of newspaper accounts on early baseball. Eventually, he would have to sell off much of his beloved baseball card collection to finance its publication.

For Burdick, of course, the real problem wasn't money —it was time. By 1962, it appears, merely writing letters had become a difficult undertaking for him. After he checked himself into Bellevue Hospital Center for treatment, unsure of whether he could write out his new address legibly, he sent a letter to Carter. "The enclosed sugar bag will show you my present address," the letter read. "Probably in for a couple of weeks for a thorough checkup and treatment. My condition was getting so unbearable that I had to do something. . . . I hope to be out about the time the shop opens at [collector Charlie] Bray's, but you can see I won't be in any condition to make the trip over unless I could do it in a private car and I don't know of anyone with a car who would make the trip. . . . I'm more sorry than I can tell you about missing the show."

In another note dated July 7, 1962, Burdick declined an invitation to Carter's home, preferring instead to devote whatever time he had left to the card project: "Don't plan on flying me to Chicago. I'm still too shaky on the feet to roam very far. Have resumed work on the cards at the museum and hope to finish the job this Fall. It's an awful mess."

Burdick was too optimistic. His work at the museum carried beyond the fall and into 1963, as he grew more and more debilitated. Finally, on January 10, he pasted his final item, number 306,353, into the last of his 394 albums and boxes. At five p.m. that day, he told the staff of the prints department that he was finished. Despite Burdick's long illness, they didn't suspect that he'd be in the hospital the very next day, or that he'd die of an exhausted heart within two months.

As Mayor later wrote, Burdick looked tired. He writhed into his overcoat and bade farewell to the curator.

"I shan't be back," he said.

5

The Great Changemaker

Inside the offices of Topps Chewing Gum Inc. in the early 1950s, there wasn't a more unlikely partnership than the one being forged between Sy Berger and Woody Gelman. The two men shared almost nothing in common, aside from their childhoods in Brooklyn and their employment at the Topps offices in the waterfront district. The straight-laced Berger was an aspiring businessman with a knack for networking and schmoozing, a recent college grad with an accountant's education and mind. Gelman, to the contrary, was an established but disorganized commercial artist with a background in cartoons, an eccentric who was drawn to people who shared his oddball interests—trading cards, pulp art, and comic books. Berger and Gelman were thrown together largely by chance, after the president of Topps, Joseph E. Shorin, decided the company would invest heavily in baseball cards. He tasked the two men with creating a radically different kind of card.

What Shorin and his underlings had in mind was a card that boys would snatch up compulsively because of its design and features, and not simply because it was there every spring. Having seen the recent success of Bowman in Philadelphia, Shorin and his three brothers, who collectively owned Topps, believed that there was a prosperous future in cardboard. The game of baseball itself was in the midst of a golden age, and the nearly perennial success of the New York Yankees and the

Brooklyn Dodgers in the late 1940s and early '50s had been consuming young boys in the Shorins' Crown Heights neighborhood from April to October. The Shorins wanted to break into the card market before Bowman ran away with it.

So Berger and Gelman started spending more and more time together as they tried to come up with a card that would appeal to children more than Bowman's offerings. After working long days at the Topps offices, they got together for late-night brainstorming sessions at Berger's apartment on Alabama Avenue in Brooklyn. As they sat on the couch or at the kitchen table, Berger, who'd collected Goudeys as a child, would tell Gelman what features he'd like to see on a card, and Gelman would sketch mock-ups. The card they ended up developing included a number of features that had rarely, if ever, turned up on earlier sports cards. For one thing, they decided to leave a space beneath each player's name where they could place a facsimile of his autograph. Beside that, they put a team logo, a seemingly obvious flourish that in fact had hardly ever been featured on baseball cards. Another innovation was the back of the new design. As a youngster, Berger, the accountant, had been obsessed with computing his favorite players' averages over the newspaper at the breakfast table. He thought that children might enjoy reading each player's statistics in a more kid-friendly format. Previously, the only time player stats had been included on baseball cards was when they were woven into a short biographical paragraph.

Perhaps the most radical departure from typical baseball cards was in size. Cards of the day usually measured around two inches by two and a half inches, in the tradition of tobacco and candy cards from the 1910s and '20s. Berger and Gelman thought that the Topps card should eclipse the others, offering more detail in the pictures and a more resilient piece of cardboard. The clear solution was to make it bigger. The mock-up they came up with measured two and five-eighths inches by three and three-quarters inches, which would become the rough dimensions of all future baseball cards, no matter which company produced them.

Berger and Gelman had created the prototype for the modern baseball card. The design elements of the 1952 Topps set would kindle not only the imaginations of baseball-loving children but also their collector's instincts. Topps was on its way to dominating the field of baseball cards for the next forty years.

Long before it became Topps Chewing Gum, Morris Shorin's family enterprise was known as the American Leaf Tobacco Company, which began importing Turkish tobacco for American cigar makers in 1890. After two decades of growth, the firm began to founder during World War I, when U.S. companies lost much of their access to Turkish tobacco leaves.

The Great Depression strained the business even more, and as hard times wore on, Morris's four sons—Joseph, Philip, Ira, and Abram— thought that they might be able to reverse the downturn by diversifying. Having noted the success of companies such as Fleer and Bowman's Gum, Inc., the brothers decided, in 1938, to start manufacturing bubble gum. After renaming the company Topps—as in "tops in the field," with an added "p" for brand recognition —they released their first dime-store gum.

Only a few years into this new line of business, the Shorins had to face yet another marketplace setback: the sugar rationing and jelutong latex shortage of World War II, which crippled gum production throughout the country. In a clever bit of marketing, the brothers managed to turn the dearth of gum to their advantage by introducing a cute wartime slogan that played on national loyalty and fears of espionage: "Don't Talk, Chum—Chew Topps Gum." The campaign helped Topps keep its brand name alive during a slow period, and as production boomed and the gum industry grew more competitive following the war, the

Shorins tried to brand Topps gum as "The Changemaker"—the perfect way to snag those couple of cents a customer would otherwise have gotten back from the cashier at the corner store.

Like other candy makers, Topps went after kids' pennies through cheap novelties such as comic strips and trading cards. Their early gum cards took advantage of the sometimes fleeting popularity of non–sports figures such as cowboy Hopalong Cassidy, real-life "collector of animals" Frank Buck, and pioneer Davy Crockett, who, as the subject of a Disney-produced television show, caused a sensation in school yards in the early to mid-1950s. Unfortunately, such trends tended to run their courses fairly quickly. One day it was Davy Crockett, the next it was Daniel Boone, and the card makers had no sure way to keep ahead of the fickle minds of gum-chewing children.

The young and aggressive Berger, however, recognized the perennial success of sports cards. "All this time, all the early days, late '40s and early '50s, we're looking over at the Bowman Gum Company," Berger once told *Sports Collectors Digest*. "And they had baseball and football cards, and it was a very fascinating thing. You could depend on it every year. You could put out a series of baseball cards, football cards, and wow, you knew they were going to sell. You didn't have to worry whether kids liked it that year or not. They liked it all the time." In 1950 alone, Topps watched Bowman disseminate 200 million baseball cards for total sales of about $1 million, then a substantial sum for a gum maker. Topps wanted a sure thing, too. Berger went to Joseph Shorin—the reputed namesake of the Topps company's Bazooka Joe bubble gum—and convinced him that Topps could not only do baseball cards but also do them far better than Bowman.

Even back then, there was a history of costly litigation surrounding the production of baseball-themed bubble gum cards. When a Boston-based manufacturer called Gum Products, Inc., put out its Double Play card series in 1941, St. Louis Cardinals first baseman and future Hall of Famer Johnny Mize sued the company for using his image without permission. Like Honus Wagner, Mize was ahead of his time. Ballplayers in

those days paid little attention to their publicity rights, tending to welcome the free exposure of such cards rather than question their legitimacy. The card manufacturer won the case against Mize, but it had to
halt the production of Double Plays because of the cost of litigation. To
avoid any legal tussles the Bowman Company thought it would be wise
to secure cheap contracts with most of the ballplayers whose likenesses it
would be reproducing.

In Joseph Shorin's view Topps needed to ink agreements with the
majority of big leaguers if the company hoped to square off against
Bowman on candy-store counters. So Shorin and a lawyer friend created a company called Players Enterprises that billed itself as a marketing firm for ballplayers. Players Enterprises delivered Topps enough
contracts for the company to roll out its inaugural baseball series. But
this wasn't the celebrated and successful 1952 set that Berger and
Gelman would devise—it was the little-known and largely disastrous
batch of cards known as the Red Backs and Blue Backs of 1951.

Along with showing a big leaguer's disembodied head, each card in
the set represents a particular baseball play—a walk, perhaps, or a fly
out—so that youngsters could "play" against each other with a stack
of cards. The Red Backs and Blue Backs therefore functioned as both
unsightly baseball cards and dreadfully boring playing cards. Worse yet,
the set suffered from a game-ending production problem. Because
Bowman's contracts appeared to grant the company the exclusive right
to market baseball cards with bubble gum specifically, the Shorins believed that they could avoid a lawsuit if they packaged their cards with
taffy instead. A problem at the printer meant that the cards were
coated with a varnish that was transferred to the taffy during packaging, making the candy taste even worse than the stick gum that came
with Bowman's cards.

"You wouldn't dare put that taffy near your mouth," Berger once
explained. "I won't mention the printer's name who printed the cards,
but we ended up suing him, and that '51 series really was a disaster."
The cards failed to turn a profit, and Topps abandoned its taffy efforts

for the time being. The company made another abortive pre-1952 attempt at baseball cards with its Magic Photos set of 1948. These diminutive cards measure about an inch by an inch and a half, and they flopped with children because the magic rarely materialized. The front of the cards feature invisible portraits of ballplayers and historical figures that were supposed to develop after the application of water and the Topps Company's patented "magic" chemical. If the player did appear—and there was no guarantee that he would—he looked more like a ghost than a flesh-and-blood diamond hero.

What the Shorins needed was a simple but attractive baseball card they could package with the only confection Topps handled well: bubble gum. But first they needed to obtain the rights to produce such cards, which meant they had to infiltrate the closed ranks of Major League Baseball.

To learn more about how Topps managed to secure its legally unassailable position atop the card world, I visited Berger one spring afternoon at his home in Rockville Centre, on Long Island, New York. When I knocked, the then eighty-four-year-old shuffled to the door wearing round glasses, a baby-blue collared shirt emblazoned with the Topps logo, and a pair of khakis hiked over his stomach. In the living room, he pulled out a ten-pound book that contained reproductions of every card Topps printed over the course of thirty-five years. Berger had retired just a few years ago, after a half century with the firm.

"Topps was a company I loved," he said. "The day I went to Topps was the first day they made Bazooka. The factory was upstairs above the offices. They didn't have room for the bubble gum up there, so they put it behind the offices. I came home every night smelling like sugar and gum."

As Berger told it, in 1951 he started hanging out at the big-league clubhouses in New York, where he hoped to ingratiate himself to enough players to allow Topps to produce a more expansive set of baseball cards than the failed Red Backs and Blue Backs. Fortunately for Berger, the negotiator charged with procuring contracts on behalf of Bowman was a woman, and she had to wait outside the locker rooms after games. Berger, however, strolled right in and chatted players up as they changed. This might seem like nothing more than a lucky break, but it's typical of the many aggressive tactics Topps used in the early '50s to establish its market control.

Berger and the Shorins understood that ballplayers didn't necessarily appreciate outsiders spouting legalese at them while they got into their civvies. As Berger later testified in court, "I spoke to the players about the agreement that we had to offer and they paid very little heed to me. I quickly found out that baseball is a very, very closed fraternity where they are quite leery of strangers. . . . I came back to Mr. Shorin and told him that I thought this was beyond me, not being part of baseball, and that it required that we have a man who was known in baseball and respected in the field to do this job."

To make the players more comfortable with him, Berger enlisted a former minor-league ballplayer turned Jersey longshoreman named Turk Karam to accompany him around the stadiums. Karam had never managed to rise above AA ball as a player, but he'd scouted in the big leagues as a "bird dog"—meaning he was a part-timer on no club's official payroll—and spent enough time in pro baseball to be well known and well liked throughout the league. With Karam's help, Berger made a simple pitch in the clubhouses. Even if players already had contracts with Bowman, he urged them to go ahead and sign nonexclusive contracts with Topps and earn $75 apiece for their signatures. Such agreements clearly conflicted with Bowman's contracts, but Topps was apparently willing to take its chances in court. If a player was willing to assign Topps exclusive rights to his picture for three consecutive years, then Berger would cut him a check for $200, twice what Bowman was offering for a similar deal.

Given the astronomical salaries and bargaining power that major-league players have enjoyed in more recent years, those sums seem like a pittance. But the typical young player was thrilled just by the prospect of having his face on a gum card. Many of them would probably have signed for free. More important, during the 1950s, baseball card contracts served as the only additional income seen by 80 percent of major-league players, and many of those who spent a moment to talk with Berger were happy to walk away with a few more dollars to supplement their generally unexceptional wages. Some players entered contracts that they must have known were incompatible. Wes Westrum, the longtime catcher for the New York Giants, managed to ink conflicting contracts with three different card companies; enticed by a watch and some money, he signed his contract with Topps just two days after signing one with Bowman. As Baltimore Orioles catcher and budding hitting coach Charley Lau later testified in court, "Back in those days, most of us were struggling, and if we felt that we were lucky enough for somebody to want to sign us, we were going to jump at it."

A lawyer for one of the gum companies was more blunt with *Sports Illustrated*: "You could walk up to one of these ballplayers and offer him $50 to sign a contract to commit suicide. He wouldn't read the contract or ask what it required him to do. He'd just grab the pen and sign. Then he'd pick up his glove and run out for fielding practice."

Berger and Gelman happened to be designing the modern baseball card during the 1951 postseason. As even casual fans know, that year's playoffs climaxed with what many consider the most famous moment in the game's history: Bobby Thomson's "Shot Heard 'Round the World," a walk-off home run that sailed over Dodgers left fielder Andy Pafko at the Polo Grounds, earning the Giants the National League pennant. With the frequent replaying of the black-and-white footage— along with announcer Russ Hodges's fevered, immortal call: "The Giants win the pennant!"—the shot has become a moment in sports loaded with cultural import. (In his brilliant novel, *Underworld,* Don DeLillo famously casts Thomson's homer as a kind of inauguration of postwar America, devoting sixty pages to a reimagining of the game and its aftermath.) As baseball historian Jules Tygiel has noted, for many fans Thomson's dinger is filled with "retrospective romance," marking the zenith of a golden age of the game that ran "from the arrival of Jackie Robinson in 1947 to the uprooting of the Dodgers and Giants from New York to California a decade later."

Perhaps Topps was nothing more than blessed in its timing. More likely, the company was reading the trends better than any of its competitors. Baseball was enjoying unprecedented popularity in the years after the war. The stadiums were setting new attendance records, with crowds hovering at around 20 million annually. Those numbers would eventually fall, but only because the number of radio stations carrying ball games would double. The 1951 season saw the first coast-to-coast telecast of a big-league game and local television stations had begun broadcasting home games regularly. As Roger Kahn writes in *The Era, 1947–1957: When the Yankees, New York Giants and Brooklyn Dodgers Ruled the World,* "The crowds watching television baseball multiplied and grew. Interest as opposed to attendance never flagged." It seemed the sport had something for everyone. Not only were the leagues being racially integrated, but some of the greatest stars of the day were the sons of German, Italian, and Jewish immigrants. And with television, you no longer had to live in the Bronx or Brooklyn to enjoy a ball game—the sport had reached the swelling suburbs, where it flourished.

Fortunately for Topps, those suburbs were populated with an unholy number of gum- and baseball-loving schoolboys. Bazooka Joe and his crew may have been distinctly Brooklynesque, but Topps would find new profits in the growing commuter pockets of places such as North Jersey and outer Detroit, where infields and dugouts sprouted along with new schools. By the early '50s Little League, which had been founded by a Williamsport, Pennsylvania, lumber clerk in the late '30s, had expanded to more than fifteen hundred programs throughout the East. Topps's new customers were the children of soldiers who'd returned home and women who were now free to leave wartime industries and resume family life. By the end of the '40s, 32 million babies had been born—8 million more than in the previous decade. Topps started rolling out its cards just as those kids began enrolling in elementary school. Baseball cards would quickly become a fixture of adolescent life during the baby boom.

The cards in the groundbreaking 1952 Topps set featured dynamic player poses and rich colors, but it was the small and novel touches devised by the Topps creative team that endeared them to baseball-jazzed children. The cards turned out to be the ideal size for flipping, and their backs offered two statistical lines against which Little Leaguers could compare their own numbers: "lifetime" and "past year." Berger told me that he omitted the specific year because he didn't want to date the cards—he had no idea whether they would catch on, so he wanted to leave the door open to selling off surplus stock during subsequent seasons.

The initial run of 310 cards sold so well that the Shorins decided another series of 97 cards was in order—another innovation that would become sports-card commonplace. This latter batch included one of pro ball's newer faces: Mickey Mantle. Mantle's 1952 Topps would become the most valuable postwar baseball card ever made, as well as an iconic image of midcentury America recognized by any baby boomer with a passing interest in the sport. For the next twenty seasons, Topps would issue up to seven different numbered series of nearly ninety cards apiece, each spaced a few weeks apart, starting in the spring and ending in the fall. Knowing that kids' minds would drift from baseball as the summer wore into fall, the company saved some of the best players for last in order to bolster late-season sales.

Berger was also careful to sprinkle the big stars throughout the set. "I thought when a kid's trying to collect a set of cards, you don't want to get too many Joe Blows," he once told an interviewer. "The first ten cards were pretty much stars, and the 0 cards would be the 100, 200, 300, 400, 500, which were for the real stars. The 10s, 20s, 30s,

40s in each group, those were the bigger stars, and the lesser stars were the 5s. In between, I tried to put the other guys."

With 407 players featured in its 1952 issue, Topps had rolled out the largest set of baseball cards in decades—an accomplishment made possible only by flagrantly violating Bowman's exclusive contracts with players, all but guaranteeing that litigation would follow. When the set hit stores, Bowman filed a suit in federal court alleging that Topps's use of certain ballplayers violated its own contracts with those players. The court originally found in favor of Topps, but on appeal a judge ruled that only one card maker could contract with a player for his photo. Bowman's rights had been infringed.

In his 1952 decision, which would become important case law affecting all athletes and celebrities who hoped to capitalize on their images, the judge found that ballplayers, just like anyone else famous, should have a "right to publicity" that only they can wield for financial gain: "For it is common knowledge that many prominent persons (especially actors and ball-players), far from having their feelings bruised through public exposure of their likeness, would feel sorely deprived if they no longer received money for authorizing advertisements, popularizing their countenances, displayed in newspapers, magazines, buses, trains and subways. This right of publicity would usually yield them no money unless it could be made a subject of an exclusive grant which barred any other advertiser from using their pictures."

The ruling might have clarified the rules of the game, but it also set up a fierce and costly competition between the two card makers after 1952. Exclusive contracts became more important and therefore more expensive to obtain. As in the tobacco-card contest of the previous century, the rising costs of producing cards would cut into the profits of nearly everyone involved. One of the few parties to benefit was, of course, the young boy, who was soon collecting some of the finest-looking baseball cards ever made. He was now getting more cards per pack, too. Between 1952 and 1955, as the birth rate was rising faster than at any other point in U.S. history, Topps and Bowman would fight for the hearts and minds of the largest crop of preteen boys America had ever offered candy makers. Within the industry the rivalry of these years would become known as the card wars.

Inside the companies' creative departments it was a period of artistic innovation and imitation. After Topps routed Bowman in sales with its oversize 1952 card, Bowman responded the following year with a card of roughly the same dimensions. Its 1953 set featured full-color photographic reproductions of the game's bigger stars, marking the first time that actual color photos were used on baseball cards. The set was so expensive to produce that Bowman tinkered the same year with a cheaper black-and-white set. Wise to all of the improvements at Topps, Bowman also included statistics on its cards for the first time. Topps countered with a 1953 set based on hand-painted player portraits, widely considered the most aesthetically refined card issue of the postwar period.

The inaugural issue of *Sports Illustrated,* dated August 16, 1954, included a feature story on how popular the Topps and Bowman offerings had become with children: "The most furious trading in the U.S. nowadays goes on not in Wall Street or the Chicago grain market but among youngsters out to collect a connoisseur's fistful of baseball trading cards."

Indicative of the heated competition, six of the expected 280 players in the 1953 Topps set never appeared, almost certainly because of contract conflicts with Bowman. Over the next few years the two firms, along with a weak Fleer, tussled for the rights to household names such as Ted Williams, Stan Musial, and Maury Wills, and when a star player showed up in one set he often wasn't found in the others. The companies' representatives jostled one another in the clubhouses and their lawyers traded threats through the mail.

By 1956 Bowman had had enough. The escalating production costs and legal fees had squeezed its profit margins to new lows. Just as the 1956 baseball season was about to begin, the company agreed to trans-

DAVE JAMIESON

fer all of its gum- and card-making machinery and, more important, all of its contract rights with players to Topps in exchange for a modest $200,000. Topps also obtained the name rights to J. Warren Bowman's beloved Blony bubble gum. After the sale went through, a Bowman executive reportedly told Joe Shorin that he had a "license to steal," and that he'd have the entire card industry "on the run" within a year. As Berger later recalled, "We went down like conquering heroes and took over the Bowman place."

Other gum makers had been waiting on the sidelines to see how the Bowman–Topps lawsuits played out, and now, with Topps in command of nearly all active contracts, it was nearly impossible to get back onto the field. The language of the contracts prevented it. Only Topps had the right to print a player's picture on a baseball card that was packaged "either alone or in combination with chewing gum, candy [or] confection." In other words, Topps's competitors had to sell the cards with *something,* and that something couldn't be the gum or sweets that card-collecting children were used to. So the Memphis-based Donruss company was forced to supplement its Little Leaguer Chewing Tobacco bubble gum not with baseball cards but with booklets explaining the rules of the game. Other companies were left to print cards that had to be packaged with costly and undesirable noncandy products such as marbles. When Leaf tried to maneuver its way into the business in 1956, Topps reminded the company of its airtight contracts and sent out a not-so-veiled admonishment to big leaguers, asking them rhetorically, "Wouldn't it be sheer stupidity for us to negotiate now with a direct competitor . . . after the blood, sweat and tears we spent to bring order out of chaos in our Industry?"

With Topps dominating the card industry, seven American bubble gum makers went out of business in the 1950s. The company's profits had doubled since it buried Bowman, riding what appeared to be a sustained school-yard craze. Baseball cards baffled candy executives as

101

the lone trading card that produced insatiable demand year after year. "The youngsters will not buy last year's," Joel Shorin, who eventually succeeded his uncle Joe as president, explained. "It's like buying last year's newspaper, yesterday's newspaper or yesterday's magazine. He wants the new series, the new averages, the new picture, the new uniform."

In the early '60s one candy company commissioned a survey of 339 boys and found that 89 percent of them collected baseball cards, putting cardboard somewhere between the bicycle and the BB gun on the list of boyhood necessities. General Foods, which printed baseball cards on the backs of cereal boxes during the 1950s and '60s, conducted a survey in which 93 percent of parental respondents said that their boys cut out the cards and saved them. More than half of those boys demanded that Mom go out and buy more of the same cereal. And when *Life* magazine inserted Mickey Mantle and Roger Maris cards into its pages, research showed that half of all boys who lived in *Life*-subscribing homes managed to find them, even without a parent's help.

Baseball cards had become so ridiculously popular that Fleer, a century-old firm with the most recognized square of bubble gum in the world, considered them absolutely vital to its survival. Topps had been chipping away at Fleer's profits for years because of baseball cards, and by the early '60s it had supplanted its rival as the top bubble gum producer in the world. To Fleer, this was an outrage. After all, Fleer was the very first company to market bubble gum successfully, and it had included baseball cards with its candy back in the '20s.

Fleer had also devised many of the mechanical processes that had made gum production easier and more profitable. As Fleer officials complained, it had taken the company nearly a decade to develop the right machinery to wrap its Dubble Bubble chunks in cheaper folded wrappers rather than traditional twisted wraps—yet Topps was able to take full advantage of the new wrapping machines that resulted. Topps had also imitated Fleer's practice of inserting a cartoon strip into its bubble gum packages. So why shouldn't Fleer be able to benefit from the baseball card boom?

When Fleer finally put that question before the Federal Trade Commission (FTC), in 1962, the agency decided that American bubble gum makers and baseball card lovers deserved an answer. Over the course of nearly three years the hearing before the FTC accrued more than seven hundred government and defense exhibits, plus more than four thousand pages of testimony from major-league ballplayers and scouts and gum executives and salesmen. The feds were hoping to prove that Topps's strength in the card market amounted to a monopoly—and, more important, that the company had kept other manufacturers out of the game through unfair means.

"Topps has wielded its monopoly power, inflicting injury in the bubblegum and picture card industries," the government's complaint alleged. "Topps has used its monopoly power to influence wholesalers to buy other products sold by Topps. Picture card manufacturers have been denied the ability to manufacture the most lucrative type of picture card, the baseball picture card. In addition, Topps has discriminated against vending machine operators by delayed deliveries of baseball picture cards, and by less favorable terms than are given to other purchasers. Topps' monopoly of baseball picture cards has resulted in the dominant position Topps now holds in the bubblegum industry."

The fifty-year-old Topps case file resides today at the National Archives research center in College Park, Maryland. What I found there isn't exactly a Wonka-worthy treasure trove of gum, candy, and vintage baseball cards, but it's much livelier than your typical government file. The reams of evidence include Topps store displays from the 1950s; internal memos from both Topps and Fleer; letters each card company sent to ballplayers trashing its competitor; gift catalogs the companies sent to ballplayers; letters between the Shorins and Stan Musial; old Topps and Fleer baseball card boxes; baseball coins and stamps; minutes from the players' association meetings; contracts between Topps and aspiring big leaguers, including the one signed in 1956 by a young Don Drysdale and his father, the witness; gum and card wrappers; and ancient pieces of Bazooka and Dubble Bubble, taped to the pages and fuzzy with mold.

The only thing that's missing from the Topps file is Topps baseball cards. Archivist David Pfeiffer said that the cards were removed from the file by staff after some "researchers" with sticky fingers pillaged the boxes during the 1980s and '90s. The thefts still rankle Pfeiffer, a dedicated fan of both baseball and the FTC's file on Topps. "It's a very sore subject with me," he told me. "They looted it. And I don't get it, because every card was stamped 'FTC' and stapled to the page. Anyone who knew anything about cards knew they were worthless. And there were some beautiful cards in there from the fifties."

What the file lacks in cards, it more than makes up for with card backstory. During the hearings, the lawyers wrangled over the "bubble-ability" of gum and the "flippability" of certain cards, and they patiently explained to the judge what it meant to flip a "leaner" against the wall. (Kids in the 1950s and '60s devised a multitude of card-flipping games, often competing for one another's stash, but the art was pretty much lost on subsequent generations of collectors.) As one attorney marveled in a filing, "A frequent sight in the vicinity of a candy store is children tearing open the packages of trading cards and discarding the gum entirely." As most children knew, the gum always tasted like the cardboard it came with: "It may be added that bubble-gum in slab form has a tendency to become brittle, and this is another reason why the gum is not highly regarded. If bubblegum is desired, rather than trading cards, it is available on candy counters in a more palatable form."

As the case file makes clear, during its first decade as a card maker Topps made a sweeping, cutthroat effort to freeze all of its competitors in the candy world out of the baseball card market. As one attorney put it, "You either sell out, as Bowman did, or you are driven out." To contract as many players as possible on the cheap, Topps went after pros before they had any bargaining power—indeed, before they were even pros. The company had at least thirty major- and minor-league scouts and managers on its payroll, to whom it gave either a flat fee or a per-contract fee for every player they got to sign with Topps. Kids scrapping it out in the farm leagues leaped at the prospect of having their faces on a baseball card someday, even if signing the contract meant they were bound exclusively to Topps for their first five seasons in the majors—and they were compensated only $5 for signing.

By far the best time to lock young players into long-term contracts was during spring training. At no other point in the season were so many young prospects gathered in the same place, so eager to fit into the squad and so reluctant to irk anyone official-looking. So it was in 1959, when Jim Bouton, then a nineteen-year-old Yankees pitching prospect, made his way south to Florida to start his first year in the minors. Sy Berger walked into the locker room one day, and one of the heads of the league told Bouton and his teammates to listen to the man's spiel and then sign whatever he put in front of them. The players, Bouton told me, "lined up like they were getting their flu shots." Foreshadowing a sixteen-year career as the league gadfly, the future *Ball Four* author paused. He didn't take the pen. "Berger said, 'Where's your contract?' I said I wanted to talk it over with my dad. He said, 'You wanna be on a card, right?' I said, 'Why can't I wait?' He said, 'Everyone signs in the minors. Whitey Ford signed in the minors.' I said, 'Let me talk it over with my dad.' I was nineteen. I called my dad, and he said, 'That doesn't make any sense. You don't need $5. If I were you, I wouldn't sign the contract.' So I told Berger I wouldn't do it. I was the only guy that didn't sign." It was a fairly bold stand, if only because Bouton's refusal stood to annoy the league's management—the very men he was supposed to be impressing. "There was a subtle pressure there," Bouton said. "If you didn't wanna be marked down as a jerk or a troublemaker, you would sign."

The trifling $5 sum they received became known among bush leaguers as "steak money," and it was allegedly pushed on them by scouts and coaches who regularly received gifts and other payments from Topps. As one minor-league manager testified of his impressionable wards, "You have to be father, mother, lawyer and everything else for them." Topps claimed that it never tried working with scouts or managers, citing conflict of interest, but company employees, Berger and Karam included, became de facto scouts, constantly prowling the lower leagues to sign talent at rock-bottom prices. "We work at this job 24 hours a day, all year long," Berger told the commission. "I will sit up at the ball park watching the boys who work out. . . . Our men are watching these boys continuously. They are constantly watching ball games."

When rising stars finally made it to the show, they were often presented with a Topps contract to be signed right alongside their Major League Baseball contract—that is, if they hadn't already signed their rights away to Topps as amateurs. The contract gave a player $125 for each year his face turned up on a card, but it also bound him to Topps and Topps alone for the next five years. Back then, the career expectancy of a ballplayer in the big leagues was only four and three quarters years.

Topps cut its costs by encouraging players to take their payments in the form of household goods, such as couches, televisions, and sewing machines, which the company bought at wholesale and featured in the annual Topps gift catalog that went out to clubhouses. "I would buy rifles and shotguns and stereos in large quantities," a former Topps officer, now well into retirement, told me. "Instead of giving the players a few hundred bucks, we gave them an opportunity to pick what they wanted out of a brochure."

Coaches and scouts who helped the company apparently received the same, according to testimony. When Topps wanted established pros to renew their agreements, it leaned on them through "player representatives" from each team who were on the company payroll. The Yankees' player rep during the late 1950s was right-handed hurler

"Bullet" Bob Turley. A letter that Karam sent to Berger from Florida during spring training of 1960 lays out how Topps used him to help sign the best roster in baseball.

> The confusion caused by Fleer at some of the spring training camps has somewhat abated and I figure it is time to strike at the Yankees for extensions. Fleer did not make any headway at all with this club. Practically all the players went along with the player representative, Bob Turley. As you know, Bob favors a short term commercial deal contract, but is not as aggressive as last year at this time about not signing the Topps extension. We will find Berra, Carey, Ford, Terry, and Turley himself hard to crack. Mantle is strictly a Frank Scott problem. [Scott was baseball's very first player agent.]

When it came to gifts that might sweeten the pot, Karam said that Turley wanted "a good portable adding machine," that pitcher Jim Coates was looking for "a good 8 mm movie projector," and that Yogi Berra was "anxious to get the gift his wife decides on before May 1st because the room is bare of furniture." Karam signed off with, "The minor league camps story is good. We are batting 1.000 to date."

The league's coaching staffs and top players rarely complained about this lopsided arrangement, perhaps because, according to Bouton, they were receiving far better prizes than your average journeyman catcher or utility infielder. "The fact that they got better gifts than others made them feel special," said Bouton. "And you felt like you couldn't complain that you got a toaster."

The trick to Topps's dominance was keeping players happy and unorganized. This task fell to Berger. His nearly endless expense reports from the era, which were subpoenaed by the FTC, recount one booze-soaked outing after another with the best players in the game.

It would seem Berger had the best job in baseball, aside from maybe playing center field for the Yankees. As the itemized reports show, one day he would entertain Sherm Lollar and Ted Kluszewski, or have lunch with Harvey Kuenn and drinks at the Hotel Roosevelt. Another day he'd have breakfast with Jim Bunning or dinner and drinks with Nellie Fox, or drinks and sandwiches after the game with Don Drysdale, sandwiches and drinks after the game with Eddie Yost, dinner with Mr. and Mrs. Gil Hodges, or beer with San Francisco Giants Willie McCovey, Hobie Landrith, and Al Stieglitz. The list goes on and on: after-dinner drinks with Phil Rizzuto; drinks with Warren Spahn and Del Crandall; drinks with Gil McDonald and Elston Howard; lunch with Early Wynn; "refreshments" for Art Fowler, Don Zimmer, and Duke Snider. And don't forget the cigars for Joe Torre.

Berger's connections within baseball have always been the stuff of legend. As he and I spoke, and as he continued to refer to this Hall of Famer or that as "a dear, dear friend," I began to wonder whether his reputation was a simple matter of self-mythologizing. (Berger has, for example, often referred to Willie Mays as his best friend.) But his claims became more credible when our conversation was interrupted by a call from former Milwaukee Braves first baseman Frank Torre, who was recovering in the hospital from surgery. For a while, the two discussed a recent losing streak suffered by Frank's younger brother, then Yankees manager Joe Torre. "I feel so bad the way things are going for Joey right now," Berger said.

By 1960 Berger's relentless networking had helped Topps secure contracts from an astonishing 414 of the major league's 421 players. Topps was nothing without the ballplayers, but no one in baseball seemed to realize it. They loved the company even as they carried it on their backs. After one of Fleer's repeated attempts to make players aware of their bargaining power, one general manager dashed off an angry response: "I must frankly state that in my opinion the Topps people have done more for professional baseball in general and the players in particular than any other concern which is not directly connected with baseball." Even if the compensation for players was trifling, the guy had a point. For a growing number of American boys, the pastime of baseball and the pastime of baseball *cards* had become one and the same, each hobby fostering the other, as it would for at least another generation.

Marvin Miller, the legendary head of the baseball players union, didn't appreciate Berger's coziness with the players, however. As Miller recalled bitterly in his autobiography, *A Whole Different Ball Game: The Inside Story of a Baseball Revolution,* "Berger wandered around the clubhouse like he owned the place. He was in there more often than I was, and I had a right to be there under the collective bargaining agreement. The only way he could have done that was with management's permission." Miller believed the gifts Topps handed out to players amounted to "subterranean deals" that long undermined any organizing efforts among the clubs.

How could the most recognizable athletes in America have accepted such lowly compensation? Perhaps they simply appreciated the way that Topps cards promoted the game and its players. When the Major League Baseball Players Association (MLBPA) was founded, in 1953, most players seemed as eager to please the card maker as they were to please team owners. It didn't help that the legal adviser MLBPA retained in 1959, Milwaukee judge Robert Cannon, bore a reputation as a shill for ownership. He called the players' pension fund "the finest in existence" and sang the praises of the almighty reserve clause, which bound a player to a team even after he had fulfilled his initial contract. The thinking of the average ballplayer, Cannon once told a congressional committee, went like this: "We have it so good we don't know what to ask for next." According to FTC records, players often called on Cannon for advice regarding their Topps contracts. He doesn't seem to have encouraged anyone to leverage more money out of the company. They simply took what was offered.

The only player in the late 1950s willing to demand more money from Topps was Ted Williams, who seemed to understand the value of his celebrity better than any of his colleagues. When it came time to renew his contract with Topps in 1958, Williams declined. Instead, he decided to give his name to the highest bidder. This put Topps in a jam—if it gave a significantly higher royalty to Williams, then other top-flight players might demand the same. So Fleer managed to secure a contract with Williams to do a one-year series for a then-substantial $12,500.

The company rolled out an all-Williams-all-the-time set that would go down as one of the biggest duds in the annals of baseball cards. Card makers rarely devoted an entire issue to just one player—a notable exception is Bond Bread's thirteen-card tribute to Jackie Robinson's crossing the color line in 1947—for the simple reason that such sets are rarely dynamic enough to continue selling throughout the season. But Fleer gambled on a series that depicts Williams not as a ballplayer so much as a Renaissance man, showing all facets of his life whether they're interesting or not: fighting as a pilot in World War II, hunting and fishing, spending time with his family, vacationing, even signing contracts. As a former Fleer executive told me, the eighty cards of Ted Williams were "about seventy-nine more cards of Ted Williams than kids wanted." Youngsters failed to see the magic in cards with such titles as "Williams Slowed by Injury," "Ted Decides Retirement Is a No-Go," and—perhaps the most yawn-inducing—"Ted Relaxes."

They laughed over at Topps. A Fleer executive described the company's losses on the series as "devastating." To make matters worse, the series further alienated Fleer from some of the best players in the game, who were insulted by the attention lavished on a single athlete. "Let them stick with Williams," one Fleer rep heard a player sneer in the clubhouse.

Fleer's follow-up efforts were an improvement in that they caused the company to hemorrhage slightly less money than the Williams set did.

After that set tanked, Fleer executives figured it wise to include more than one ballplayer in any given series. Unfortunately, Topps had nearly 99 percent of all current players under contract. Fleer decided to go after retired ballplayers who had never signed with Topps, and so the ill-fated old-timer set known as Baseball Greats was born.

Fleer's roster for the series was unassailable: Christy Mathewson, Connie Mack, Clark Griffith, Eddie Collins, Mickey Cochrane, Joe Tinker, and Hal Newhouser were all accounted for. The problem was, none of these names meant anything to the average seven-year-old boy in 1960. These guys had been out of baseball for so long that Fleer had had trouble tracking them down to pay them the $125 for the rights to their images. Quite a few of the former players turned out to be long dead—in which case Fleer saved $125. Nonetheless, the company lost money on the set.

After Baseball Greats ran its course, Fleer had just enough active major leaguers under non–gum card contracts to roll out a set that might interest kids. The 1963 Fleer cards were an attractive and colorful set showing off sixty-six different players, many of them All-Stars. But this time the rub was in the packaging. To skirt the gum clause in the Topps contracts Fleer bundled its cards with a cookie in each pack. To make sure that this treat didn't violate the confectionery clause in those contracts, Fleer chose a cookie with an abysmally low sugar content. As one Topps salesman joked, the cookie tasted like a dog biscuit.

Wholesalers and drugstore clerks reported seeing children tossing the brittle cookies to the floor and leaving a mess behind as they made off with their cards. Part of the problem, of course, was that for thirty years children had been accustomed to their favorite ballplayers coming with bubble gum, whether they liked the gum or not. As a Detroit wholesaler testified to the FTC, the only place Fleer's cookie cards sold well was in the poorest neighborhoods of the city, where kids understood the value of something cheap and nourishing. The cookies also proved far more expensive to make than gum—and more prone to spoilage. Fleer again logged a loss.

As Fleer started to pressure ball clubs, Berger worked hard to sell players on the idea that a card monopoly was in their best interest. In 1959 he wrote a letter to players, arguing, "Two gum companies can't live on the same picture card item any more than two movie houses across the street from each other can play the same picture at the same time. By giving two gum companies the same rights in the same field, you divide the business in half—what was good for one becomes worthless for two and the ballplayer's value to either company is destroyed."

The folks at Topps might have genuinely believed what Berger said. Some players might have, too. But no child could believe that having just one set of baseball cards to choose from was a good thing. As the Topps monopoly became impenetrable, kids saw a decline in the quality of the cards. This institutional complacency first appeared in the mid-1960s, when designs started to lose their pop and Topps became comfortable with cutting corners. When a player was traded to another team during the production process, rather than pay for a photo of him in his new uniform, the company simply had its artists superimpose new logos on the old hat and shirt. (This tweak may have curried favor with tobacco-card collectors in the 1880s, but by the 1960s and '70s it was considered a cheap cost-cutting move.) Most of these airbrush jobs were hopelessly cheesy-looking, even when they were done by the celebrated pulp-magazine artist Norman Saunders, who was touching up Topps baseball cards well before he rendered the Mars Attacks series. Topps also had no reservations about running the same photo on certain players' cards year after year, which its adolescent customers discovered with annoyance.

Such shortcuts were indicative of a sameness that would settle into Topps baseball cards for years to come, and the outcome of the FTC case didn't help. After an original ruling that Topps was violating the

Sherman Antitrust Act, an appellate court reversed the judge's decision, finding that there was nothing "inherently unfair" about the company's lock on exclusive contracts with players. "Given the large influx of new players into the minor leagues every year," the court decided, "it should not take Fleer or some other firm long to shake [Topps's] hold."

Topps would keep the market all to itself for nearly twenty years.

6

Down in the
Sub-subbasements

Sy Berger has often been referred to as the "father of the modern base-ball card." The man had half a century of influence at Topps, and many collectors have come to assume that he was solely responsible for the look and design of the company's celebrated issues of the 1950s and '60s—the sets that hooked a generation of boomers on collecting and sent baseball cards on their way to becoming a billion-dollar industry.

But Berger was a tremendously busy man, scouting the minor-league camps, and working the big-league clubhouses for contracts, schmoozing with front offices and management. It's hard to believe that such a man, especially one with no artistic background whatso-ever, had time to design and produce a massive and often captivating set of baseball cards year after year. As I tried to learn more about who was behind the classic Topps sets, former employees kept telling me that I should look into the man who sat at Berger's kitchen table draw-ing mock-ups for the 1952 set that started it all: Woody Gelman.

As it turns out, Gelman's fingerprints aren't merely all over those subsequent Topps issues—they're all over our popular culture. After coming to Topps in the early '50s, Gelman became the driving creative force behind the company's major products for more than two decades, having a hand in everything from the Bazooka Joe strip and the first Topps baseball cards to the Mars Attacks cards of the '60s and the Wacky Packages of the '70s. An accomplished collector and a visionary in the world of popular art, Gelman did more on the artistic end to popularize trading cards as a children's pastime than anyone before or since.

His keen eye for talent contributed immeasurably to his company's successes over the years. As the head of the Topps product-development team, he had a knack for discovering and nurturing creative types who operated on his oddball frequency, most notably a fourteen-year-old comic-strip obsessive named Art Spiegelman. Thirty years before winning the Pulitzer Prize for his graphic novel *Maus,* Spiegelman called the Topps offices to ask if he could see some of the original artwork from the company's trading cards. He got a call back from Gelman, who invited the kid to lunch, gave him some cartoons that had run on the backs of baseball cards, and eventually hired him. Spiegelman began producing art for Topps when he was still a teenager, and he remained on staff for more than two decades.

When I contacted Spiegelman, he told me that his next book would be dedicated to Gelman's memory, and that his time at Topps under Gelman's tutelage was the most formative experience in his life as an artist. "He was a catalyst for a lot of what happened in the junk arena of culture that he championed," Spiegelman said of Gelman. "He was working in these sub-subbasements of our culture, like animated cartoons and baseball cards and ephemeral publishing, and he both salvaged and preserved it and encouraged it into being."

Before taking his job with Topps, the Brooklyn-raised Gelman had worked as an animator on early episodes of the *Popeye* and *Superman* cartoons, which were produced by Fleischer Studios in Miami and distributed by Paramount. He was effectively run out of the gig when he tried to unionize illustrators against the studio, according to his friend Len Brown. Gelman then enjoyed a brief stint with DC Comics, creating Nutsy Squirrel, the star of the company's animal-themed *Funny Folks,* before he and his illustrator friend Ben Solomon started their own art-and-advertising agency in New York City in the late 1940s.

One of their first jobs was to design a memorable character to serve as the figurehead for the Popsicle ice-pop brand, owned then by the New York–based Joe Lowe Company. They came up with Popsicle Pete, a wholesome, half-moon-eyed redheaded boy who had a sidekick pony named Chiefy. In varying forms, the character would last for half a century, pushing flavored ices in television, newspaper, and comic-book ads. Impressed by Gelman and Solomon's ability to create designs that spoke to children, Topps contracted them in hopes of boosting their modest bubble gum brand and wresting some of the growing postwar market from the likes of Fleer and Bowman.

Like cigarette smokers during the original card-collecting fad of the late nineteenth century, the preteen gum chewers of the 1940s and '50s demanded that their consumable product come with something a little more lasting. Inexpensive comic strips seemed the perfect solution. Single pieces of Topps Bazooka Bubble Gum were sold in patriotic red, white, and blue wrappers, and each came with a kid-friendly comic strip to compete with the Fleer Corporation's Fleer Funnies. But Topps's uninspired flagship character, Bazooka, the Atom Bubble Boy, had failed to stir the young imagination.

Topps charged Gelman and Solomon with developing a new strip, and in 1953 the pair gave them a classic advertising character: Bazooka Joe. In each strip, blond all-American-looking Joe, with his ball cap and rolled-up jeans, engaged in predictably cheesy banter with sidekicks such as Pesty, who sported a flashy yellow cowboy hat, and Mort, who wore a red sweater that rode up to his nose, as they romped through what looked like a postwar Brooklyn neighborhood. Even in the '50s the gags and one-liners in the *Bazooka Joe* strip were staler than the gum itself: "You know, Joe, lots of girls don't like to go out on dates." "How do you know, Mort?" "Because I asked them." Yet when wrapped around chunks of Bazooka, the innocuous strip helped move pieces of penny bubble gum by the tens of millions.

In typical Gelman fashion, the strip was cribbed from a then under-appreciated piece of popular culture: the "kid gang" genre of comics that reigned supreme in the prewar funny pages, especially the *Reg'lar Fellers* strip that featured neighborhood wanderer Jimmy Dugan and his associates Puddinhead Duffy and Pinhead. But Bazooka Joe could be distinguished from the all-too-reg'lar Dugan boy and his nondescript ilk by one particularly inspired detail: an eye patch. A slight augmentation, for sure, but what could be more disturbing than to suggest that this lovable kid from the block had recently lost some of his eyesight, if not an entire eyeball? Len Brown, who came to Topps in the late '50s, told me that the character's slightly sinister vibe was also typical of Gelman. "Popsicle Pete was a wacky-looking guy, and even Bazooka Joe was kind of scary—to think of a kid with one eye out. . . . Pete and Joe were kind of like first cousins, both a little weird."

The strange accessory was something of an inside joke: Gelman and Solomon were lampooning the famous "Man in the Hathaway Shirt" magazine advertisement, in which a debonair-looking Baron George Wrangell endorsed the C. F. Hathaway clothing line with one eye conspicuously covered. "They said, 'Let's make Joe more identifiable—kids will remember the eye patch,'" said Brown. But the patch lent Joe a worldliness that in a modest way ran against the innocent tone of the strip in which he starred. And it probably wouldn't have thrilled Topps executives to learn that the man hired by Gelman to draw the character throughout the '50s, Wesley Morse, had in the 1930s cut his illustrator's teeth on so-called Tijuana bibles, also known as "dirty little eight-pagers." Among the earliest pornographic comic books, they were sold illegally during the Great Depression.

In this hidden fashion, Bazooka Joe represents Gelman's creative ethos. It seems that for every card of a straitlaced sports hero Gelman would put out in coming years, he also wanted to create something as ingrained with subversiveness as the Mars Attacks set. Joe is also typical of Gelman's Topps work in that the character has proved remarkably long-lasting. There is perhaps no other marketing creation in the candy industry that has successfully plugged a product for as long as Bazooka Joe has. Even today, according to Topps, 97 percent of adults and 89 percent of children can identify his face. (The company also claims that psychological studies have proved Bazooka Gum to be "one of the most frequently identified 'smell memories'" among Americans.) It never mattered how dreadful the strip itself was—in fact, that was largely the point. "The appeal of it," longtime Topps artist Jay Lynch suggested, "is that it's so bad it's good."

Over the years, Gelman's pliable creation has survived a number of tweaks and overhauls, courtesy of the Topps marketing people, who have strived to keep Joe hip to the latest generation and clear of any controversy. But his dark side is apparently irrepressible. "Now it's *Bazooka Joe and His Gang,* but for a time it wasn't '*gang*' because they didn't want to encourage gangsterism," said Lynch. "Some PR firm Topps hired was worried about that. With Mort, there was a dictionary of underworld lingo that came out once, and it said that Mort meant 'uncircumsized penis' in prison because of the way his turtleneck was pulled up. Topps heard about it and changed his name to Red and pulled down his shirt. And in the Bronx, the common term for street crack was 'bazooka.' But Bazooka Joe doesn't live in New York anymore. Now I guess he's in some university town somewhere."

In spite of his gift for creating comic-strip personalities, Gelman would make his most lasting mark in the gum-card arena. The baseball cards his team designed in the '50s were not only unusually attractive but also some of the most fun and innovative trading cards that had ever appeared. His 1953 set included the first-ever baseball trivia questions to be put on the backs of cards. The 1954 set was the first to use two player poses on each card—a portrait and an action shot. And the backs of '50s and '60s Topps baseball cards were the first to include complete comic strips, many of which were drawn by *Mad* and EC Comics veteran Jack Davis. When they weren't designing baseball cards, Gelman's artists were preparing the nonsports cards that would help make Topps an institution on dime-store shelves: Hopalong Cassidy, Frank Buck's Bring 'em Back Alive, Look 'n See, Who-Z-at Star, Tarzan and the She Devil, World on Wheels, Elvis, the Beatles, Isolation Booth, Robin Hood, Space Cards, and Target Moon.

"Gelman wasn't just a creative genius with cards," auctioneer and card expert Bill Mastro said. "He was behind the wrappers and the boxes, all the color, a whole kaleidoscope of things. He was responsible for everything innovative with Topps in those years."

While much of the scuffling between Topps and Bowman was about player contracts, the rivalry was also about aesthetics. Which company had the creative team that could design cards that spoke to the American child's imagination? In this respect, it was Woody Gelman who would win the card wars of the 1950s. And once they were over, even the Topps brass could no longer pretend that the firm was actually selling bubble gum and not cardboard.

As Topps honcho Joel Shorin put it to a reporter after the FTC case was put to rest: "The cards wag the gum."

The looks of those sets came from Gelman's encyclopedic knowledge of the history of card design. An enthusiast of all paper ephemera, Gelman spent his life accumulating tobacco and gum cards, early comic books, pulp magazines, and silent-movie posters. When libraries were unloading back issues of periodicals in favor of microfilm versions, Gelman was there to scoop up the unwanted volumes. Whether it was cards or comics or newspapers, he was constantly trying to file and order the things he kept either in the basement of his home in Franklin Square, New York, or in a nearby storage space. "It was like going into a library at a university and going through the stacks and old publications," Topps colleague Brown said of the basement. "All paper from the turn of the century through the 1940s."

Gelman started collecting cardboard as a child, in the 1920s, when he became enamored with cheap strip cards that were sold two for a penny. As an adult, he became what's known as a "type collector," meaning he tried to obtain at least one card from every set ever made. Completion of any given set wasn't as important—Gelman wanted an example of the design. The approach was "less Peggy Guggenheim" and more "Collyer Brothers," said Spiegelman, referencing the famous pair of hermitic Manhattan hoarders who died amid more than a hundred tons of their own rubbish, and whose story, friends say, Gelman loved.

"His interest in old paper was enormous," recalled Spiegelman. "At his place was the first or maybe the second time that I'd ever seen those old cigarette cards. He was a collector of them before they were even a category. Back then, it was the equivalent of bending down and picking up bottle caps. Everything [he designed] was informed by that massive collection at the core of his interest, like collecting Sunday comics when nobody cared. A lot of his projects grew out of these things from the nineteenth century. He was interested in cataloging everything. His place was a sea of paper goods, almost filled solid."

Gelman's step-father, who shared his passion for postcards and trading cards, started a mail-order card-collecting business in 1951 and left it to Gelman upon his death. It was called the Card Collector's Company, and many longtime baseball card hobbyists believe that the concern made Gelman and his father-in-law the first card dealers in America. When a collector called Topps in search of a particular card he didn't have, the company would refer him to Card Collector's, where Gelman and his son, Richard, would sometimes have to climb a ladder to sort through the massive inventory and fill orders.

For the price of a quarter and a fifteen-cent stamp, Gelman sent his card catalog to hard-core collectors scattered around the country, including Jefferson Burdick, with whom the designer became friendly. "I bought my first T206 Ty Cobb from Gelman for twenty-five cents," recalled Mastro. "If I got to choose who I wanted, it was a quarter. If I didn't care, it was fifteen cents. So I taped my quarter to a piece of cardboard and I wrote a letter: 'Dear sir, I want Ty Cobb. I'm enclosing my quarter as your catalog says. I don't want anybody else.' Next thing I know an envelope arrived."

Appropriately, the mail-order company's ever growing stockpile was housed in what used to be a U.S. post office. In the 1970s a good portion of the Gelmans' catalog of thirty-five million cards was damaged or destroyed in a massive fire. But even today, their former inventory will surface at card shows with telltale singed borders and water damage.

Gelman's drive to collect stemmed from a fascination with mass-produced images from earlier periods of American life. He once told an interviewer, "The growth of pop art is simultaneous with the growth of the nation." He was so enamored with a 1902 Sears Roebuck catalog he discovered that he had it reprinted in its entirety. "It was fascinating," recalled Brown. "It was the size of a phone book, completely illustrated, with everything from telephones of the time to furniture and lingerie." The book, published in 1969, sold quite well, with people around the country giving Gelman's concentrated dose of nostalgia a place on their coffee tables. His old tobacco and gum cards similarly served as artifacts of expired popular culture that could be summoned at any time from a breast pocket.

"He kept samples of everything in albums," said Mastro. "Wrappers. Salesman samples. Pins. Postcards. Stuff that was mailed to people for whatever reason. He had a collection, a shelving unit filled with albums, and it went all the way back to the nineteenth century. Little uncut sheets of things, original artwork, even photos showing things as they were when they were issued. A lot of what we know of cards came from those albums."

As prescient as it seems today, Gelman's collecting was, in the 1950s and '60s, considered a curiosity at best, an abnormality at worst. According to colleagues, even Gelman's wife didn't understand the nature of his compulsion. Few people aside from Burdick seemed willing to make their childish-seeming passions a matter of public record, and the trading cards and comic strips that Gelman collected held little value beyond their potential as pulp or fish wrapping. The one time that Gelman professed his love for cards to someone outside of his tiny subculture, he was burned for it. In 1967 he showed a reporter for the *New York Times* around his home for what he probably thought was an innocuous story on collectors of nostalgic ephemera. Instead, the article amounted to a rather condescending hit piece on fringe collectors, whom the writer called "a specific kind of nut."

"There is one New Yorker, Woody Gelman, who has spent years peacefully accumulating gum cards, greeting cards, cartoons and a number of other irrelevancies which simply piled up around his wife's washing machine in the basement and gave him great pleasure," the article read.

Gelman tried to explain how the collector's mind operates. "Most of them have a disease," he was quoted as saying. "You start instinctively, as a child. Part of collecting is the desire to complete something, to find everything in one category. Part of it is a recapturing of the past. You discover again how to play. You go back with a vengeance." Gelman apparently never made the intellectual dimension of his pursuit clear to the reporter, who brought the collector's folly into sharp relief by devoting ample space to a rubber-band ball that had been growing for some time in Gelman's basement. According to Topps colleague Bhob Stewart, who drew comic strips on the backs of baseball cards in the late 60's, Gelman felt deeply embarrassed and misunderstood when the story appeared. "He'd told everyone to look for it. But on Monday, Gelman was in his office with the door closed, and the entire day no one really spoke to him. Nobody knew what to say, it was so horrendous. He never mentioned the article again."

Friends recall how Gelman had a habit of renewing two subscriptions to *Life* every year, back when the publication was a humor magazine. Each month, he would tear one issue into individual pages and file the images according to subject or artist. He would keep the second issue intact as an artifact unto itself. It was all a part of his interest in what he called "image retrieval." In a predigital age, he dreamed of a time when artists and researchers would be able to conjure all the recorded images of a certain subject in an instant. "What he envisioned was kind of like what you have with Google nowadays," said his son, Richard. "He wanted to be able to put in 'gum cards of the twenties,' press a button, and have every possible thing come up and be able to retrieve history right at home."

He filed away cards and photos as if such an ability were always on the horizon. In the back of the Topps offices was a loading dock where Gelman kept pallets of bound newspapers. He paid someone to come into the office and go through those newspapers page by page, clipping images and filing them accordingly.

Topps Wacky Packages had their genesis in Gelman's fascination with print advertising. Specifically, they grew out of a collection he'd put together of early-twentieth-century die-cut advertising cards, which were shaped like the products they promoted. Originally, Gelman wanted to obtain permission from the companies whose products were on the cards and simply reprint them. There was nothing ironic or satirical in his concept. "Len Brown and I said, 'Yeah, but we'll do it as a parody,'" Spiegelman recalled. This had never occurred to Gelman. Such was his love of outdated ephemera that he assumed his youthful customers would share his interest.

In the days before a thriving secondary card market, the folks at Topps viewed their various series as no different from the generally worthless cardboard of past generations: the young collector would assemble them; the mother would later dispose of them. Naturally, Gelman saw things differently. He had a hard time throwing away anything made of paper, let alone illustrations done by artists he respected and commissioned. "None of those guys saved cards, and I think that pissed him off," Gelman's son said of Topps brass. "All you had to do was save one set a year, and they didn't. If we didn't take them, they destroyed them."

So Gelman started an informal Topps archive, stowing away not only the original artwork to many of the company's card series but also copies of the cards themselves. After each set came to fruition, Gelman and his team would take two copies of each card and glue them into a three-ring binder, displaying both the front and the back. That way, his creative department would have something to refer back to when designing future sets and the company would be able to keep a running history of all the cards it had created. Friends say that Gelman wouldn't have had it any other way.

"There's something very satisfying about finding and ordering, and it animated Woody's entire life," said Spiegelman. "It was what made him want to run that Card Collector's Company. He understood the collector's brain. If you have Numbers One and Three and Four, then Number Two becomes very important, even if it's a player who left baseball after a year to become a stockbroker. I think that that's what collecting can offer therapeutically, more for boys than girls—a way of understanding the world. Woody's life was devoted to making some kind of coherent order out of it."

Gelman's gathering of cardboard and print art served another function. He wanted to preserve the work of the artists, contemporary and deceased, who weren't receiving the attention Gelman believed they deserved. He revived the work of cult illustrators such as

Alex Raymond (*Flash Gordon*), E. C. Segar (*Thimble Theatre,* which featured Popeye), and Hal Foster (*Prince Valiant*) before they were canonized, reprinting their work under his Nostalgia Press banner beginning in 1967.

The generation of comic-book authors who came of age in the 1960s and '70s is indebted to Gelman for also rescuing from obscurity the comics auteur Winsor McCay, whose fantasy *Little Nemo in Slumberland* is considered by some the most important strip to have run in the first half of the twentieth century. *Nemo* tells the story of a seven-year-old boy who drifts off each night to Slumberland, a marvelous yet sometimes frightening realm ruled by King Morpheus, only to awaken each morning to realize that his adventures were merely dreams. McCay combined his surreal and occasionally disturbing plot lines with a visual style that employed wild colors and unusually detailed backgrounds, taking full advantage of the then generous space in the color comics pages. *Nemo* has become arguably the most influential of the medium's early works and still, many believe, one of its very finest. Yet most comic-book auteurs would know nothing of McCay if not for Gelman.

He discovered many of McCay's original strips at a cartoon studio where McCay's son had been working in the late 1940s. Because nobody thought that the strips should be saved, they were being used as scrap paper under roughs of new cartoons, where they protected work surfaces from razor-blade cuts. Gelman snatched up every piece of McCay's work the studio had. In 1966 some of McCay's original drawings were put on display at the Metropolitan Museum of Art, under the curatorial direction of none other than Jefferson Burdick's compatriot, A. Hyatt Mayor.

In 1973, Gelman published a collection of *Little Nemo* strips in Italy, having found insufficient interest to publishing the material stateside. Children's author and illustrator Maurice Sendak, writing about the book in the *New York Times,* said that all the credit for its existence belonged to Gelman, "collector, editor and the best friend

Winsor McCay ever had," despite the fact that McCay and Gelman had never met.

In many ways, the coherence and order that Gelman applied to his card and comics collections eluded him in his everyday life. To family and colleagues he seemed perpetually harried, his head filled with book projects and inchoate card series, most of which would never see the light of day. Gelman's anxious, manic nature became something of a running joke at Topps, where artist Larry Riley, who had also worked as an illustrator at Paramount, once drew a picture of Gelman that he shared with coworkers. In it, Gelman was running off to nowhere in particular, fumbling for his belt as his pants pooled around his ankles. Above his head was a thought bubble: "I have no time to shit . . ."

As much as the higher-ups at Topps might have appreciated Gelman's work, his friends got the impression that he was never quite viewed as a grown-up in the workplace. "He would get too enthusiastic," laughed Spiegelman. "When he started liking something, you'd see his face beaming and he'd be bouncing on his toes, talking about all the great things that could happen. That didn't seem like executive body language."

One of Gelman's grandest schemes was to produce a large hardcover magazine that would be filled with journalistic articles laid out as tiered comic strips; he visualized it as the ultimate in pop design, but he never went beyond commissioning a few stories. He lived in perpetual dread of disappointment, and he once told his son that he failed at the first nine things he tried in his life. Even his career working at Topps was something of a concession. He had the talent and the desire to be an artist like those he hired, but he didn't have the will to endure the vocation's financial uncertainties.

Gelman, who was born in 1915, grew up in poverty, his divorced mother taking the family from one temporary living arrangement to another in Brooklyn during the early years of the Great Depression. As much as he loved spending time in museums and galleries and drawing as a boy, he didn't want to live in penury as an adult, especially once he had a wife and children. "He was a guy who had a tremendous brain but not the ability or the confidence to make it happen for himself," is how his son put it.

Rather than risk a life of possible destitution, Gelman stayed in the safe employ of Topps and became a patron of others. He recognized the genius in unconventional illustrators and offered them Topps work so they could make a little money and keep their pens moving. Before Fritz the Cat and Mr. Natural became counterculture icons, Robert Crumb was working on the Topps catalogs that illustrated premiums for gum salesmen—essentially, internal publications. "I had to draw this big mountain of prizes: electric coffee pots, toasters and blenders and sports equipment," Crumb once grumbled in an interview. "That was awful working for them . . . a real sweatshop."

Soul-sucking as it was, such work paid the bills. In the late '60s, after Spiegelman had a drug-induced breakdown and, he said, "went quite nuts, first going to a mental hospital, then a commune," the twenty-year-old returned to the Topps offices a humble, strung-out wreck in need of work. Gelman walked off and returned with a cashier's check for $1,000 and an offer to write some gags. Gelman also commissioned legendary illustrators Jack Davis, Basil Wolverton, and Wally Wood when they were relative unknowns.

Many of the talents Gelman corralled at Topps would form the core of the underground comix movement of the 1960s and '70s. Yet the work they were doing for him was meant for children, and Gelman spared no effort to attune himself to that notoriously unpredictable audience. He was known to stop in at Brooklyn candy kiosks to see what was selling well among the elementary-school set, and he would also dispatch Brown to a local school yard to test new card designs. The then twenty-five-year-old Brown was admittedly "very self-conscious" about showing artwork to prepubescents in the neighbor-hood playground, but Gelman considered it a necessary step in creating a product that spoke to youth.

Though the Topps brass trusted his proven methods, Gelman didn't necessarily make the final call on each baseball design. Rather, he and his team brought forth a handful of possibilities after days or weeks of tinkering. "Woody would come up with a couple of thumbnails or our group of young artists would visualize maybe a dozen designs," recalled Brown of working on Topps baseball cards in the late 1950s and '60s. "Then we would weed it down to three or four and give them to the heads of the company. The vice president and the sales guys would come in—it was a big deal—and everyone would pick the design from that handful of cards. This was in the old days, when you could look at a baseball card and say, 'That was a 1962.' Now they're so generic, there's no longer a sense of style or design. I think that's a loss. But in those days, of course, we were designing them for kids. It was always with the kids in mind."

Contrary to what children at the time might have imagined, the Topps offices weren't exactly a place where elfin men chewed bubble gum and cheerfully designed next season's baseball cards. Instead, picture a batch of poorly dressed artistic cranks toiling away in a dilapidated plant in an industrialized part of Brooklyn.

"It was just a beat-up old factory," remembered David Saunders, who as a child visited the office regularly with his father, famed pulp artist Norman Saunders, and had free reign to rummage through the uncut sheets of cards. "It had this antiquated cage elevator where an operator sat with a spittoon. He'd slam the cage shut, just like you were in a factory. The place stunk like ink, and there was saw-dust on the floor and heavy oak furniture all over. They all wore those green visors. It had a totally industrial feel to it, like a filthy, dirty factory. They were all drinking or smoking, spitting on the floor into the sawdust. It smelled bad. They all wore ugly neckties, like they were from the twenties or thirties. There was cigar smoke everywhere. But they always had something to hand out for free, candy or cards."

Behind the wholesome veneer of Topps baseball cards was a Gelmanesque sense of the offbeat, what Saunders described as the art department's general inclination toward all things "nutty, kooky, silly, mad, and cracked." Gelman himself was certainly no prude. When Topps was putting together a series of Batman trading cards, Gelman drew a card for his son that would never make it to the printer: the Caped Crusader taking a crap.

In a 1960 letter to the *New York Times,* Gelman rebuked the paper's film critic for penning a review lamenting a growing depiction of sex in the movies. "A little bit of questioning makes one wonder where we picked up our ideas about immorality in sexual matters. Are the sexual mores of the Puritan, or of the Church of 2,000 years ago to remain our eternal guide? Is there something evil about the discussion of sex? Is the picturization of the undraped female morally degrading or is it actually healthy?" In the 1960s Gelman went on to draw illustrations for a series of then racy sexual-humor books. The one copy that I managed to track down was at the Library of Congress, and although it had been translated into French, understanding the punch lines wasn't crucial to enjoying the illustrations. Page after page showed silhouetted feet—sans bodies—tangled in different lovemaking positions: in a car, underwater, in space, in chains, in a maternity ward, in an igloo, in a therapist's office. The book was published under the coy title *Sam, the Ceiling Needs Painting.*

Each year, Gelman's creative department enjoyed a couple of relatively short down periods between designing next season's baseball cards and designing next season's football cards. During this time, employees were free to pursue more unconventional projects. Under Gelman, these tended to be frequently satiric and sometimes violent.

In the early '60s, around the start of the Civil War centennial celebration, a Topps executive thought it would be a good idea to cash in with a card series commemorating notable figures of the conflict. In the vague concept laid out by higher-ups, Gelman recognized the likelihood of a truly dreadful issue: portraits of stodgy generals on one side, dreary one-paragraph biographies on the other. "We were devastated," Brown recalled. "Who wants to see pictures of Grant and Lee?" Gelman told his team that it would take some liberties with the concept. Rather than give children a tiresome history lesson, Topps would give them a brutally graphic depiction of war.

Ceding to his love for pop-cultural pastiche, Gelman modeled the issue on Gum, Inc.'s Horrors of War series. As his artists were mocking up their Civil War cards, Gelman hauled his own Horrors of War collection down to the office. "They even had pictures of hands being cut off by the Japanese and other cruelties of war," said Brown. "Woody laughed. He said, 'We'll make it like this. The kids will love it.'"

The set's eighty-eight cards were conceived by Gelman and Brown and painted mostly by Norman Saunders. They have point-blank titles such as "Painful Death" and "Savages Attack" and show scene after scene of mutilation and destruction. Packaged as an instructive and edifying series —each wax pack came with realistic-looking Confederate money printed on parchment-like stock—the cards would collectively become known as the Civil War News because of their newspaper-style backsides, which recount important moments in the war with varying degrees of accuracy. "It wasn't really educational," admitted Brown, who authored the capsules. "I embellished it so much there was probably no truth to it." Topps executives initially balked because of the series' graphic nature, but they eventually relented.

Issued in 1962, the cards were a hit. Gelman had earned some creative capital and he intended to use it.

The next war Gelman wanted to show children was interplanetary. He and his team dreamed up a preposterous fifty-five-card story line about cruel Martians who descend upon Earth shortly before their own planet is due to explode from internal atomic pressure. The concept drew on H. G. Wells's *The War of the Worlds* and a host of sci-fi flicks from the 1950s, such as *Invaders from Mars* and *It Came from Outer Space*. But it was probably inspired most of all by Hugo Gernsback, the creator of the pulp rag *Amazing Stories,* which, launched in 1926, is considered the first science-fiction magazine. Gelman, unsurprisingly, had started collecting issues as a child.

Wildly popular among schoolkids, the 1962 Mars Attacks set was like a lurid underground comic book in trading-card format, full of bug-eyed aliens, voluptuous women, and burning human flesh rendered lifelike by Wally Wood and Bob Powell, who did the pencil roughs, and Saunders, who did the final paintings. Saunders painted the original images on four-by-six-inch cards at his home, where his wife, children, and neighbors posed as earthlings watching in horror as much of America was vaporized. In one illustration, entitled "Destroying a Dog," a young boy despaired as a Martian incinerated his yowling puppy. Saunders modeled the character on his eight-year-old son, David, who posed in the kitchen with the family mutt, Cindy. The original art for that card, along with that for about a dozen others, was so disturbing that Topps executives sent it back to Gelman demanding it be toned down. (On the edited card, the dog isn't yet incinerated—the beam is merely on its way to his belly.)

To brace for the public outcries that would surely be inspired by such sets as the Civil War News and Mars Attacks, Gelman always made sure to have some boring yet undeniably educational card series in the pipeline, such as one depicting the flags of all nations and another showing off Detroit's many different automobiles. He also chose to publish Mars Attacks under the company name Bubbles, Inc., rather than Topps, so his employer's moniker wouldn't be associated with the gory images. It was a clever but futile preemptive move. Parents were horrified upon the cards' appearance, and Brown remembers Joel Shorin having to field an angry call from a prosecutor in Connecticut who wanted to know why the company felt compelled to scare the hell out of children. Although the cards sold briskly, the uproar was enough to spook Topps executives into canning the series after only a limited release. The choice was completely voluntary, for although the world of comics was governed by the Comics Code Authority, which had been established in 1954 in response to political crowing from conservatives, the world of trading cards had no formalized mode of censorship.

In the larger context of Topps children's products, nightmarish sets like Mars Attacks served as the perfect foil to the dream-inspiring baseball cards, and some kids seem to have appreciated getting a look at this darker world. "They were the first bits of pop culture that told me about the dangers in the world," said David Saunders, who was famous on the playground as the son of a Mars Attacks artist. "I felt personally addressed as a kid looking at those cards. There was an attitude of naughtiness in those cards in a world that otherwise was squeaky clean, kind of Bozo the Clown"—kind of Bazooka Joe and baseball cards, really. "Civil War News and Mars Attacks were the first things I saw on the shelves that were directed at children, not adults, that said, 'You better look out. There are people out there that want to fucking kill everybody.'"

Gelman continued running the creative department at Topps well into his sixties. After the company established its monopoly in the baseball card market, it formed a sports department to handle all of its baseball and football issues, which became increasingly photo-driven and less imaginative. But it left the nonsports cards to Gelman and his artists.

During the early 1970s Gelman enjoyed some unexpected success with Wacky Packages. The cards had fizzled during their original run in the late '60s, but they were so popular during the next go-round that *New York* magazine made them the subject of an October 1973 cover story, calling them "the middle-class little kid's answer to subway graffiti." "In their minor art form, Wacky Packages are revolutionary. Gone are the jocks and rock stars, the traditional card ploys. Wacky Pack puns are the *Mad* magazine effect leaking sideways into the under-culture. Watergatian Weltschmerz is nibbling the collective unconscious, and Wacky Packages are selling rampant with their put-downs of products that kids have had thrown at them and into them daily by TV and Mom."

The article was actually a sore point with many Topps artists, because it made no mention of them. To the creative department, it seemed that the company brass had always gone to great lengths to pretend that their products sprang from the ether, rarely, if ever, referencing their artists by name in print. (Apparently, the company still operates under the code of *omertà*. When I asked a Topps spokesman for some interviews with long-time Topps employees and executives, he told me that he could offer no such access, aside from a referral to the retired Berger. After all, he suggested, Topps might want to do a book of its own someday.)

Wacky Packs were the last big hit Gelman oversaw at Topps. He died of complications due to a stroke in 1978, after leading the company's product development for a quarter century.

The artwork and cards that Gelman saved remained at Topps. A decade after his death, once baseball cards had established themselves as a massive industry, Topps decided to unload much of the product sitting in what it called its "vault." In 1989 the company consigned most of its trove of old cardboard—sports and nonsports issues alike—

to the Guernsey auction house of New York. Many card dealers and industry leaders hoped that the sale would put up numbers high enough to place sports collectibles alongside fine art in the auction world. The card company consigned some twenty-five thousand items, and Topps executives were hoping that the trove would top $1 million.

The Guernsey auction was like a Woody Gelman retrospective. On the block were the original artworks to series he and his team designed, sheet after sheet of uncut vintage cards from the 1950s and '60s, and lots filled with original Wacky Pack art and Mars Attacks production sheets—everything he'd overseen during his time with the company. Most of the presale buzz focused on the player portraits used for the 1953 baseball set, among them oil-painted depictions of Mickey Mantle, Willie Mays, Roy Campanella, Bob Feller, and Jackie Robinson. Guernsey estimated that the Mantle painting could fetch up to $20,000. But once the bidding was over the price had reached $110,000. Mays fetched $80,000, Robinson $71,000.

At the time, the Topps Guernsey auction seemed like insanity. "The business and romance of collecting and dealing baseball cards has turned corporate," the *New York Times* noted after the sale of the Mantle painting. "The transaction saddened most of the spectators. Some said they missed the days when they flipped cards against the wall. But the sale cheered the more than 300 professional card dealers, who seemed to welcome the instant inflation." Any doubts that the secondary baseball card market was serious business had been put to rest once and for all.

Even some of the more peripheral items, such as baseball card contracts and canceled $5 Topps checks to players, earned bids in the hundreds and thousands of dollars. Apparently, there was great collector interest not just in baseball cards but also in the history of baseball cards. A release that allowed Mantle to have cards created by manufacturers other than Topps, signed by both parties, went for $16,000. Mantle's original 1951 contract with Bowman sold for $13,000.

"Almost everything went beyond expectations," Guernsey president Arlan Ettinger, who ran the auction, told me. "I remember one letter written by the great Willie Mays to Topps. We laughed about it when we saw it. Mays was complaining about the fact that the toaster he had received from Topps kept burning his toast. He wanted to know, Could they please get it repaired in some way? To think of someone who was as sensational as Willie Mays, and realize he's a person like all of us, complaining about burned toast. The letter had nothing to do with sports. It sold for about $2,000, which in those days was a very healthy sum."

Topps reached its magic number and then sailed beyond it. Total auction sales came in just under $2 million, which hobbyists hailed as monumental. For the creative team and Topps at large, there was a certain validation in the stratospheric results. The company had made its contribution to popular culture—at least a handful of wealthy collectors who'd grown up with Topps had come to believe so.

Yet the auction also embittered some of the artists who'd worked under Gelman. Spiegelman, for one, had shown up at the sale in hopes of taking home some Wacky Package art, but he suffered the indignity of being outbid on most of his own pieces. To compound the insult, after the auction, some winning bidders asked him to sign the artwork that he couldn't afford. "This grave robbing, this selling of the company out from under itself—that was appalling to me," the artist said. "And they'd said they would never do that." Spiegelman left Topps shortly after the auction.

Many of the items in the Topps vault, Spiegelman said, never would have been available for sale if Gelman hadn't bothered to tuck them away. Even several of the loose-leaf binders into which Gelman had pasted Topps cards over the years—the creative department's unofficial archive—were offered in the auction. (Other binders from Gelman's archive still come up for sale periodically, offered inside the Topps Vault, a storefront that the company maintains on eBay.) The write-up in the

Guernsey catalog praised the binders as "an extraordinary collection." And that they were: vintage cards pasted into albums by the very man who ushered them into being, then thought them worth saving before anyone else did.

Even so, the text made no mention of Gelman—and the binders sold for just a couple of thousand dollars apiece.

7

Nostalgia Futures

When Marvin Miller was elected head of the Major League Baseball Players Association, in 1966, the union's total resources amounted to a $5,400 account with Chemical Bank and a cabinet full of case files stashed in someone else's office in the New York Biltmore Hotel. Miller had just given up his influential post as chief economist for the Steelworkers Union in Pittsburgh for this apparently unpromising job representing professional baseball players. But he was a dedicated labor man, and he'd come to consider ballplayers to be just as poorly compensated and exploited as any group of blue-collar workers who toiled in a mill or mine.

By the time the forty-eight-year-old had accepted the players' union job and arrived in New York, he'd learned that pro players, in spite of their massive celebrity in postwar America, were decades behind steel and coal workers when it came to wielding the power of collective bargaining. In the twenty years since World War II had ended, the minimum salary in the big leagues had gone from a measly $5,000 to an even more measly $6,000; when adjusted for inflation, the modest raise turned out to be a decline. Massive ballpark draws like Willie Mays and Mickey Mantle could command around $100,000 from owners, but among the plebes the average salary remained south of twenty grand.

The problem wasn't just a feebly funded and impotent trade organization. It was also the attitude of the people that organization ostensibly represented. The average player despised the very concept of a strong union. Many hailed from small towns that had been engulfed in labor strife at one point or another, and they feared that racketeering and strikes would poison a beloved pastime if the likes of Miller got involved. Before he even had a chance to sit down with players, Miller was reading antiunion blather in the papers directed at him from the very men he'd soon be representing. According to Miller's autobiography, California Angels first baseman Joe Adcock expressed the prevailing view succinctly to newspapers during 1966 spring training: "Pro sports has no place for unions."

Miller's first order of business, then, was to instill a union consciousness in players, to make them recognize that as a group they could push back at team ownership enough to improve both their salaries and their rights as laborers. But before the revolution could begin, Miller needed to fund his organization. To do so, he looked to baseball cards.

The fight Miller was about to pick with Topps marked the beginning of a dramatic restructuring in the business of baseball. Within a few years owners would no longer have a clear upper hand in their dealings with players, and Miller would have refashioned his anemic little union into one of the most formidable in the country.

During his first few weeks on the job, Miller pored over the union's contracts and agreements inside the office in the Biltmore. He kept coming across the name Topps. The more Miller learned about the players' arrangement with the Brooklyn firm, the more appalled he was at what he considered the unconscionable structure of the deal. He was also surprised to learn that many ballplayers never received copies of their contracts with Topps even after they requested them, and that they'd been told if they wanted to see the documents, they needed to trek to the Topps offices in person.

"When you considered what the compensation was, and the fact that it was an exclusive deal, it was absolutely one of the most outrageous things I'd ever seen," the ninety-one-year-old Miller told me. Miller had quickly come to believe that the relationship between major leaguers and Topps was a "microcosm" of the players' decades-long subjugation to team owners through the all-important reserve clause. In the days before free agency, this clause allowed team owners to "reserve" players for the following season, effectively binding them to their current teams and preventing them from relocating in search of better salaries. The rule had been introduced in 1879, when each of the National League teams was permitted to hold on to five players for the following season. In 1885 New York Giants shortstop John Montgomery Ward formed his Brotherhood of Professional Base Ball Players, the first players' union in American sports, largely in response to the reserve rule. When, in 1922, the Supreme Court ruled that professional baseball was an "amusement" not subject to the laws of trusts and interstate commerce, the ownership-favoring rule was entrenched in the sport for decades to come.

Miller quickly came to believe that players were as fettered to Topps as they were to their teams. When he heard about Fleer's futile attempts to break into the baseball card market, he called the company's president, Donald Peck. "Competing with them is like running in quicksand," Peck said of Topps. By hustling at minor-league and spring-training camps, Fleer had managed to sign a fairly substantial number of players to nonexclusive deals, but the contracts were worthless until the exclusive arrangements obtained by Topps expired, which wouldn't be for years.

"I'd learned enough about licensing to know that in a program like that the players were entitled to a percentage of the revenue, and they were getting zero on that," said Miller. "They were getting fixed payment, and that was it. Topps's value was still rising. And the other part that outraged me was the way they had organized it. They actually had scouts in the minor leagues, figuring out who was most likely to make the majors. And these were the ones they signed up even as they were in the minors, getting five-year agreements for five dollars with no other payments unless you made it to the majors. You've got to remember how young these kids were."

"Most players didn't realize they were being taken advantage of," Jim Bouton, who was something of an activist in the union, told me. "The attitude was, *Here's a guy who's gonna put us on cards, isn't that great? And we can get a gift from the S&H Green Stamp catalog, too!* Back then, players recognized no value in themselves as ballplayers. Most players were even content with the salary structure. There were very few people who fought that, and I was considered a pain in the ass just for holding out for an extra thousand dollars."

In Miller's view, Topps needed the players more than the players needed the card company. He planned on leveraging the players' promotional value into a new contract with Topps that would finance the union for the time being. (Miller had already convinced owners and players to deduct union dues from player salaries, but the money wouldn't be available until after the 1967 season was under way.) He called Joel Shorin to restructure the deal. The Topps president was polite but unyielding. He didn't plan on giving the players a penny more than their $125 per year.

"There will be no changes," he told Miller, "because, honestly, I don't see any muscle in your position."

With Topps refusing to budge, Miller made a proposal to Fleer. For $600,000, he offered, the company would receive the same exclusive rights that Topps enjoyed, starting in 1973. Miller also offered to sell Fleer the rights to produce baseball cards packaged with any product except bubble gum. Fleer turned down both offers, figuring that 1973 was too far off and that only bubble gum paired well with cards.

So Miller urged players not to renew their contracts with Topps. "The only leverage you have is not to sign renewals," he told them. "Eventually Topps will have contracts with no one." Most of the players agreed, even though it cost them a few hundred bucks apiece in the short run.

In the 1968 preseason Sy Berger made his usual rounds of the club-houses on behalf of Topps, but to no avail. Shorin called Miller back.

"I see your muscle," he conceded.

According to Miller, the negotiations over a new arrangement between Topps and the players' union were so heated that one of the card company's lawyers had a heart attack in the middle of a meeting and died on the spot. There was, of course, potentially a huge amount of money at stake. Miller's people wanted more than just larger contract fees paid to players—they also wanted a piece of the Topps pie, in the form of royalties. This was a line that Topps officials were surely loath to cross. If the company conceded, then the more money it pulled in at stores, the more money the union would pull out of the company.

In the end, the union got its way. Under the new deal, Topps doubled its flat fee to $250 annually per player. More important, the company agreed to pay out 8 percent on card sales up to $4 million and 10 percent on all sales above that. Group licensing by ballplayers—by any organized American athletes, for that matter—was born.

The game's biggest stars remained free to sell their faces and person-alities to anyone they wished, but only the union had the right to nego-tiate ballplayers' contracts as a group. And as Fleer's disastrous Ted Williams set had proved, individual star power went only so far—it was as a unit that ballplayers wielded the most marketing power. Within a few years, hundreds of companies would seek to market their products through the union, and its licensing program would put hundreds of millions of dollars into players' pockets. The restructuring of the Topps deal was the first of a raft of negotiations in the 1960s and '70s that would lead Hank Aaron to describe Miller as someone "as important to the history of baseball as Jackie Robinson." Any lingering suspicions of Miller among the players evaporated after he struck the Topps deal.

"It was important on two levels," Bouton said. "One, it showed how powerful Marvin Miller was and how smart he was. It gave him instant credibility. But also, the players' association became immediately self-funding."

The union began selling baseball card rights to companies who agreed not to step on Topps's toes by packaging their cards with gum or candy. New card sets were rolled out by firms such as Chevron, Milton Bradley, and Kahn's Wieners, all of which seemed to realize that baseball-loving kids had at least some control over the family finances. The Shorins fought most of these new card ventures, accusing the players' union of licensing "sham products" such as toy rings and iron-on patches. When Miller struck a deal with Kellogg's to put out 3-D cards of ballplayers, Shorin threatened to sue, even though the cards didn't violate the Topps contract. Dealing with Topps and the growing licensing program became "almost a full-time job" in itself, according to Miller. At the same time, a slew of unlicensed cards and novelties began to find their way into kids' hands as well.

To complicate matters even further, the folks at Fleer decided that they wanted to get back into the baseball card market. The company had sold its pool of player contracts to Topps for $400,000 years before, but once the accompanying noncompetition agreement expired Fleer went after the Brooklyn firm. Fleer executives had been attending baseball card shows in secret and had convinced themselves there was more room than ever for a competitor. First they tried to get a license to sell five-by-seven-inch photos and patches depicting players, but, under Topps's contracts with players, Topps had the right of first refusal on any such products. Shorin argued to Miller that the patches would flop—retailers with full shelves of them would take a pass on other union-licensed products, and the baseball card market on the whole would be diminished. Though he generally thought Shorin overcautious when it came to the prospect of competition, Miller understood the reasoning, and so did the players. The union turned down the proposal. Fleer sued.

Although Shorin and Miller had been butting heads for nearly a decade, the two were named as coconspirators in a 1975 antitrust case brought against Topps and the union in federal court. (This case was entirely separate from the Federal Trade Commission's probe into Topps's alleged monopoly.) Ted Taylor, a collector and hobby columnist, testified on behalf of Fleer. "Fleer was very antsy and knew there was money to be made there," Taylor told me. "I thought there was a real market for more than one card company and more than one card set. I had even suggested that if Topps wants the market for itself, they should make different sets. The cards came out in series, and waiting for the next one just wasn't very exciting for kids."

For twenty years, Topps had maintained that baseball cards are no different than any other type of swapable cardboard, and that the company therefore couldn't possibly be operating a monopoly. This time, the court rejected that argument. Baseball cards were a rite of American boyhood, the judge determined, and no other candy-store offering—certainly not the stuff showing *Dukes of Hazzard* or *Star Wars* characters—could serve as a substitute. In a sometimes passionate ruling the judge wrote, "Even if the product was merely a casual idea of a long-forgotten promoter in the 1880s, and even if there are hundreds of variations and substitutes which logically might exist, the concept is now so embedded that baseball cards literally define themselves." A kid, he went on, "knows if he has not yet found Dave Winfield, Keith Hernandez, Robin Yount or Ron Guidry. . . . Baseball cards are the only product on a typical candy rack to set forth baseball statistics. They are, in other words, an education in baseball."

Topps and the union, the court ruled, had conspired to shut Fleer and other candy companies out of the card world. Topps was prohibited from forming any long-term exclusive contracts with players, and the union was required to grant a license to at least one other card manufacturer by 1981. Fleer was awarded $3 in damages by the court, but the company stood to gain much more money in the future as it was free now to go ahead and print baseball cards. The twenty-five-year Topps monopoly had come to an end.

Baseball cards had been a niche product distributed by a single company, but they would soon develop into a thriving industry. Because of changes set in motion largely by Marvin Miller, baseball cards would soon become more popular and more profitable than ever before.

For years the brass at Topps had insisted that the market for baseball cards could sustain only one card maker. Joel Shorin, in fact, had often told Miller that market research he'd commissioned demonstrated just that. So it was probably with a degree of horror that Shorin watched as two companies rushed to sign contracts with the Major League Baseball Players Association to produce their own card sets for the 1981 season: Fleer and Donruss, the former manufacturer of Little Leaguer Chewing Tobacco Bubble Gum.

Even though Fleer had been waiting two decades to compete with Topps baseball cards, the company had only a few weeks to produce its set and get it into stores. Donruss was operating on a similar schedule. Due to the time crunch, the two firms' premiere sets looked even less inspired than a lazy Topps offering. With just three months to get its bearings, Donruss had trouble finding suitable photos for some players, resorting to using pictures that were out of focus or had shadows cast across players' faces. The company's cards were also riddled with errors, at least thirty-one in total—statistics were botched and, more commonly, names were misspelled. In the first printing for the year, the Angels' Tom Donohue was "Don Donahue," the Minnesota Twins' Glenn Adams was "Glen Adams," the Kansas City Royals' Paul Splittorff was "Paul Spittorff," the Cleveland Indians' Duane Kuiper was "Dwayne Kuiper," and the Oakland Athletics' Rob Picciolo was "Bob Picciolo," among others. Worse, Donruss didn't even bother to pull out the airbrush to account for off-season trades, so a player's team name at the bottom of his card often conflicted with the uniform in his photo. And on the back of the cards, Donruss offered a measly two lines of statistics —"1980" and "lifetime"—even though Topps had been giving the season-by-season breakdown for a decade.

Fleer's set was so slipshod that the production department went back to press twice in an attempt to correct the errors. Donruss, meanwhile, couldn't get enough of its cards out the door to satisfy dealers, and kids who did get their hands on Donruss cardboard often grew disgruntled: the same card could turn up as many as five times in one wax pack. In the growing number of card shops in small towns everywhere, collectors were wondering whether the two companies had intentionally inserted the haste-induced errors into their sets to create buzz.

A strange thing happened. In spite of Shorin's worst fears, and in spite of the new cards' low quality, sales of baseball cards rose across the board. Topps had tallied sales of $9.2 million in 1978, but sales of Fleer and Donruss cards alone reached $20 million in 1981. The breakup of the Topps monopoly proved to be a boon for all card companies, as well as for baseball players, who now received royalties from several different card manufacturers.

When presented with a choice between three different card designs, children apparently wanted to buy all three.

By the time Fleer and Donruss rolled out their first sets, a small cabal of collector speculators had grown wise to the fact that some cards, whether new or vintage, had become relatively valuable. Cards had almost always had prices attached to them, even when Jefferson Burdick began sending out his *Card Collectors Bulletin* in the 1930s, but cards that had been worth a few cents were now worth a few bucks. Some of the rarer specimens, such as the T206 Honus Wagner, were commanding hundreds and occasionally thousands of dollars apiece, and the growing number of trade shows sprouting up in the East and the Midwest testified to a growing market.

In the mid-1970s the most aggressive collectors started crisscrossing the country in search of private hoards of cards that could be snatched up at bargain prices. Burdick had done much the same but, unlike the earliest card lovers, this new generation of collectors was well aware of baseball cards' status as a commodity—albeit an undervalued one. Many of these enthusiasts could credit their early transactions with turning them into wealthy men later in life. One of them is San Diego collector Kit Young, whose mail-order card business now has an annual sales volume well into the millions of dollars. Back in the '70s Young could see that vintage-card values were rising, sometimes exponentially, and that out on the road he might be able to snag a collection worth $1,000 for a fraction of that.

"We'd pick an area of the country—say, Ohio—and take about a ten- or fifteen-day road trip," recalled Young. "You'd take eight or ten grand for a four-city hit. We'd rent a car, go around the towns, and we'd have ads in the local papers saying OLD BASEBALL CARDS WANTED— just throw it in the sports section. We'd say, 'We'll be at the Holiday Inn. Ask for Kit Young.' And you'd wait for someone to show up. Someone would come stumbling in with a cigar box or shoe box, and you sat down on the bed and you made an offer. You'd get one crack at them, and you paid by cash. You're hoping for the holy grail to walk in. For a lot of people it was just found money. The cards were sitting in the closet, and then all of a sudden they've got $500 in their pocket from us." Not all customers were content to leave Young's room with a small wad of cash, however. One night in a rough part of Oakland, California, Young and his traveling companion, Chicago collector Pat Quinn, scooped up a pile of '60s-era baseball cards from a pair of locals, who returned to the hotel later that night, visibly drunk, and robbed the card dealers at gunpoint.

For most of the "rogues of the road," as Young refers to the early itinerant collectors, the unknown and the unpredictable—preferably not accompanied by guns—were the whole point of their travels. "I can't describe the enjoyment of going on a buying trip and wondering what would walk in the door," recalled Gar Miller, a Young colleague from Wenonah, New Jersey. "It could be a young guy with an old box

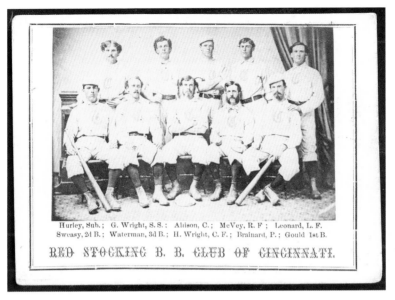

The 1869 Cincinnati Red Stockings trade card from Peck & Snyder, arguably the first baseball card. Courtesy Robert Edward Auctions.

Left. A signed portrait of sporting goods mogul Andrew Peck dated April 1873, about four years after he issued some of the very first baseball cards.
Courtesy Robert Edward Auctions.

Center. Duke's 1888 "Terrors of America," one of many tobacco card sets put out by marketing visionary James Buchanan Duke. Courtesy Robert Edward Auctions.

Right. Duke's Algeresque "Histories of Poor Boys Who Became Rich."
Courtesy Robert Edward Auctions.

Left. An 1887 Kalamazoo Bats cabinet card of A's infielder James B. "Chippy" McGarr. Courtesy Robert Edward Auctions.

Right. An Old Judge card of Boston Hall of Fame hurler Charles "Old Hoss" Radbourn. Note the middle finger slyly extended on Old Hoss's left hip. Courtesy Robert Edward Auctions.

Left. Slugger "Big Ed" Delahanty looking mysteriously skyward on his Old Judge card. Courtesy Robert Edward Auctions.

Right. Hall of Famer and vaudeville performer Mike "King" Kelly, shown in his 1888 card from Allen & Ginter. Courtesy Robert Edward Auctions.

Left. The fabled T206 Honus Wagner card. Courtesy Robert Edward Auctions.

Right. The ultrarare T206 "Slow" Joe Doyle error card. There are less than ten in existence, and the finer specimens can command a half-million dollars or more. Courtesy Robert Edward Auctions.

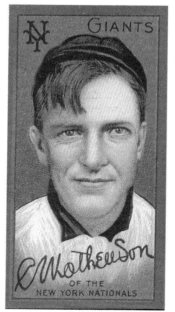

Above. Collector Mike Gidwitz with a couple of his baseball card-style portraits. Gidwitz sold his T206 Wagner for $1.27 million in 2000. The portrait to the left was painted by Gerry Dvorak; the right by Dave Hirsch. Courtesy Brett Nadal.

Left. A 1911 American Tobacco card of Christy Mathewson, based on a portrait shot the previous year by baseball photographer Paul Thompson. Courtesy Robert Edward Auctions.

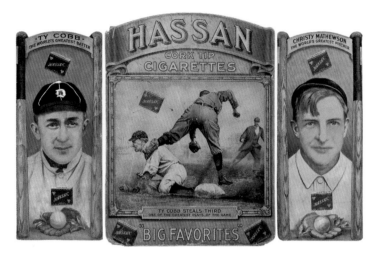

A large store display advertising Hassan Cigarettes "triple folder" cards from 1912. The center panel on this card, which shows Ty Cobb sliding into third-baseman Jimmy Austin, is based on the famous shot by lensman Charles Conlin. Courtesy Robert Edward Auctions.

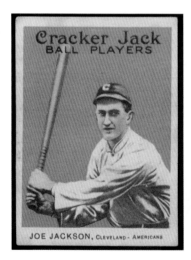

Left. Shoeless Joe Jackson's Cracker Jack card from 1914. Because they came in boxes of Cracker Jack, many surviving cards are stained with caramel. Courtesy Robert Edward Auctions.

Right. A 1911 Turkey Red Ty Cobb card. Many collectors consider this American Tobacco Company issue to be the most attractive of all tobacco sets. Courtesy Robert Edward Auctions.

  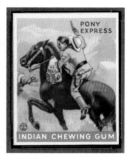

The Goudey Gum Company's Indian Gum started a schoolyard craze in 1932.
The cards were based on portraits of Native Americans at the Smithsonian.
Courtesy Robert Edward Auctions.

Left. The controversial Nap Lajoie
card that duped countless boys into
buying more and more Goudey cards.
Courtesy Robert Edward Auctions.

Right. Hank Greenberg's 1938
"Heads-Up" card from Goudey.
Courtesy Robert Edward Auctions.

Circa 1935 Diamond Stars. Courtesy Robert Edward Auctions.

A section from an "uncut sheet" of Goudey cards from 1933. The cards were never cut individually and put into circulation, making such sheets rare and valuable. Modern collectors covet the sheets for their singularity and attractiveness.

Courtesy Robert Edward Auctions.

Left. "Ras Seyum's Bodyguard Defends Palace," from Gum Inc.'s notorious "Horrors of War" series, created by gum mogul J. Warren Bowman and ad man George Moll. Courtesy Robert Edward Auctions.

Right. "Spanish Volunteers Swim Icy River." These renderings were almost certainly the work of artist Charles Schumacher. Courtesy Robert Edward Auctions.

The

American

Card Catalog

A comprehensive listing, with values, of what is known in American Cards; designed to assist in their classification and to facilitate their sale and exchange among collectors and dealers.

Acknowledgment

Appreciation is extended to the many collectors throughout the world who have cheerfully assisted in assembling the data in this Catalog. With their help, it is possible to present these listings in a form which, to most classifications, will need little further amending. Errors and omissions should be reported so that they may be corrected for the benefit of all. Sample cards will be returned with thanks.

Price 75c from

J. R. Burdick, 439 So. Crouse Ave., Syracuse 10, N.Y.

In Great Britain, orders of 5 may be forwarded to

C. Glidden Osborne, Highfields, Marlow, Bucks, England

Left. The title page of Jefferson Burdick's self-published American Card Catalog, the foundation of the card hobby.

"JOE" DI MAGGIO

Right. The 1941 Play Ball card of Joe DiMaggio, issued by Bowman's Gum Inc. Courtesy Robert Edward Auctions.

Left. Satchel Paige's rare 1949 rookie card from the Leaf Gum Company of Chicago. Courtesy Robert Edward Auctions.

Right. The 1949 Bowman Roy Campanella. Courtesy Robert Edward Auctions.

Left. The 1951 Bowman Willie Mays. It would be the last year Bowman had the field to itself. Courtesy Robert Edward Auctions.

Right. A World War II-era matchbook showing Topps's wartime slogan. The gum shortage crippled production for most companies at the time.

Sy Berger, the man who put Topps on top in the '50s and '60s, at home in Rockville Centre, New York, in 2007. Courtesy Dave Jamieson.

The iconic 1952 Topps Mickey Mantle, the most hallowed baseball card of the postwar era. Berger didn't list a specific season on the back, instead opting for the vague "previous year," because he didn't want to date the cards if they failed to sell in 1952. Courtesy Robert Edward Auctions.

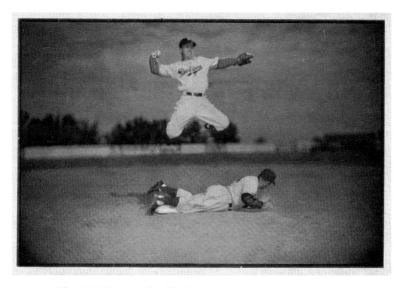

The 1953 Bowman Pee Wee Reese. Courtesy Robert Edward Auctions.

 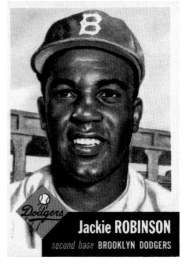

Left. The 1952 Topps Andy Pafko, #1 in the historic series. The Pafko card is extremely difficult to find in good condition. Many collectors believe that's because boys in the '50s put the #1 card at the top of their stacks and wrapped them in rubber bands. Courtesy Robert Edward Auctions.

Right. Jackie Robinson. Topps's 1953 cards were based on hand-painted color portraits. The fierce competition with Bowman in the early '50s led to some of the finest cards ever made. Courtesy Robert Edward Auctions.

Left. A 1957 Topps wax pack. The price changed over the years but the packaging stayed more or less the same. Courtesy Robert Edward Auctions.

Right. The 1958 Topps Hank Aaron. Courtesy Robert Edward Auctions.

From Fleer's ill-conceived 1959 all-Ted Williams set. Williams was the only player Fleer could steal away from Topps, so the company chose to depict its star in all facets of his life, whether they were interesting or not. Courtesy Robert Edward Auctions.

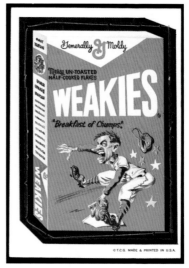

Left. Woody Gelman, the artist who helmed Topps's creative department for more than two decades. Courtesy Richard Gelman.

Right. Topps's Wacky Packages, launched in 1967, lampooned popular commercial brands with elementary-school humor. Courtesy Robert Edward Auctions.

The Norm Saunders painting that was used for the first card in Topps's 1962 "Mars Attacks" set. For this renowned series, Gelman and his art team were inspired by Hugo Gernsback and the trashy sci-fi films of the 1940s and '50s.
Courtesy Robert Edward Auctions.

Original artwork from Topps's 1962 "Civil War News" set. This rich and explicit series was conceived by Gelman and protégé Len Brown.
Courtesy Robert Edward Auctions

ROBERTO CLEMENTE
Pittsburgh Pirates—Outfield

Left. The 1963 Fleer Roberto Clemente. Courtesy Robert Edward Auctions.

Right. Marvin Miller, long-time head of the baseball players union, in a 2003 photo. Miller's negotiations with Topps in the 1960s changed the business of baseball forever. Courtesy Larry Goren.

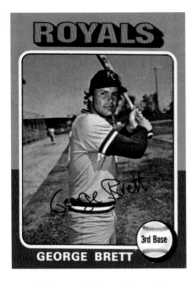

Left. The 1975 Topps George Brett rookie card. Courtesy Robert Edward Auctions.

Right. The 1984 Topps Don Mattingly, the card that started the rookie card craze and helped launch the card boom of the 80s.

Left. A sample from Topps's 1987 "woodie" set, the author's personal favorite from childhood.

Right. The 1989 Upper Deck Ken Griffey rookie card, the most famous of its era. This was the inaugural card in Upper Deck's inaugural set, and it revolutionized the card business.

BILL RIPKEN
SECOND BASE

FLEER

Left. The infamous Billy Ripken error card from Fleer's 1989 set. Note the obscenity on the knob of his bat. Courtesy Ben Goetting.

Right. Ethical card doctor Kevin Saucier, at work in his alteration "lab" in Harbor City, California. Courtesy Dave Jamieson.

Left. Bill Mastro. Courtesy Bridget Montgomery.

Right. Card auctioneer Rob Lifson. Courtesy Rob Lifson.

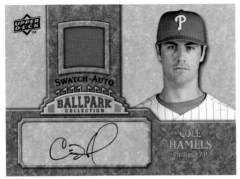

Left. Philly hurler Cole Hamels's 2009 Ballpark Collection card from Upper Deck, featuring the player's signature and a swatch of his uniform. As the industry has struggled in recent years, card companies have tried to enhance cards with autographs and pieces of memorabilia.

Right. A 2008 "Hair Cut Signatures" card from Upper Deck, featuring Abe Lincoln's autograph and a piece of his hair. This bizarre curio sold for $17,500 on eBay.

Left. A 2009 Johnny Damon Goodwin Champions card from Upper Deck. Like other recent offerings, this modern card borrows its look from one of the earliest tobacco sets, in this case the cards put out by Goodwin & Co. in 1888.

Right. The 2009 Topps Jason Bartlett

of cards or an old guy who had his grandson's cards that were worthless —you just never knew. You might find some beautiful collection that had unopened packs of cards. It was just thrilling." For the wandering hobbyist it wasn't difficult to get a great deal from the noncollector who walked through the door, because there were no price guides to govern transactions. As Gar Miller told me, "You didn't know what anything was worth."

This loophole in the hobby would soon be closed by a professor from Bowling Green University named James Beckett III. Beckett had grown up in the 1950s collecting early Topps cards, although his father had allowed him to pore over his trove only when it was too rainy to play outside. Like many young cartophiles, Beckett eventually put aside his collection. But he got back into baseball cards while pursuing a PhD in statistics from Southern Methodist University. Like Young and Miller, Beckett started checking into Holiday Inns around the country during the '70s. The more hotel-room dealings he had, the more he understood that no one had any firm notion what the cards' market value was, including the most knowledgeable collectors.

As a professor of statistics, Beckett was the ideal candidate to "bring some order out of the chaos," as he would later say. In 1976, he launched a poll in the hobby newspapers asking dealers and collectors how much particular cards had been selling for in recent months. Because collectors were inclined to juice the value of cards they had in hand, Beckett sought several hundred respondents so that especially high (or low) numbers could be averaged out. The following year he published a rudimentary price list whose valuations seem cut-rate next to today's: the Topps Mantle rookie was listed at $50 and the American Tobacco Wagner at just $500. By 1979 Beckett and a partner, Dennis Eckes, released the *Sport Americana Baseball Card Price Guide,* which they started updating annually. Eventually, Beckett would launch a monthly magazine and employ a team of ten full-time baseball card analysts who would travel to card shows and shops, examine auction data, and sift through major-league box scores to determine card values.

Until Beckett came along, card prices had shown up in newsletters but usually only in large groupings—cards of a certain tobacco set, for instance, might be worth roughly $3 apiece. Beckett's detailed list of individual card values essentially reflected a baseball player's worth in the eyes of fans. As one academic study would find, looking at the value of baseball cards served as an excellent way to determine a ballplayer's "star power," or how strong a draw he was for his team's owner. Beckett also made collector investors more condition conscious by including in his magazines one of the first card grading systems, providing definitions for what he considered "mint," "excellent," "very good," "good," "fair," and "poor" cards.

Beckett pronounced himself a born-again Christian right around the time he launched his price guides, in the early 1980s, and he viewed the assigning of values to baseball cards as something of a religious calling. "Would it be sacrilegious to say that we want to be a source for wisdom?" he once asked an interviewer. "We want to be representing some good ideals. We're not going to hit people over the head with the fact that me and a number of the leaders of the company . . . well, lets just say we have high moral standards. We don't promote people because they're Christians or anything. But they must have good ethics and moral character. It isn't what you say you are, but what you demonstrate."

Beckett's publishing empire now claims about a dozen titles, and it was acquired by Apprise Media in 2005 for a reported $20 million. (In addition to being deeply religious, Beckett is an intensely private man. When I asked him for an interview he politely declined, telling me he was "in the process of deciding how and where I want to tell my story.")

Like the magazine's founder, American boys approached *Beckett Baseball Card Monthly* with something like religious reverence. It was the first magazine I bought and the only one I leafed through regularly as a child. Among the ranks of elementary- and middle-school-age kids, I certainly wasn't alone. The magazine's circulation eventually reached about one million, with many of those issues no doubt destined for the book bags of young boys. We walked the school hallways in the '80s with our *Becketts* sandwiched between our textbooks, and we followed the price fluctuations of our favorite players with slavish devotion, tearing into the latest issue to see whether the little arrow beside Don Mattingly's name was pointing up or down. Jim Beckett's valuations served as the foundation for all card trades, and his name became familiar to so many who came of age in the 1980s.

What none of us understood at the time, however, was that Beckett's guides were probably creating card prices just as much as they were reporting them. When Beckett successfully sued a competitor over copyright infringement in 1979, claiming that a rival publication had stolen his data, even then the judge noted that because Beckett's guides were "regarded as the authority in the field, it is entirely possible that the prices in [his] publication not only reflect market prices, but in fact can determine market prices." Beckett eventually gave up card dealing himself to avoid the perception of a conflict of interest—and the prices in his publications continued to climb. Old-school collectors who once simply enjoyed amassing cards found that, by the '80s, values were rising well beyond the average hobbyist's means.

Jim Beckett did as much as anyone to turn baseball cards into a billion-dollar industry. In a less conspicuous way, so did television super-producer Aaron Spelling. Bear with me.

From 1979 to 1984, Spelling produced an hour long prime-time mystery series for ABC called *Hart to Hart*. Similar to other inanely implausible Spelling offerings, this show featured Robert Wagner as Jonathan Hart, a dashing self-made millionaire and amateur sleuth, who, each week, enlisted his beautiful wife, Jennifer Hart (Stefanie Powers), in solving an intrigue-filled whodunit. The May 4, 1982, episode of *Hart to Hart*, "The Harts Strike Out," revolved around baseball cards.

A dead man leaves behind nothing but a trove of "valuable, untraceable baseball cards," appraised at a quarter of a million dollars, instigating a violent family squabble. At the episode's climax Jonathan Hart finagles his way into a high-stakes card-flipping game at a card show, only because he knows the password: "Ebbets Field." Cue the beyond-bad dialogue.

> Jennifer: "Ebbets Field? Flipping? What's going on?"
> Jonathan: "Let's get down to the convention floor so
>   I can buy some cards and get in the game of flip."
> Jennifer: "Darling, I think you've already flipped."

As ridiculous as it may seem, Kit Young, who followed the pulse of the hobby more closely than most, insists that the episode's airing was a watershed moment in the world of baseball cards—the closest thing to a genuine "coming out" moment as you'll find. "There were millions of people watching," he told me. "It was really the first time the hobby had national attention."

Of course, there were other, less anecdotal signs that baseball cards had reached the mainstream. The same year that "The Harts Strike Out" was aired, Topps struck a deal with retail giant Kmart to manufacture cards for its stores. Topps had previously made cards for companies such as Burger King and Coca-Cola, but here the cards weren't promoting some other product—they were the main attraction, and they were now taking up valuable shelf space in one of the country's largest retail chains. A few months later the Wall Street private equity giant Forstmann Little & Company bought Topps for $94.5 million with the intention of taking it public. Soon after, the Finnish company Huhtamaki Oy bought Donruss from General Mills for a rumored eight-figure sum. As these well-heeled outside investors sought to tap into the hobby's vast potential, it became clear that baseball cards were no longer an industry to be run by a couple of candy-biz families generation after generation.

* * *

As more card sets and hobby publications poured into drugstores and card shops, a new term emerged among schoolboys: "rookie card." In years past, collectors had never made much of a fuss over whether a particular card was the player's first to appear. Things changed in the early '80s after Mickey Mantle's 1952 Topps rookie card sold for around $3,000, then a staggering sum for a postwar piece of cardboard. Such sales marked the beginning of a long nostalgia boom, as the boys who'd collected those early Topps sets grew into professionals with income to throw around.

The Mantle rookie card benefited from more than just the Mick's status among fans and his Hall of Fame numbers. Compared to other Topps cards of the era, his was extremely difficult to find in top condition, thanks in large part to a disposal of cardboard carried out by Sy Berger years earlier. In the early 1960s, Berger told me, he was tasked with ridding the Topps office of its back stock of cards that had never sold in the '50s. Normally, such refuse would simply be thrown into the trash. But the boxes contained expired coupons that had been given to wholesalers as incentives. Berger worried that, if he left them to the janitors to dispose of, the outdated vouchers might make their way into circulation and cause confusion.

The bulk of the cards were from the "high series" of the famous 1952 set, numbered 311 to 407—perhaps the most coveted sequence of baseball cards ever made, containing Mantle, Jackie Robinson, Pee Wee Reese, and Roy Campanella among others. The fact that these cards had never sold was no big surprise. Mantle hadn't yet achieved superstardom, and the high series had been introduced as an afterthought late in 1952, when the attention of American boys had already drifted to football.

So Berger hit up a few carnivals, hoping the booth workers would take the cards off his hands for cheap and use them as prizes. Yet nobody wanted them. Berger was no collector, and he saw no use in holding on to them. He decided to dump them into the ocean. There were several hundred cases of old product, each with thousands of cards apiece, that went into three garbage trucks. Berger pulled a favor with a friend who owned a garbage scow, and they loaded the cache onto the barge in Brooklyn and hauled it out to sea by tugboat. A few miles off the coast of New Jersey, Berger sent to the ocean floor a few tons of mint-condition Topps cards, including perhaps thousands of those iconic 1952 Mantle rookies.

As card collecting became a mainstream pursuit in the early '80s, more and more vintage cards like the Mantle found their way out of attics and into circulation. But this influx of cards didn't, as one might expect, drive prices down. Vast numbers of new collectors were entering the market at the same time, so demand easily outpaced supply. These new collectors looked at the gains made by the '52 Mantle card and began to snap up the rookie cards of unproven players, creating a speculative frenzy. Jim Beckett began making note of a player's rookie card in his guides and assessing them at several times the value of the same player's later cards, a price structure that dealers were glad to support. As one hobbyist wrote at the time, "Essentially, the entire rookie card phenomenon began as nothing more than dealer hype, a way to sell more new baseball cards than ever before at unprecedented prices." The frenzy would drive sales of new product for years.

Perhaps no one helped fuel the rookie-card fad quite like Pete Rose, whose 1963 Topps card began rising exponentially as he approached Ty Cobb's all-time hit record in the early 1980s. The Rose rookie climbed from $65 in 1981 to $375 just two years later, and demand was so high that the hobby's first substantial stock of counterfeit cards made their way into the market. A Los Angeles Police Department detective, who happened to be a dealer and a collector himself, spearheaded an investigation that found a pair of California men had printed more than ten thousand sham Rose rookies on thin cardboard stock. The cards had been selling at trade shows for around $100 each. Although the men were convicted the counterfeits never made it to the shredder, and a lawyer for the guilty parties successfully petitioned that the cards be returned. The judge ruled that the cards be stamped "original counterfeit" by the LAPD. In a testament to how insatiable the demand for Rose rookie cards was, the stamped fakes went back on the market and sold accordingly for about $25 a pop.

Buying rookie cards became a way for fans to legally gamble on a player's future. Yankee Don Mattingly's spectacular 1984 season, in which he hit 23 homers, had 110 RBIs, and captured the American League batting crown at the age of twenty-three, propelled his Donruss rookie card to $100 by the 1987 season. "That's why I make an argument for Don Mattingly to be in the Hall of Fame," Jay McCracken, a former Upper Deck executive, told me. "He's the one that bailed out the card industry in 1987." That year, a fourteen-year-old boy in Florida was disseminating counterfeit Mattingly rookies among credulous adult card dealers. The boy had about a thousand of them printed in high quality at a local copy shop after reportedly convincing the clerk that he was Mattingly's cousin. The boy initially sold them at school, including to one classmate who ponied up about $1,200 for more than three dozen of them. The counterfeiter foisted another $1,800 worth on a shop owner who thought the $38-apiece price tag was a steal. "As far as the state is concerned, if it's a juvenile, it's not fraud; it's an act of God," the owner complained to a reporter. "And what am I going to do? Break the kid's legs?" Another card dealer said he'd been hoodwinked by the same boy running a different scam. "This kid just called me up and said, 'My mother just put down a deposit on some 1987 Donruss cases. Would you like a couple?" the dealer explained. "He goes around to three, four, ten different dealers and gets them to put two-thirds down. Then he skips town."

Baseball cards were being touted as a legitimate investment alternative to stocks, with reputable financial publications referring to them as "inflation hedges." Newspaper editors started running feature stories with headlines such as "Turning Cardboard into Cash: These Are Boom Days for Baseball Cards" (*The Washington Post*), "A Grand Slam Profit May Be in the Cards" (*The New York Times*), and "Cards Put Gold, Stocks to Shame as Investment" (*The Orange County Register*).

Even the *Wall Street Journal* and *Money* fueled the speculation, reporting that few investments in the previous decade had demonstrated the fabulous rate of return on baseball cards. A hobby bulletin called the *Ball Street Journal,* claiming entrée to a network of scouts and coaches with major-league clubs, promised collectors "insider scouting information" that would help them invest in the cards of rising big-league prospects. Kids bought books with titles like *Making Money with Baseball Cards: A Handbook of Insider Secrets and Strategies* and *The Top 100: The Best Baseball Cards to Own, Ranked and Rated for Collector and Investor.* But the secret was already out, and buying into cards by the early 1990s violated a fundamental rule of investing: never rush into a market that's already mobbed.

In one of several articles the *Wall Street Journal* ran expounding the liquidity of baseball cards, the newspaper employed an apt term to describe this mode of investing: "nostalgia futures." In the world of baseball cards, the report went, "the key player isn't really Rose or Gooden or even Honus Wagner, but rather Paul Volcker, the rangy Federal Reserve Board Chairman. His nifty squeeze play against high inflation has made card-collecting a whole new ballgame. These colorful pieces of cardboard haven't dived in value like some of the collectibles that became popular inflation hedges." And why would they?

Perhaps because each card was being printed in astronomical numbers. The card companies were shrewd enough never to disclose how many cards they were actually producing, but even conservative estimates put the number well into the billions. One trade magazine estimated the tally was 81 billion baseball cards per year in the late 1980s and early '90s, or more than three hundred cards for every American annually. The 81 billion figure included so-called vanity baseball cards, which were printed for everyone from Little Leaguers to fledgling actors looking to publicize their credentials, but in all likelihood the major producers were collectively churning out millions of cards for each big-league player.

Precious few investor collectors seemed even to ponder the possibility that baseball cards could depreciate. As the number of card shops in the United States ballooned to ten thousand, dealers were filling their storage rooms with unopened cases of 1988 Donruss sets as if they were T-bills or bearer bonds. Shops were regularly burglarized, and local newspapers and hobby publications carried headlines such as "Las Vegas Card Shops Raided" and "Mantle, Schmidt Cards Taken in Armed Robbery" with surprising regularity.

And as if to prove that *Hart to Hart* really does imitate life, the body of a card dealer was found slumped behind a display case in his San Luis Obispo, California, card shop in early 1990. Frank Gove had been bludgeoned to death, the thief making off with $10,000 worth of his sports cards. "I mean, baseball is supposed to be the all-American game," a detective working the case told a reporter at the time. "This is really the dark side." A few weeks later the hobby gained some unfortunate national attention with the sad story of Bob Engel. A respected veteran umpire in the National League, Engel was arrested for allegedly stealing more than 4,180 Score baseball cards, worth $143.98, from a Target store in Bakersfield, California, and attempting to steal another fifty packs from a Costco. Engel, whose own face had appeared on cards, was suspended indefinitely from Major League Baseball.

For those disturbed by such unseemly tales, the baseball card hobby had begun to resemble the game of baseball itself: an American institution that appeared to have strayed from its noble and innocent beginnings. Never mind that baseball cards, much like the game, had always been big business and always been a revenue machine. There had been nothing guileless about the Topps monopoly, and nothing particularly dignified about using baseball cards to shill cigarettes to grown-ups and children alike a hundred years earlier. As outspoken hobbyist Lew Lipset wrote in an issue of his *Old Judge Newsletter* in 1990: "Try to make a living in this hobby and you'll learn about . . . deceit, unfair business practices, the lack of truth in advertising, price manipulation, collusion, restraint of trade, insider trading, patronage, extortion, payoffs and bribes, graft, plagiarism and, last but not least, hype."

8

Cardboard Gold

In September 1987, Paul Sumner walked into a baseball card shop in Anaheim, California, called The Upper Deck. At the time, Sumner understood little about the growing world of baseball cards, aside from the fact that there appeared to be a lot of money in it. Not entirely satisfied with his day job as a salesman at a nearby printing firm, Sumner was looking to moonlight with some sort of hobby business. He was tired of earning profits for other people. He'd been exploring the worlds of rare coins, comic books, model trains, and even doll houses when he learned that the Topps Mickey Mantle rookie card, which Sumner had had seven copies of as a child, was selling for $4,500 and more at card shops. He was at The Upper Deck to do some industry research.

Like thousands of other men around the country, Bill Hemrick, the owner of The Upper Deck, had recently opened his shop in hopes of riding the card boom to prosperity. It hadn't been an easy road so far. Hemrick had attended a baseball card convention at a Holiday Inn in Anaheim, spending $4,000 on what he believed was about $8,000 worth of 1984 Donruss Don Mattingly rookie cards, Sumner told me in an interview. After selling most of them, Hemrick, along with many of his customers, learned that the cards in fact came from the notorious batch of Mattingly counterfeits. Hemrick kept one of the counterfeits encased at The Upper Deck as a conversation starter.

He called over Sumner, and placed two Mattingly rookies in front of him on the counter.

"What do you think of these?" he asked.

Sumner took a close look at them. "This one looks real," he said. "But this one looks like a fake."

Hemrick was startled. A customer who wasn't even familiar with the major card companies could tell in a matter of seconds that he'd bought $4,000 worth of junk. Sumner explained how he knew. He'd been in the printing business for much of two decades, and it wasn't difficult for him to tell when something on cardboard had been copied. He actually carried a jeweler's loupe with him, and through it he could see a minuscule amount of red, yellow, and blue ink bleeding out beneath the black type on the fake; those colors shouldn't have been there. Someone had clearly scanned the original.

Offering up the woeful tale of his Mattingly deal, Hemrick asserted that card counterfeiting was a growing problem in the industry. Printing equipment and scanners were getting cheaper just as baseball cards themselves were getting more valuable. Other fake rookie cards, such as those of rising stars Eric Davis and Danny Tartabull, had also turned up at shows and in stores. Buyers couldn't be completely sure that what they were buying from even reputable dealers was real.

Sumner had a solution for the market's uncertainties. "I can print a card that looks as good as *Architectural Digest* magazine," he told Hemrick, "and I can put a hologram on every single card to keep them from being counterfeited."

He knew what he was talking about. Though he worked as a salesman, Sumner had a strong grasp of the printing process, as well as of the science of holography, which wasn't much more than a couple of decades old. Sumner had been fascinated when he saw his first hologram, in 1969, at the Museum of Science and Industry in Chicago. On the museum wall hung a hologram of a chess board, and Sumner was so confounded by it that he had to lift it off the wall before accepting that it wasn't a real board. Three years later he was studying at the art school of California State University at Long Beach, at a time when there was a small movement afoot to bring arts students toward the fundamental sciences. Sumner soon found himself establishing the school's holography lab, working on developing what's known as the white-light-projection hologram.

For years, holography was considered the proverbial solution in search of a problem. By the early 1980s, however, it had been put to excellent use on credit cards. The people at Visa discovered that a hologram is a simple and cost-effective way to prevent their plastic cards from being counterfeited. In order to credibly duplicate a hologram, a counterfeiter requires both holographic training and prohibitively expensive equipment, sometimes running into the millions of dollars. The use of holograms drastically reduced the counterfeiting of credit cards. And on top of that they looked cool. Not long after Visa's now famous dove appeared in three silver dimensions, Sumner's clients at the graphics firm were asking him to put holographic images on their brochures.

By using holography on baseball cards, Sumner thought that he could end whatever counterfeiting existed in the hobby. And he wasn't joking about making the cards look like *Architectural Digest*. Sumner's company, Orbis Graphics, had been doing work enhancing photographs for the glossy authority on interior design, so he had a good handle on the process needed to put high-quality photographs on paper stock.

Not only could he create a more secure baseball card, he could create a higher-quality one.

Sumner visited more card shops to do market research. He found that when the kids got out of school, they poured into the shops in groups, sometimes with their mothers in tow. He was shocked at how much money these kids were willing to spend on cards. "Mommy would give the kid a twenty-dollar bill. It was insane," he said. He started asking collectors and dealers the same two-part question: "One, do you want a better baseball card? And two, do you want a card that is counterfeit-proof?" He grew convinced that both kids and adults wanted more serious-looking cardboard, while price-conscious companies like Topps and Fleer seemed unwilling to give it to them. The cards he had in mind might be twice as expensive to produce as traditional ones, but he saw a clear market for them.

Hemrick, the shop owner, jumped at Sumner's vision for a new card company. In January of 1988, they incorporated under the same name as Hemrick's shop, Upper Deck, hoping to connote both a deck of cards and high-end cachet. They found another partner in Sumner's boss at the graphics company, Boris Korbel, who knew nothing of baseball cards but saw the potential. Korbel, in turn, reached out to his friend Richard McWilliam, a well-connected accountant, to round up investors. Jay McCracken, a well-known hobbyist in Southern California, left his job in management at Nestlé to join the team.

Sumner wanted to break the mold of the traditional baseball card. He fashioned himself an inventor and a Renaissance man—he'd either studied or worked in mathematics, aeronautical engineering, laser sculpture, printing, and marketing. He drew on much of what he'd learned in his undergrad and postgrad years to design his cards. "Everything I'd been in my life went into that first year of Upper Deck cards," he told me.

For starters, he decided to use higher-grade cardboard and ink than his competitors, hoping they would lend the photos more definition. (Upper Deck's cardboard, Sumner told me, technically wasn't even paper; he declined to explain, saying it was a trade secret.) He also drew up plans for a new machine that would cut cards without dinging the corners and edges and then shuffle them in a random order. This would solve one problem he'd been hearing about from collectors, that cards were packaged in sequences that dealers were able to determine after opening up enough cases. Dealers could therefore break open the packs they knew held the money cards, replace them with commons, and reseal them. And as he flew back from a meeting in Minnesota where he'd discussed the shuffling machine with engineers, Sumner thought of a novel way to package his baseball cards. He was struggling to open his foil bag of airline peanuts when it hit him. He could put Upper Deck cards into tamper-proof foil packaging. When Sumner got home he called an executive at Planters, who put him in touch with their package maker. That way, unscrupulous dealers and collectors wouldn't be able to reseal Upper Deck packs at all, as they could with wax packs. (Upper Deck would adopt this packaging method for its second major card issue, in 1990.) In a stroke of luck, Sumner also found a German press manufacturer who'd recently designed a new machine that could affix holograms to paper without leaving an imprint on the other side. It seemed everything was falling into place, as long as he could keep expenses within reason.

The Upper Deck team had to set a firm cost ceiling for each part of production, for they knew they needed to meet a magic number for the store price: ninety-nine cents per pack, after tax. That certainly wasn't cheap —it was twice the price of competing brands. But Sumner was sure that kids wouldn't care so long as a buck got them "a pack and a penny back," even though marketing people were telling him he was crazy. "They said it was like putting out a cola that would cost double what Coca-Cola did. Everyone said, 'You can't do that.' But collectors were screaming for it."

As slick as they might be, the cards would never see the light of day unless Upper Deck scored a contract with the baseball players' union. For help in this they turned to De Wayne Buice, a journeyman reliever coming off his unlikely rookie season with the Angels at the age of thirty. Not long after logging his seventeenth and final save that year, Buice wandered into Hemrick's card shop while searching the strip mall for a Chinese restaurant. Hemrick quickly enlisted him in a baseball card signing. Though Buice was hardly a household name even in Southern California, in a testament to the popularity of baseball cards he managed to draw a few hundred fans to The Upper Deck one afternoon. In Buice, Sumner and Hemrick saw their much-needed connection to the baseball fraternity. They offered him a stake in the company if he could get them access to players and help fast-track a license with the players' union. Buice later said he never wanted anything from baseball cards except to get his picture on one, but it was the cards rather than the game that would make Buice a millionaire.

Ever since the Topps monopoly had been busted, revenues from baseball cards had become the union's gravy train, accounting for some 90 percent of the Major League Baseball Players Association's earnings from licensing. From 1986 to 1989 the players' union quadrupled the money it made from licensing, much of it going into the players' rainy-day "contingency fund," the emergency cash they would use to pay themselves if the owners forced a lockout. When Upper Deck came knocking, the union had just doled out its fourth coveted license to produce cards, to the Score Company, from which it would extract its standard 11 percent of the wholesale price of all card sales. Though the union was rightfully leery of oversaturating the market, they came around after meeting with Upper Deck's founders in New York. Sumner and his partners pitched themselves as serious marketing experts breaking into a world of small, family-run gum-and-candy outfits. "We were the first company in baseball cards to be run by businessmen rather than food people," Sumner said. "We told them, 'We're different. We have marketing plans. We've been to school for this stuff.'" They didn't want Upper Deck cards to be in the gum or candy aisles; they wanted them standing alone in groceries and drugstores, front and center on prime real estate. And unlike Topps, they wanted to do it all with the hardcore collector in mind. As McCracken, the company's former head of sales, put it to me, "When your product comes into Price Club and a pallet's gone in half an hour, that's not Mrs. Smith buying cards for Johnny. It's the dealers."

The union recognized the moneymaking potential of a slick, high-end card, which is precisely what Upper Deck unveiled in early 1989. McCracken believed at the outset that the company was engaged in "niche marketing"—catering to a small sliver of collectors, primarily adults, who were driven by investment rather than fun or nostalgia. The entire hobby was headed toward the investment side, children included. Even elementary and middle schoolers took part in what might be called aspirational acquisition. Trading primarily in Upper Deck cards as opposed to Fleer said something about a kid's standing on the playground. Upper Deck's sleek appeal was readily apparent at the National Sports Collectors Convention in 1988, held in Atlantic City. Sumner and Hemrick had nothing but card prototypes of Buice and teammate Wally Joyner to give out, and they were mobbed for them. "Three times over the course of two days, the people that run the show had to come to our table and clear people out of the way," Sumner recalled. "There were so many people waiting they blocked the aisle. It was absolutely amazing." Soon they had $19 million worth of preorders. They also had a cocky expression for the cards they hadn't even manufactured yet: "Cardboard gold."

In the end, Upper Deck's splurging on production paid off with an unusually attractive card. Though they didn't have the charm or imagination of a vintage Topps set, the cards had a crisp elegance and simplicity to them. Sumner, who had sketched the design on a napkin at a pizzeria, wanted the pictures to do all the talking. And so the only design embellishment was on the right side of each card, which had been mocked up to resemble a first-base line. (On Upper Deck's second annual set, the line would run along the top of the card, from first to second; on the third set, it would run along the left side of the card, from second to third.) "On the front I wanted as big a picture as possible," Sumner said. "And I wanted an action photo, with as little graphics as possible. I wanted you to be able to see the detail of the photo."

Sumner's team didn't scrimp on the action shots. They contracted the small company of V. J. Lovero, the celebrated *Sports Illustrated* baseball photographer and clubhouse regular who would go on to shoot more than thirty covers for the magazine during his career. (After the photographer's early death in 2004, at age forty-four, longtime *SI* baseball scribe Tom Verducci eulogized that "baseball never looked so sweet as it did through the lens of V. J. Lovero.") Lovero's team shot a quarter of a million photos for Upper Deck that first year, weeding it down to twenty-five thousand upon delivery, according to Sumner. Of that batch, about fourteen hundred photos ultimately went onto cards; the backs of the cards came in full color—a rarity in baseball cards—and with an extra player photo. In the end, the high-grade paper and artwork re-sulted in rich color and unprecedented detail in the action shots. Upper Deck cards looked practically like color photographs.

At the very bottom of the back of the card was a holographic dia-mond, small enough to be covered by a dime, bearing the Upper Deck name. Given the splashy premiere, it would come as no surprise when Upper Deck soon headed down the road of limited-edition autographed cards seen by many collectors as investments. Baseball cards were less and less something to play with—or, for that matter, to be touched. Even Upper Deck's common cards of unremarkable players looked as if they belonged in a lucite case. Though Sumner may have built his business plan upon some honorable precepts—giving cardboard lovers a better product, eliminating counterfeiting, preempting dishonest dealers—his company's products called up that old demon of the baseball card hobby: speculative collecting. Of course, this part of Upper Deck's appeal was no mistake, as the company made clear with it's advertising motto: "Upper Deck: For the kid on the street and the Wall Street investor."

When the first Upper Decks were released, kids flocked to them. A lot of the company's early success could be traced to a lucky gamble made by a teenage employee: the choice of an unestablished player to be no. 1 in the series. For years, Topps had carried on a less than scien-tific system for reserving the choicest numbers in their sets, such as no. 1 and no. 100, for some of the biggest stars of the game. (When Topps finally lured Ted Williams away from his exclusive contract with Fleer, in the late 1950s, the Brooklyn firm compounded the insult to Fleer by putting Teddy Ballgame in the no. 1 slots of both its 1957 and 1958 sets.) After all, card no. 1 kicked off the year in collecting. So in late 1988, Upper Deck decided it should put a hot rookie at the front of the pack. The decision was made by a college student named Tom Geideman. Geideman knew the company's founders from hanging around Bill Hemrick's card shop, where he'd earned the respect of other collectors by accurately predicting which prospects' cards would rise in value. His understanding of the minor-league system went well beyond the average fan's, and he seemed well suited to figure out which minor leaguer might turn into the season's breakout star.

According to CNBC sports reporter Darren Rovell, Geideman put some serious thought into the inaugural set's numbering, just as he would with every set that followed. (His creativity would peak with the 1992 set, when he set aside the numbers ending in "69" for the players with the most porn-flick-sounding monikers, such as Heathcliff Slocumb, no. 569, and Dickie Thon, no. 769.) After poring over an issue of *Baseball America,* Geideman figured that the honor of being no. 1 should go to either Gregg Jefferies, Gary Sheffield, Sandy Alomar Jr., or Ken Griffey Jr.—all of them abnormally talented and exciting young stars. The safest of this lot was Jefferies, whose stellar play for the Mets in the latter half of the previous season had sent his 1988 rookie card into an inflationary gallop.

Geideman being a Seattle Mariners fan, Upper Deck went with the riskier choice of Griffey, whom the team had snatched up as the top pick of the 1987 draft. Son of a veteran outfielder still playing in the bigs, Junior hadn't yet turned twenty. The Seattle franchise was banking its future on a center fielder barely out of high school. Manager Jim Lefebvre proclaimed of Griffey, "When he does take over in center, it will be for the next twenty years." The mounting buzz and pressure were such that Junior swallowed more than 270 aspirin in a suicide attempt before he even put on a Mariners uniform. (He recovered and didn't speak of the incident until 1992.) The hype proved warranted during 1989 spring training, when he set preseason team records for hits (32), RBIs (20), and total bases (49). Looking like an established All-Star, he batted .360 and hit successfully in fifteen consecutive games. Lefebvre decided to put the nineteen-year-old in center field on Seattle's opening day. He roped a double in his first major-league at-bat, and within a matter of weeks he'd revealed himself as a once-in-a-decade kind of player.

Yet Griffey was anything but an obvious choice for Upper Deck. Geideman had hammered out the set's lineup in November 1988, before he could even have known whether Junior would play anything above AAA ball the following season. The company couldn't get its hands on a shot of Griffey in a Mariners getup before the cards would go to press, so it had to alter a photo of him in a San Bernardino Spirit uniform. "I ran into Griffey the next winter in Nashville, where he was doing a card show," McCracken told me. "I introduced myself, and he said, 'Where the hell did you get that photo of me?' He had no clue what had been done." The Griffey gamble paid off for Upper Deck as well as it did for Seattle, largely because the minds over at Topps hadn't had the wherewithal to include Junior in their initial 1989 offering. There was precedent for such costly neglect. In 1986, when Topps failed to create a card for then rookie star Jose Canseco to include in its standard set, collectors turned to Fleer and Donruss for pictures of the A's steroidal beefcake, draining Topps sales. Griffey's absence was another deep embarrassment for the longest-running name in baseball cards, and collectors quickly turned to the new start-up for the hottest young face in the game.

Kids and adults alike pursued the Upper Deck Junior as if it held the key to their financial independence, but what was considered a desirable piece of cardboard in fact wasn't very scarce at all. More than a million of the cards had rolled off the presses, and because no. 1 resided in the top left corner of Upper Deck's print sheets, it was more liable to be cut poorly or have its corners dinged than other cards in the set. Whenever someone complained about a damaged card coming out of a fresh pack, company policy was to replace it to keep the customer happy. "And what cards were they sending in? The Griffeys," McCracken explained. "Eventually you're going to run out of Griffeys. So there were sheets printed with just a hundred Griffeys on them."

The Upper Deck Griffey rookie would become the most-graded card of all time, with Professional Sports Authenticator, the largest card-grading company, evaluating and encapsulating more than fifty thousand of them and Beckett's grading service another twenty-five thousand.

*　*　*

There were now at least four major manufacturers on the block—Topps, Fleer, Donruss, and Upper Deck—rolling out hundreds of millions of cards apiece. But no matter how many baseball cards were on the market, they were snapped up as fast as they could be printed. In 1989 the industry was poised to cross the billion-dollar threshold for new-card sales. To executives at Fleer, this was a shocking state of affairs. It was only a few years earlier, in 1980, that the company had gained the right to print baseball cards at all. In the years since, Fleer had blossomed into a nice little company. Its longtime owners, the Mustins, came from a long line of Pennsylvania Quakers, and they were proud to be providing a wholesome enjoyment for American kids.

Just two weeks after rolling out its 1989 set, however, Fleer and its baseball cards weren't looking so wholesome. The tumult at its Philadelphia headquarters started with a call from a *Baltimore Sun* sports reporter. He wanted the company's comment on Fleer's card no. 616. Fleer execs had no idea what the reporter was talking about. They went scrambling through their files to find the card of Baltimore Orioles second baseman Billy Ripken. The twenty-four-year-old stood expressionless with a bat resting over his right shoulder. On the knob of the bat, in small but clear black writing, were the words FUCK FACE.

The folks at Fleer were suddenly wise to what had already managed to explode on playgrounds across the country. Kids outside of Baltimore received a dual shock. Here was the mother of all expletives and, hey, who knew that Cal Ripken had a little brother? The card immediately became a sensation, and any boy who managed to score the rarity discovered that it was quite the commodity at school. Classmates begged just for a peek.

The Ripken card was part of a long tradition of camouflaged obscenity in baseball cards. The first mischievous piece of cardboard had surfaced a century earlier, when Charles "Old Hoss" Radbourn, the legendary hurler for the Boston Beaneaters, covertly unfurled a middle finger on his Old Judge card of 1887. (Radbourn managed to flip the bird in a number of baseball photos over the years, including in his 1886 team picture, which some believe is the first photograph of any kind to depict the obscene gesture.) In 1972 the Detroit Tigers' hothead manager, Billy Martin, took up Radbourn's torch, offering kids the middle finger on his Topps card. But the Ripken card was different for one reason. Fleer executives managed to halt its distribution within two weeks of release, making it an "error" card. (Cards with typographical or statistical mistakes abound, but they qualify as more valuable error cards only if they are corrected.) So the card was not only naughty; it also appeared to be scarce. As collectors scrambled for the Ripken, the card's value multiplied again and again over the course of days.

What surely would have been a common card worth a few cents was accruing value at an exponential pace. Within a couple days of the story's breaking nationally, the card had jumped from 10 cents to $2. Then it went to $5, to $10, and to $50. People who'd never collected baseball cards bought the Ripken as a novelty. By late January it was fetching $100 and more. Dealers found themselves raising its price during the course of a card show, sometimes hawking it for twice as much at the end of the day than at the beginning. Fleer executives disclosed little about the card publicly—except to say that it was rare, which only increased the frenzy. Unopened cases that guaranteed a few Ripken errors were selling for as much as $1,700 apiece. Ripken apparently couldn't wait for the hysteria to die down. "If people are crazy enough to spend that kind of money on a card, it doesn't concern me," he said. Donald Peck, the company's vice chairman, summed up the mood at Fleer thusly: "We're all paranoid."

Only paranoia could explain Fleer's scatterbrained handling of the controversy. The simple solution would have been to blot out the obscenity before any more cards reached the marketplace. But the company couldn't settle on just one method of concealment. On some cards, FUCK FACE was covered with a light airbrushing. On others, with a darker airbrushing. Some cards sported a black box with hard edges, others a black box with rounded edges. Sometimes the box wasn't black at all—it was white. And, most baffling of all, the card sometimes came with a cut along its bottom, apparently from a paper trim-mer. Rather than calm the storm, Fleer's seemingly endless variations created a Billy Ripken submarket, replete with its own nomenclature and pricing. There was the original FUCK FACE, the FUCK FACE Double Die, the FUCK FACE Double Die Saw Cut, the Whiteout, the Black Scribble Loop, the Black Box Square Edge, and so on. Perhaps the most prized was the FUCK FACE with Ripken Autograph. Distraught as he was, Ripken was happy to let a dealer escort him to a Jersey City card show, where he signed some of the cards for paying customers about two weeks after it first appeared.

The slew of different versions has led many collectors to believe the FUCK FACE card was an intentional publicity stunt. These conspiracy theorists point to the fact that Fleer sales skyrocketed after the news broke. They also like to ask how the card could have gone through so many production stages without anyone at Fleer having noticed the expletive. Ted Taylor, who came on board as a Fleer executive after the incident, told me that no Fleer employee would have knowingly done something to tarnish the company's reputation. The Mustin family ownership, he said, was embarrassed and livid. "*Mortified* wasn't the word. Some people who'd been working there said it was like hell on earth afterward. They fired people. They just went crazy. The atti-tude was, *You destroyed our good name.*"

The photo was taken in Boston before an Orioles–Red Sox game during the 1988 season. Ripken put on an O's home jersey expressly for the shoot. Back at his lab, Fleer's Boston-based photographer, who was one of the company's top lensmen, failed to notice the expletive when he developed his slides. He passed them on to the Fleer production team, who pushed the FUCK FACE photo through mock-ups. When the company sent blue-line proofs back to the photographer, he didn't no-tice anything amiss then, either. The photo went off to the printer.

After the card appeared, suspicion quickly turned to Ripken himself. After all, the infielder was known as the O's prankster in residence. But that distinction also sometimes made him the butt of his fellow players' jokes. He'd taken a cream pie in the face during an on-field interview two years earlier, and he claimed that he'd been handed a bat before the shoot. He fumed that he was a victim, embarrassed and angry at his teammates for their brazenness and at Fleer for its sloppiness. "I had no idea that word was on the bat when the picture was taken, and I don't know how it got there," he told a reporter. "I know I'm kind of a [jerk] at times. I know I'm a little off. But this is going too far."

Ripken's embarrassment may have been genuine, but his indignation was not. He withheld the true story for twenty years, finally breaking his silence on the matter to Rovell in 2009. (The fact that baseball fans still wanted answers after two decades says quite a bit about the FUCK FACE legend.) Ripken had actually penned the phrase himself, in an admittedly odd attempt to distinguish one of his practice bats from the rest of the lumber in the O's bat room; that he held that bat in particular for his Fleer photo was a complete accident, he maintained, and he told Rovell he was still upset that Fleer's production staff never spotted it.

Ripken went on to play twelve major-league seasons, putting up a respectable .247 career batting average as a reliable utility player. Nonetheless, his greatest legacy, aside from his relation to his brother Cal Jr., and his father, Cal Sr., is his place on the ignominious FUCK FACE card. The incident was no boon to the Mustin family, either. While the Ripken affair may have boosted the company's short-term sales, the need to stop the presses cost the company around a quarter of a million dollars. Worse, lingering humiliation helped expedite the company's sale during the 1989 season. After fifty years with the firm, Fleer paterfamilias Gilbert Mustin chose to step down. "The Ripken card was the straw that broke the camel's back," said Taylor. A leveraged-buyout group picked up the century-old candy maker for an undisclosed sum.

Three years later, at the height of the card market, Marvel Entertainment would buy Fleer for a handsome $265 million.

* * *

The prime beneficiary of the FUCK FACE affair was the card industry at large, particularly Upper Deck, which had positioned itself perfectly to benefit from a speculator-driven market.

The Ripken story ran in major newspapers across the country, attracting even the sports-ignorant to card shows in search of the curio. Newspapers launched new baseball card columns in their sports pages to capture more readers. A card columnist for New York's *Newsday* declared the Ripken "perhaps the most significant sports card of the 80s." The card, he opined, "deserves no praise, but it helped turn a red-hot boom into a supernova that sucked in football, basketball and hockey, too."

The card signified that hype ruled the market. In those days, a company might print a million copies of a single player's card. Fleer wouldn't put a number on it, but *Beckett Baseball Card Monthly*, the hobby's leading publication, estimated that anywhere from eighty thousand to one hundred thousand FUCK FACE cards were at large in the market—certainly a smaller number than your average player's, but by no means qualifying the card as a rarity. Within a matter of months of having sold it for as much as $300, card dealers were having trouble unloading the R-rated Ripken at $15.

The illusion of scarcity, of course, is a powerful marketing tool. The card companies all seemed to grasp this around the same time, with the number of "error" cards, by one calculation, growing fivefold during the 1989 and 1990 seasons. Among the more notable flubs were a 1990 Donruss card for John Smoltz that pictured Tom Glavine, a 1990 Donruss card for Juan Gonzalez with a reversed photo, and a 1990 Topps card for Frank Thomas on which the player's name was missing. Though some of these were certainly innocent mistakes, in some cases the companies may have done sloppy work for the very same reason that Goudey had skip-numbered its card sets some fifty years earlier. For collectors it made the thrill of the chase all the more thrilling.

Dealers began picking up a dozen or more cases of about ten thousand cards at a time, breaking them down into player lots. An investor would then be able to purchase, say, a thousand-count lot of Frank

Thomas rookie cards, effectively turning the White Sox first baseman into a penny stock. A hot or cold month for Thomas could swing the collectors' investment a few thousand dollars either way. The company that pioneered this baseball-cards-as-securities form of investing was Cherry Hill, New Jersey–based Score Board, Inc., run by the father-son duo of Paul and Ken Goldin, who began buying massive stocks of cards from Topps in the late 1980s. Their business model turned the younger Goldin into a multimillionaire by his midtwenties, the executive vice president of a company logging more than $30 million in annual sales, much of it to baseball card investors.

The frenzy peaked around 1991 when, an industry researcher determined, dealers and investors spent about $1.4 billion on wholesale sports cards for the year ending in June. But that number represents only what dealers paid directly to the card companies; after the sale of vintage cards and the resale of new product, the actual figure is probably twice as much or even more. During the National Sports Collectors Convention of that summer, more than a hundred thousand collectors mobbed the Anaheim Convention Center.

This speculative atmosphere made the founders of Upper Deck wealthy men. "I have a lot of good memories and a lot of bad ones," said Sumner, adding that he worked so hard in Upper Deck's first three years that he often slept on the office floor and rarely saw his wife. He stepped down as head of the company in 1992, at the height of Upper Deck's success, probably knowing that as a major shareholder he'd never have to worry about money again. (When Sumner and I had lunch together in Newport Beach, he remarked casually that he'd like to earn another $20 million someday. Now he spends his days trading futures, primarily as a hobby.) "Upper deck was a concept that developed at the right time at the right place," he said. "The price was right, the market was right, the climate was right. Everything was right for that to happen. It couldn't happen now."

According to reporter Pete Williams's 1995 book *Card Sharks: How Upper Deck Turned a Child's Hobby into a High-Stakes, Billion-Dollar*

Business, the company logged sales of a quarter of a billion dollars in 1991, more than half of which came from the staggering 4 billion baseball cards that it rolled out the door that year. (The rest of the sales came from the company's other sports card lineups.) It had supplanted Topps as the market leader. The largest of Upper Deck's shareholders each took home about $18 million for the year. (There was no need to pity the old-line Brooklyn candy company, however; the inflated market drove Topps's own sales to a record $200 million.) Upper Deck's cards had become so valuable that employees were smuggling them out of its Yorba Linda plant, then selling them on the black market in Southern California, according to Williams. When shareholder and cofounder Bill Hemrick filed a $10 million lawsuit against the company, in 1993, he made Upper Deck sound less like a baseball card company than an intrigue-filled Wall Street investment house. The company's executives, Hemrick alleged, took part in "the secret manufacture and distribution to themselves" of certain high-priced baseball cards and, more bizarrely, in reprinting additional copies of a valuable Dale Murphy error card, in which the Atlanta Braves outfielder was the victim of a reversed negative. Hemrick claimed that 13,500 of the Murphy errors, which had been selling for up to $100 each, went to a cabal of Upper Deck insiders. Hemrick, tangled up with Upper Deck in a separate lawsuit, later dropped his case, issuing a statement saying his allegations were based on faulty information.

The hobby's growth had become unsustainable. It was one thing for dealers and kids to believe that they could buy a crate's worth of rookie cards, stash them in their basements, and wait for them to turn into pay dirt. It was quite another for Upper Deck board members to give themselves the right to buy cases of baseball cards at wholesale prices, running up tabs in the tens of thousands of dollars, as Williams detailed at the time. The card companies believed that they could effectively print money, and as much of it as they wanted. For a few more years, they were right.

9

Gem Mint Ten!

By mid-October 1994, Joseph "Papa Joe" Chevalier, a syndicated sports talk-show host based in Northbrook, Illinois, had spent two months reaming Major League Baseball owners and players for the labor strike that had scuttled an especially exciting season. The players had walked off their jobs on August 12 after months of bitter and fruitless negotiations, much of it revolving around the dreaded possibility of a salary cap. At a time when fans normally would have been gearing up for the World Series, Chevalier and his callers instead were fulminating over the greed to be found on both sides of the dispute, and ruing the season of broken records that never was.

During one particularly impassioned broadcast, Chevalier solicited his listeners for ideas on how to voice their disappointment and anger to the world of professional baseball. The phone lines lit up with bile-filled callers, but the most novel scheme came to the studios by way of fax. *How about hosting a mass burning of baseball cards?* one listener proposed. Chevalier loved the idea. He went on the air and told his audience to mail him their cards.

"'If you are as outraged as you say you are on the phone, then send me your baseball cards and I'll burn them,'" Chevalier, who still hosts a sports show, told me he said on the air in 1994. "This, to me, would be the ultimate sign of true outrage, because people love their baseball cards." Afterward, his program director said, "Cute. But no one will send you their baseball cards." Looking back, it's hard to say what the program director underestimated more—the diminishing value of many baseball cards or the extent of fan disillusionment with players and ownership. Perhaps not since the infamous Black Sox scandal of 1919 had baseball lovers held their game in such low esteem.

The dispute between the union and the owners was rooted in Major League Baseball's deteriorating financial outlook. From the owners' perspective, player salaries had been growing at an ungodly rate ever since the reserve clause was struck down, in 1975, when the average big leaguer was pulling in about $45,000 a year. By 1994 the average salary was just south of $1.15 million. Adjusted for inflation, player pay had grown roughly ninefold in just twenty years. By 1994 salaries were swallowing up 58 percent of the league's annual revenues—compared to 43 percent just four years earlier—a state of affairs that owners argued was unsustainable. And though it was true that the league was raking in more money than ever from licensing fees, revenue from national television broadcasts had fallen off in recent years.

Worse, there was a growing payroll gap between big- and small-market teams. Many owners believed that the Montreal Expos and Kansas City Royals of the world couldn't survive alongside megamarket teams such as the New York Yankees and Los Angeles Dodgers without some fairly monumental changes. Under their proposal, all teams would share broadcasting revenues—and all players would be subject to a salary cap. Having watched earnings compound ever since the start of the Marvin Miller days, the now robust players' union was terrified by the prospect of anyone's putting a ceiling on individual salaries. It didn't help that labor relations had been poisonous ever since Major League Baseball commissioner Fay Vincent stepped down in 1992 under pressure from ownership. A decisive leader and able negotiator, Vincent had in

1990 defused a thirty-two-day spring-training lockout that prefigured the more severe work stoppage of 1994.

Acting commissioner Bud Selig canceled the rest of the season on September 12. The last time the World Series had been scrapped was in 1904, and never before had an American sport been forced to cancel its entire postseason because of labor issues. At the moment the players walked, three-quarters of the way through the season, San Francisco Giants third baseman Matt Williams was on pace to break Roger Maris's thirty-three-year-old single-season home run record, and San Diego Padres right fielder Tony Gwynn was flirting with a .400 average for the year, an accomplishment not seen since Ted Williams hit .406 in 1941. Editorials deeming the strike an enduring disaster for business proved true: it would be a decade before fans started filling stadium seats again at prestrike levels.

In Northbrook, the baseball card business was facing a catastrophe, too. Just a few days after Chevalier made his on-air announcement, the cards began to arrive at his studio. Well attuned to fan anger at the time, he was expecting as many as ten thousand cards. He was shocked when the haul soared past that number and moved closer to half a million. Chevalier received two shipments from FedEx and UPS each day, with packages seeming to come from all of the three hundred cities across the country where his show was broadcast. His affiliates set up boxes at their stations so that locals could also drop off cards in person. Envelopes with single cards in them poured in, but there were also factory sets and sealed card packs that had never been opened—the owners had simply put shipping labels on them. The overwhelming majority of castoffs were commons, but plenty of once valuable rookie cards had also been thrown into the mix.

"One Little League did a drive and collected something like three thousand cards," said Chevalier. "The outrage was real."

In fact, there were so many cards that he couldn't burn them as promised; when the local fire marshal grasped the immensity of the trove, he declined to give the studio a permit for the bonfire. Chevalier went on the air in search of an alternative. One of his listeners offered up his wood chipper. In November, the mass burning was changed to a mass churning, as five hundred thousand and more pieces of cardboard were shoveled into the machine's maw during a live show. Even afterward, the cards continued to come in, though Chevalier begged his listeners to stop sending them. Whatever was left went to a Chicago boys' home.

The strike led plenty of fans to pledge they'd never watch another game—and, to the growing horror of the card companies, plenty of collectors to pledge never to buy another pack. But the fact is the card industry had been headed for an epic crash ever since the speculative era of collecting had begun. The question isn't whether the strike killed the baseball card industry. It's whether the baseball card industry had much life in it by then anyway. Why is it that, by 1994, children were ready and willing to send their once cherished cards off to the incinerator, with bitter notes addressed to Chevalier such as the one that read, "Burn them, Papa"?

The strike didn't cause the decline of the baseball card business. It merely aggravated a situation that had been worsening ever since card production peaked in the early 1990s. Everyone who made a living off of baseball cards had come to anticipate increasing wealth and prosperity. Manufacturers expected a steady stream of dealers to place orders. Dealers expected a steady stream of customers to buy their product. And adult collectors and even kids expected steady returns on their investments.

"If there was one thing that spelled the downfall of the hobby boom, it was greed," Ted Taylor, who tracked the pulse of the hobby as a Fleer executive in the early '90s, told me. "The Players Association, the league, the card companies—everyone wanted more. And the guy they were trying to get money from ran out of money. I could never get my colleagues to understand: *There's not as much money and interest as you think there is.*"

The worst culprits were the powers that be in professional baseball. As the sole licensors, Major League Baseball and the players' union determined who could produce cards and under what conditions. Because the Major League Baseball Players Association functioned as such a powerful gatekeeper, a lot of minds in the industry believed that the most influential people in the hobby weren't Jim Beckett or the Shorin brothers so much as Don Fehr, the union's leader, and Judy Heeter, the head of the union's licensing program. In less frenzied times, the union was careful never to sanction a weak set of cards that might diminish the baseball industry as a whole—it was worth giving up short-term revenues to keep the long-term cash flowing in. But as the card market grew more profitable in the early '90s, Fehr and the union let more and more companies inside the gates, wringing more royalties out of each one. During the first half of the decade, the number of companies producing sports cards grew fivefold.

Just as Marvin Miller had used baseball cards to empower the union, Fehr used cards to make it flush with cash. In the decade leading up to the strike, the amount of money the Players Association pulled in through licensing had grown by a startling 2,500 percent, much of it through the sale of cardboard. Leading up to the strike, the union's cash pile was doubling each season, making the players arguably as powerful as the owners. The assets amounted to about $100,000 for each player, coach, and trainer.

For years, the millions the union pulled in through baseball cards and other merchandise went straight back to the players as a "refund" on the dues they'd paid. But as the relationship between players and owners grew increasingly sour, Fehr started exacting a large chunk of the licensing revenue and dumping it into a "strike fund," a pool of money from which players could receive income while they weren't playing ball. By the time they walked off the field the strike fund was rumored to be a hefty $175 million.

When the 1994 season ended abruptly in August, baseball cards simply stopped selling. Card-shop owners—the number of whom had doubled in just two years—were sitting on product they couldn't move. Many of the stores closed. And though they'd distributed their '94 product, the card companies had to prepare for a '95 season not knowing whether it would arrive. The outlook was so dire that they considered creating cards for likely replacement players, an idea the players' union was less than excited about. In the end, the companies drastically cut production but still managed to sell only about half the cards they made for the upcoming season. Card sales were at about half their high from just three years earlier. A simultaneous strike in the National Hockey League further devastated the card makers, especially Donruss, which was sold during the work stoppages.

Of course, the card companies had already inflicted a lot of damage on themselves. As the industry preened, manufacturers drifted from their family origins and grew increasingly corporatized. Topps had gone public in 1987, not long after a leveraged buyout, and Fleer did the same in 1990, after the Mustin brothers sold it. In a symbolic break with its humble roots, Topps ditched its original, pre–World War II offices at the dingy Brooklyn warehouse in 1994, swapping it out for some fancy new digs at 1 Whitehall Street in lower Manhattan. The new headquarters was a short walk from the New York Stock Exchange. Around that time, Topps was trading on the NASDAQ exchange at $20.25 per share, its highest price ever.

Topps saw a rich future in branding, as if it were a cardboard-peddling Walt Disney Company. Rather than pouring energy and capital into improving its card line, the firm created *Topps*, the magazine, which covered, well, Topps the company. As the three-hundred-thousand-circulation publication was launching, Topps's director of new product development called it a "marketer's dream," telling the *New York Times* that "the possibilities are mind-boggling" when one considers the recent expansion of the card world. Topps began distributing its magazine to thousands of card shops that would soon be shuttering. The magazine itself would cease publication within just a few years.

In its 1990 annual report, Topps told investors how it planned to stay atop the card world: "The Company competes in the collectible picture card market by designing products which it believes will especially appeal to adult collectors, in addition to children." Though kids had been the lifeblood of baseball card sales for generations, the company had decided to target grown men, most of whom would be buying new cards only as long as they saw juicy returns on their so-called investments.

Topps and its competitors showed little in the way of long-term strategy or self-restraint as they pursued grown-up wallets. The preferred modus operandi was to get as many different cards onto the market as quickly as possible. In the early '90s Topps, Fleer, and Upper Deck alike began producing increasing numbers of sets, many with gaudy names evoking Upper Deck's concept of a "premium" card: Topps Stadium Club, Fleer Flair, Upper Deck Silver Sluggers. Having seen cards like the Mickey Mantle rookie sell for tens of thousands of dollars, manufacturers created a vintage-card aura around new products, touting "limited editions" and an ever growing number of collector-baiting bells and whistles. Packs that had sold just a few years earlier for a quarter or two suddenly jumped to $2, then to $5, then to $20, and eventually to as high as $250 for the most exclusive issues. Cards were decked out with holograms and metallic foil, and bubble gum was excluded from packages so it wouldn't damage the precious cardboard inside.

Rather than trekking down to the school yard to run ideas by children as Woody Gelman had a few decades before, baseball card–industry leaders increasingly relied on consumer-marketing specialists to guide their product lines. Taylor, who told me he "never met a pack of cards I didn't want to open," was something of an odd man out on Fleer's executive board, insofar as he understood the collector's mind and had more than a clue as to what children actually wanted. As Taylor explained, his colleagues looked at the market as if they were hawking "cars or shoes" rather than collectibles with a particular niche. In 1996 Topps went so far as to abandon cardboard altogether for its football CybrCards. Each "card" was a $20 CD-ROM. "Our research shows that card collectors tend to have a higher proportion of CD-ROMs in their computers than other people," a PR rep explained at the time.

As Topps and others flooded the market, the sales of new cards tumbled—along with Topps's share price. "In the late 80s and early 90s, when everybody wanted to play these stocks, we were recommending them," an industry analyst told *Sports Illustrated* in 1996. "Now I tell investors to sit on the sidelines and watch." By then, Topps stock had fallen to $4.25, a fraction of its 1992 high. Late that year the company was forced to shutter its gum- and card-making plant in Duryea, Pennsylvania, eliminating nearly six hundred jobs and outsourcing its manufacturing. Topps cards had rolled out of the small, former mining town for three decades. The following year, Topps put up a loss of nearly $11 million.

"It's a shame there weren't more hobbyists involved at high levels," Taylor told me. "There should've been more than just corporate types to scream, 'No, you're making too many!' But they just wouldn't believe you. More might be better when you're selling toothpaste. Not baseball cards."

A lot of the adult collectors Topps had come to rely upon headed for the exits, having realized that new cards couldn't hold their value. In 1999 a Houston-area neurologist told the *Wall Street Journal* that he'd spent $70,000 on baseball cards since 1985, all in the hopes of one day financing his daughter's college education. He dumped the cards in 1995. "My wife still gives me a hard time," he said. "It clearly wasn't the best way to invest."

Indeed, the idea of baseball cards as investments gradually became a pop-culture joke, unintentionally embodied by late-night television pitchman Don West. Competing with the nocturnal peddlers of kitchen gadgets and home fitness equipment, the broad-shouldered, goateed former knife salesman became a notorious fixture on the Shop at Home Network, where for most of the 1990s he hawked baseball cards and other sports collectibles to the uninformed, the desperate, and the sleep-deprived. According to West's trademark hyperbole, the rookie cards he offered weren't in merely mint condition —they were "gem . . . mint . . . ten!" He hinted at a prosperous future for anyone who called in to his *Sports Collectibles* show, credit card number at the ready. "Be dialin', people!" he would implore. "Buy more than one!" Though such bombast was ridiculous enough to earn West a lampooning on *Saturday Night Live* courtesy of Will Ferrell, it was a crucial part of the act, given that much of what he sold were the overproduced common cards of the '80s and '90s, pooled and repackaged into lots.

Even though the cards were wildly overpriced, West managed to move an awful lot of them. At the end of his stint with Shop at Home he claimed to have raised his show's annual sales from $3 million in 1993 to around $150 million by 2001.

For decades the most devoted card collectors had believed that too many cards were being put out, even when they weren't. "There are too many baseball cards being issued," Jefferson Burdick complained in a 1959 letter. "In the early days, it was bad enough when they put out a 250-card set. Now it's four times that, or almost, between the gums, cookies, meats, and a few other things. I gave up."

When Burdick penned that grievance, there were perhaps three nationally distributed baseball card sets and a handful of regional ones. In 1994 more than 350 sets poured into convenience stores and card shops. Like any consumer, a collector enjoys having choices. But the goal is almost never unbridled accumulation, especially for children. This deluge of cards had a devastating effect on the hobby. Kids lost the common experience of collecting the same sets their friends did, and all of the rituals that entailed. After all, it doesn't make much sense to swap cards if you and your buddies aren't working from the same pool.

So, like Burdick, the kids gave up.

By 1996, a Fleer survey of children turned up some disturbing, if unsurprising, news. Compared to just a few years earlier, kids were vastly more interested in video games than in cardboard. By the late '90s baseball cards had largely disappeared from school desks and lockers. "When a pack of cards went from $1.45 to $3.45, I just stopped collecting—my allowance is $5," a twelve-year-old New Jersey boy told the *Wall Street Journal* in 1999. "Now I go on the Internet a lot and play Nintendo." A fifteen-year-old in the same story was more blunt. Cards, he said, "just stopped being cool. . . . No one I know collects them anymore."

Hobby publications wondered aloud where all the kids had gone. "Children were the lifeblood of the sports card industry," *Sports Collectors Digest* declared in 1997. "But, as we all know, the gum is gone— and, to some extent, so are the kids." Even so, the magazine managed to round up twenty-five children "who indicated they owned sports cards" and, through a survey, laid out "some notable trends": the youngest collectors don't know or care what their cards are worth; they aren't that impressed with holograms or gold foil, even if that stuff is "kinda neat"; they don't mind if the corners of their cards get dinged when they play with them; and they don't seem willing to buy a pack of cards priced at $5. Almost everything the card companies did seemed to run counter to this conventional wisdom. "Dealers who sponsor 'trading nights,'" the digest noted, "often spend a lonely evening in their hobby shop."

During the 1980s and early '90s surveys showed that the average age of a baseball card collector had been around thirteen. After the strike that age skyrocketed. The typical attendee of the 1996 national baseball card show was a wheezing thirty-eight years old. Boys who grew up with Nintendo found a ready alternative to baseball cards in less expensive Pokémon cards, a cardboard spin-off from a video game that just so happened to be about collecting. Others gravitated toward Magic: The Gathering or another of the legion of collectible card games that hit toy store shelves in the '90s. Kids were still into cards, it seemed—just not baseball cards.

Once the industry started to tank, the card companies flailed about in search of sales-boosting gimmicks to keep them afloat. They took advantage of one particularly toxic stunt over and over again: the insert card. Insert cards had been around in one form or another since the 1960s. The original idea was to take a regular wax pack of five or so cards and insert something novel—say, a rub-off tattoo or a peel-off sticker—to spice things up and maybe pull kids away from competing brands. But when it was revived in the '90s the insert card wasn't a sideshow in the pack so much as the main attraction. Billing them as "prizes," the companies used inserts to create the illusion of scarcity, suggesting to collectors that any card that comes in only a fraction of packs must be unusually valuable.

The diabolical idea of the high-end insert came courtesy of a card dealer turned executive named Don Bodow. According to Pete Williams, *Willy Wonka and the Chocolate Factory* was a favorite movie of Bodow's son, so the Upper Deck vice president of sales was forced to watch the thing repeatedly. Bodow saw the obvious parallel to his own line of work. Just as chocolate-loving children tore through one Wonka Bar wrapper after another in search of one of five golden tickets, so did collectors tear through pack after pack in search of prized rookies. Bodow wanted Upper Deck to create a new kind of golden ticket, something that would produce a buying frenzy. So in 1990 the company had Reggie Jackson autograph a limited run of cards and dropped them into late-season packs of Upper Decks. (After the stunt proved successful, the enterprising Jackson launched his own golden-ticket project, hoarding away as many copies of his 1969 Topps rookie as he could find. His plan was to sign 563 of them—one for each of his career dingers—and market them upon his induction into the Hall of Fame. Before he could cash in, many of the cards were lost during a fire at his Bay Area home.)

By 1996, the sports-card manufacturers were putting out a staggering eight hundred insert sets each year, all reputed to hold precious, big-ticket items such as cards that had been slathered with twenty-four-karat gold foil. "I can tell you that the people making these decisions were consumer-products people who never, ever grasped the concept that collecting 600 or 700 different cards could be as profitable as making collectors buy whole boxes of cards to find one or two inserts out of a 10- or 12-card insert set," Taylor told *Sports Collectors Digest,* trying to explain the insert phenomenon. "The marketing geniuses (with their Ivy League MBAs) wouldn't know a utility infielder from an electrician."

Eventually, the card makers didn't dare put out a set that didn't include such cards, and collecting itself started to look a lot like a scratch-off lottery. The few kids who remained in the hobby tore through packs with trembling hands, hoping to find something like a Michael Jordan "refractor" card, which had a chrome reflective device built into it and was fetching thousands of dollars in card shops. Some dealers started using metal detectors to ferret out the packs that contained this and similarly tricked-out cards.

Because of how aggressively children pursued them, these habit-forming pieces of cardboard became known as "chase" cards. Kids were buying $5 packs with the hope of finding a $50 card, and disconcerted dealers complained that youngsters were buying packs, rummaging through them, and tossing away all the normal cards when they didn't find the most valuable prize. Collectors no longer tried to build complete sets of six hundred or seven hundred cards, because most of the cards had become trivialized. As one dealer astutely observed, it was as if the slick inserts had become the regular cards and the regular cards had become the expendable bubble gum. In New York the city's consumer-affairs department eventually forced the card makers to state on their packaging the long odds of scoring a chase card.

Not surprisingly, class-action lawsuits popped up, spearheaded by fuming parents who'd watched their little collectors turn into little gamblers. A group of parents filed a racketeering lawsuit against Topps and Marvel-owned Fleer in 1996, enlisting doctors and experts to bolster their claim that the companies' chase cards led to compulsive gambling and, ultimately, amounted to an illegal lottery. Apparently, many adults were just as addicted as children. "I had a guy in his 40s who used to spend $200 a week, then he came in twice a week, spending $500," a dealer explained at the time. "He'd open the packs right here. You could see the sweat on his brow." The lawyer in a suit filed against Upper Deck, who was seeking damages for any kid who'd bought cards in search of insert cards, compared the card companies' new fad to Joe Camel: "They're selling a dangerous product to kids."

Of more than a dozen suits none was successful.

In the late 1990s the companies' attempts to produce baseball cards with investment appeal reached a new low when they began carving

up game-used equipment. Hoping to entice collectors with something jazzier than just plain autographs, they diced up the bats and
uniforms of big leaguers, affixed the pieces to cards, and marketed
the resulting "rarities" mostly as insert prizes in high-priced packs.
Manufacturers liked to sound a populist note as they pursued this
bizarre new gimmick. By divvying up these major-league mementos
into thousands of packs, they claimed to be making high-end collectibles available to the working man—not just to Cooperstown and
the wealthiest of collectors.

No one cried foul when companies disseminated the minced jerseys of contemporary All-Stars such as Frank Thomas and Barry Zito.
Eventually, though, card makers set their sights on some of the
game's more hallowed relics. In 2003 Donruss dropped more than a
quarter of a million dollars on a Yankees home jersey that Babe Ruth
had worn in 1925—one of just three known to exist—and then cut
it into twenty-one hundred square-inch swatches. "This just happens
to be a wonderfully historic relic of the greatest player who ever
lived," Donruss president Bill Dully said defensively. "What we're
doing is re-creating Babe Ruth's legacy—we're not shredding or destroying it."

Donruss would give one piece of the very much shredded jersey to
Ruth's eighty-six-year-old daughter, Julia Ruth Stevens, and a few
others to its various departmental employees of the year. The rest of
the fragments of pinstriped cloth would be inserted into packs of
Donruss cards for the next three years, at prices ranging from $2.99
to $150 per pack. Protesters of the move included baseball fans,
sports-memorabilia collectors, and the curator of the Babe Ruth
Birthplace and Museum.

Though it eluded Donruss executives, observers grasped the fact
that even a wonderfully historic relic doesn't contain much history
once it's been atomized. Card companies had once chronicled the
game; now, it seemed, they were simply exploiting it. In spite of his

best efforts at spin, Dully couldn't hide the fact that the shredding of the Ruth jersey was, in the end, simply about his company's bottom line. "There's always going to be controversy," he told ESPN.com. "But something like this is just the reality of the free market and the reality of capitalism."

10

The Ringmaster

In early 2007 Lionel Carter, the old friend and colleague of Jefferson Burdick, consigned his entire collection of vintage gum and cigarette cards to Mastro Auctions, then the largest baseball card and sports memorabilia auctioneer in the country. For the Burr Ridge, Illinois–based company, the consignment was no small coup. Carter, at ninety, was a legend among cardboard lovers—a "hobby pioneer." Few collectors had ever seen his haul in person, but almost all knew it by reputation. Carter had started accumulating baseball cards during the Great Depression, when he was fifteen years old, and he'd never let the demands of adulthood get in the way of his hobby. Even during World War II, when he was serving in the Pacific theater, he'd had packages of cards shipped to him. He opened them in the barracks bathroom, beyond the view of his fellow soldiers.

By the time Carter's trove was being prepared for sale, hobby experts agreed that it was one of the greatest original collections of baseball cards still in private hands. It contained some fifty thousand cards, all of which had been kept safely away from grubby fingers in leatherbound albums, into which they'd been carefully mounted with art corners. Carter's trademark as a collector, as a Mastro Auctions press release put it, was "insane mint condition."

His was a collection after the heart of company founder Bill Mastro. Mastro, who'd been running his auction house for a decade, wielded condition-consciousness as a powerful marketing tool in the sale of vintage baseball cards. Due partly to the auctions Mastro had been holding, a card graded an 8 out of 10 could be worth five times as much as the same card graded a mere 5—a marketplace fact that made the unsullied Carter collection all the more valuable. Mastro had seen Carter's card albums twenty-five years earlier, but looking at them again as an experienced auctioneer he was stunned by the sharp corners and vivid colors on the seventy-year-old cardboard. "These cards are in a class by themselves," he said before the sale. "There is simply no comparison."

In typical Mastro fashion he turned the sale into a major hobby event. The cards went off to a grading company and came back with stellar marks, each encased in a special holder stamped "Lionel Carter Collection." In the end, the cards netted nearly $2 million, helping Mastro solidify his reputation as an auctioneer whose semiannual sales of baseball cards and memorabilia usually came in at around $10 million each. Carter, a retired bank manager from rural Illinois, became a rich man overnight. Mastro, already worth at least $5 million, became an even richer man.

What was surprising about the Carter auction, however, wasn't the astronomical prices; it was the fact that Mastro had scored the consignment to begin with. As an old-school collector, Carter resented just about all the recent developments in his hobby: the card grading, the lavish auctions, the investment-minded buyers. In short, he resented everything Bill Mastro stood for. Carter had known Mastro in the 1960s, when the teenager was proposing card deals with older collectors by mail and telephone. Even then, Carter disliked his aggressive style. "You should see the letters he wrote me when I was a kid," Mastro said. "He hated me."

But just as in the art world, the most accomplished collectors of baseball cards often find dealers and auctioneers circling them in their golden years. In the years before the auction, Carter was paid several visits by Mastro's friend Doug Allen, the president of Mastro Auctions. The courtship apparently paid off. When Carter decided to sell his cards after an attempted robbery at his house, he must have realized what other hobbyists already had: that no matter how tightly they're held on to, the most valuable and sought-after baseball cards in the world eventually passed through the hands of Bill Mastro.

"The idea was to create a service," Mastro told me of his company not long after the Carter auction. "Because we're really in the service business. Nobody really needs a Willie Mays baseball card. But when you talk to these guys, you'll think they do—you'd think it was like air."

Like him or not, Mastro eventually became one of the card world's key players, a charismatic and outsize personality who freely admits that his enemies within the hobby have good reason to hate him. There was no dealer more cutthroat when it came to edging out his competitors, and no dealer more adept at harnessing the neediness of wealthy, fanatical sports collectors. The story of how the baseball card business was transformed from a vanishing kids' pastime into a thriving trade geared toward wealthy adult fetishists is in many ways the story of Mastro himself.

"We're more in the business of psychology than in collecting and hobbies," he said of baseball card auctioneers. If his record-breaking auctions were any indication, then Mastro had clearly mastered the psychology of the collector. But along with the brisk sales came mounting controversies. Mastro was accused of trading in doctored baseball cards, as well as of selling game-used uniforms and equipment of uncertain provenance. Most seriously, collectors alleged that his auction house had engaged in shill bidding.

When I visited with Mastro, in 2007, he was in the midst of an impressive sales run. His company had recently engineered a private deal in which a complete set of 1914 Cracker Jack cards went for $800,000, the most money ever paid for a single set of baseball cards.

Later, he auctioned off a collection of 1912 Pirate cigarette baseball cards for just under $1 million. And after unloading Carter's collection, he got his hands on one of the hobby's most unusual and valuable finds ever: a rare haul of 145 Colgan's Chips "tintop" cards. These small, circular cards were inserted into aluminum tins filled with "chip" gum in the early years of the twentieth century. An anonymous noncollector had recently inherited them from his father-in-law, and when he set out to find a seller he was steered inevitably to Mastro. With the help of the tintops, Mastro put on a series of auctions pulling in several million dollars apiece.

Then Mastro's luck took a turn. During the summer of 2008, on the very day he sold a Honus Wagner T206 for $1.62 million, Mastro and his employees, while tending their booth at the National Sports Collectors Convention outside Chicago, were paid a visit by agents from the Federal Bureau of Investigation. Mastro and his people were issued subpoenas in a federal grand-jury hearing. Nearly all of the hobby's most prominent dealers were manning booths at the convention, and many of Mastro's colleagues were aghast, if not entirely surprised, to see the feds swarming.

Within nine months Mastro Auctions, the most formidable baseball card business of its kind, would crumble.

Mastro first recognized the irrational impulses of the collector in 1965, as a twelve-year-old growing up in rural Bernardsville, New Jersey. Pouring all of his allowance money into drugstore baseball cards, he'd gotten his hands on every player in the 1965 Topps set—save for Bob Schmidt, a backup catcher with the Yankees. Mastro bought hundreds more cards in his search for this forgetful common, until the World Series came and went and the five-and-dimes stopped selling baseball cards for the season. His efforts to secure that last card taught Mastro that a passionate collector will ignore all logic, financial and otherwise, in pursuit of a personal prize.

The search for the Schmidt led Mastro to the back pages of the *Sporting News,* where a handful of dealers advertised their wares. Mastro mailed his dimes to the dealers and in turn received their crude, mimeographed auction listings, which opened up a new world to him. He discovered the loose-knit network of men that had grown around Jefferson Burdick, and he had no compunction about pestering these aging collectors for their cards. Mastro broke with collector's etiquette by making relentless phone calls to men like Carter, who preferred to write long letters about card trading rather than spend money on long-distance calls. "They're saying, 'What are you doing? Why are you calling me?'" Mastro recalled. "Well, I'm calling you because I want the cards. I want to know, *Can we do this deal?*"

There was one older collector who took a shine to the pushy teen: Frank Nagy, a pipe fitter and after-hours card auctioneer from Detroit. Nagy taught Mastro everything he needed to know about baseball cards and business. One lesson was in leverage. Nagy, somewhat famously, once used his family's entire life savings to buy every last card belonging to Walter Corson, a former pro ballplayer from Pennsylvania who'd amassed one of the largest baseball card collections in the world. Outside Corson's home, Nagy loaded hundreds of pounds of boxes into the family station wagon, which barely made it back to Michigan. The move nearly destroyed his marriage, but it also made Nagy's collection perhaps the largest and most valuable in the country. Nagy wrote the young Mastro long letters, sharing his thoughts on which sets were prized and how to make smart trades.

At the end of Mastro's first visit to his house, Nagy sent him home with a complete set of Goudeys, along with a complete set of 1911 American Tobacco cards, both of which were then worth about $1,000. (Today, it's closer to $100,000.) Nagy simply told Mastro to send him some cards in return whenever he got the chance. In the years to come Mastro would spend weeks at a time at Nagy's home, the two often engaging in all-night card-trading marathons. Nagy had little mercy when it came to trading, approaching it like a game of poker: never

expose your line of thinking, and break your opponent through a series of clever tactics. Sometimes, by morning, Mastro would discover
that he had only a third of the cards he'd started with the night before. "I don't know if it's an appropriate credit to him," Mastro later
wrote of Nagy, "but he became my mentor in this hobby."

In addition to being a mentor, Nagy eventually became a client. After
Nagy's death, Mastro sold the T206 Wagner the older collector had left
his family for more than $450,000 in 2005.

Nagy, like Mastro, believed that inflation was good for the hobby.
It might make the cards more difficult to obtain, but card collecting
couldn't grow unless the values of the cards themselves grew. Mastro
started to take advantage of escalating prices once he got to tiny
Moravian College in Bethlehem, Pennsylvania. He bought and sold
cards as much as he studied, becoming the only one among his friends
who drove a nice car and always had beer money. "The values started
to rise and there was an opportunity," he said. "But it was about me
being able to make more money so I could buy cards. If I had nothing
but cards, then that was all that mattered to me. I just kept funneling it
all back in. All the deals were made to increase the quantity and quality
of my own collection."

Mastro foresaw a lot of money eventually pouring into the world of
baseball cards, which is why he quickly left his postcollege career as a
respiratory therapist. He started brokering deals for high-end vintage
cards, either functioning as an intermediary or speculating on his own
behalf.

He'd developed an encyclopedic understanding of baseball card history, knowing exactly what was out there and what it might be
worth. "He's at the top of the heap as far as knowledge goes," one
of Mastro's competitors in the auction world told me. "There aren't
many people with the experience he has." Mastro epitomized a new
kind of business savvy in the hobby, combining a card nerd's expertise
with the deal-making instincts of an investment banker. "I wanted to
do everything out of a briefcase," he recalled. "I wanted to be lean,

mean, and like a machine with a cellular phone. If you wanted high-end stuff, I was the guy you had to talk to."

Of the fifty to one hundred T206 Wagners known to exist, dozens have passed through Mastro on their way to new buyers. One of the first he handled was the most treasured of them all: the 8-of-10-graded Wagner eventually owned by Wayne Gretzky and then Michael Gidwitz, a card that quickly validated Mastro's vision of a booming, high-stakes hobby for the well heeled. In 1985 he bought the now legendary piece of cardboard from a Long Island dealer for $25,000, money that was put up by his auctioneer friend Rob Lifson. Mastro paid Lifson back with a less-desirable T206 and set out to find a buyer for his new acquisition.

He'd recognized the T206's dollar-making potential years earlier, by the simple fact that it was the first card Jefferson Burdick had separated from the pack and attributed a higher value to. Mastro considered it the one card that could drive the hobby into the consciousness of the mainstream, so he hyped its myth as much as he could.

Within about a year Mastro found a buyer for the T206 card: James C. Copeland, the wealthy owner of a California chain of sporting-goods stores, whom Mastro had been counseling on memorabilia investing. He sold the card to Copeland for $110,000, the most money ever paid for a single card. After he closed the deal in San Luis Obispo, Mastro called an Illinois Mercedes dealership from the airport. When he got off his plane, he headed straight to the lot and picked up his new 560SL. He drove it home with the $50,000 balance from the Wagner deal in his pocket.

That card would eventually command $2.8 million, but Mastro would never regret selling it when he did. After all, the deal made a loyal client out of Copeland. By 1989 Copeland was looking to unload many of the items he'd amassed over the previous five years, and he wanted Mastro to broker the largest sale of sports memorabilia in history. But Mastro realized that there could be no single buyer for the haul. "There was nobody in our hobby who could buy a collection for five million dollars," he said. "This was 1989. For five million bucks you may as well have said, 'I want to sell you downtown Chicago.' There was just nobody that could do that."

It could be accomplished only at auction, though Mastro had never organized one. He imagined that the right kind of sale would be a conspicuous opportunity to do what he'd always wanted to do: introduce the hobby to new, wealthier customers—and boost prices accordingly. He called on a friend who was an executive vice president at Sotheby's. Though the auction house had typically shunned pop-culture items for the fine arts, it had taken notice of the numbers Topps had pulled in with its recent Guernsey auction. Sotheby's designated Mastro special consultant to an auction of Copeland's 873 items in the spring of 1991.

By then a small professional auction industry had already sprouted up around baseball cards. Mastro nonetheless viewed the Copeland auction as something akin to an anointment. "This was the first time that anybody really credible said, 'Hey, we think you have a respectable auction here,'" he recalled. "By Sotheby's saying, *We'll do an auction of your stuff*, it was like, *We're in the big leagues now. Our hobby counts. We're not in the closet anymore*." As a competitor put it, "That was such an important auction, and it put Bill on the map."

Mastro, however, suspected that the auctioneers still turned their noses up at baseball cards. As a steady flow of children passed by to view the items before the sale, a company vice president asked him, "Are these the big bidders?" Mastro replied, "Take them seriously—they're with their fathers." Collectors packed the bidding room in Manhattan, often breaking with Sotheby's usually decorous auction procedure by shouting out bids a few grand above the current one. At one point, Gidwitz stood from his seat in the front row and yelled at a bidder in the back who was competing with him for an uncut sheet of Bowman cards. All told, the lots raked in $4.6 million, setting a sports-memorabilia record.

The highlight, however, was the sale of Copeland's Wagner card for $451,000 to an anonymous bidder—who turned out to be Gretzky backed by Los Angeles Kings owner Bruce McNall, who'd made his initial fortune in coin collecting. McNall, who would later face bankruptcy and be convicted of financial fraud, offered this rationale for his and Gretzky's splurging: "If you buy something that is absolutely the best in the world, you'd be okay because there is always another buyer for something at the top end."

At the time, frustrated would-be buyers grumbled about a market peak. They couldn't have been more wrong. Values for vintage cards would continue to rise for years, making the Copeland numbers look like fire-sale prices in retrospect. But it was only the rarest and finest-condition cards that drew steady demand, as well as singular pieces of memorabilia such as bats, balls, and uniforms used on the diamond by Hall of Famers. As savvy investors and dealers like Mastro began to realize, the surging popularity of baseball artifacts could help boost the hobby even as sales of new cards were starting to plummet.

When Mastro launched his own sports-specific auction house, in 1996, he believed that the hobby had taken a decisive turn. "I could see the handwriting on the wall," he told me. "Nobody liked the guy with the briefcase and the cellular phone anymore. They liked the auctions. I knew that this guy was going to be extinct if I didn't do something."

As much as Mastro admired the studious cartophiles Burdick and Carter, with their checklists and letter trading, he wanted to leave the collector's collector behind. He geared his business explicitly toward investors who could afford the most costly of baseball cards. "I understand that the Ritz Carlton is not for everybody. Tough shit. Everybody can't drive a Mercedes. Tough shit. I'm going to do it for the guys who have money," he explained. "The rest of the guys—and hey, some of them are my friends—but sorry, you're going to get sucked up into the wake. That's the way it is."

What Mastro had in mind were people like Barry Halper. A minority owner of the New York Yankees, Halper had turned his North Jersey home into a vast baseball museum. Deeply admired by Mastro, Halper had been at the forefront of memorabilia collecting, scooping up the game's most storied relics for a song long before they were considered anything more than curios. His acquisitiveness was so well known that, during a news conference after Mickey Mantle's 1995 liver transplant, the legendary slugger spotted Halper in the crowd and shouted, "Hey, Barry, did you get my other liver?"

"When they renovate Yankee Stadium, in 1973, he takes all the stuff home," Mastro said admiringly of Halper. "All the black bats, all the contracts, all the checks. They just gave it to him. By today's standards they gave him fifty million dollars. He turned it into a collection. He was a very polished, very respectable guy, and he really brought a dignity back to our hobby that few people before him had ever done. And so I credit him with the tremendous growth in our hobby."

To cater to exclusive clientele like Halper, Mastro believed that he had to lose money at first to make money later. Most vintage-card sellers worked out of home or through hotel and convention-hall card shows. Mastro rented an office in upmarket Oak Brook, Illinois, spending $175,000 a year on his lease. Most baseball card auction catalogs had been cheap and crude publications, high on misspellings and short on information. Mastro created slick catalogs that were keepsakes unto themselves, filled with glossy photographs and backstories on card sets and game-used memorabilia. And he didn't make collectors pay for them, as was often the case. He put them into as many hands as possible for free. His company also took out costly ads in *Variety,* the kind of outlet no sports-card dealer would have thought to venture. Mastro wanted to reach wealthy people whether they knew they were sports collectors or not. One year he even paid his way into the gift baskets given out at the Academy Awards. He dropped $75,000 on 150 baseballs signed by the late Joe DiMaggio, all of which eventually went into the hands of Oscar attendees, along with a business card for Mastro Auctions.

Unlike the vast majority of card dealers, Mastro knows that there's no logic to the most rarefied kinds of collecting. "If you don't collect anything or have that collector gene, then it's hard to understand the insanity of what these guys do," he explained. "They would abandon their wives, families, fortunes—everything—for the pursuit of this stuff." Mastro took full advantage of the fetishist-collector mind-set by refusing to hold live auctions in the classic sense. His earliest were done by telephone, and he quickly moved online, creating a secure bidding system for cartophiles on the Web. Mastro preferred to have his bidders alone at home, hashing out the auction over the course of hours or days. Their own psyches would eventually get the better of them, he reasoned.

"If they have thirty minutes, they have to envision themselves not having it—the *loss* of it. I know it sounds crazy, like the loss of a relative, but give them thirty minutes, and most people will take that next bid. And across the board in an auction scenario, you'll get more money." For all of his elaborate presale preparation, Mastro held his actual auctions according to one simple principle: "Just let guys bid and let them beat the shit out of each other."

Not long after Mastro Auctions first got collectors to hunker anxiously over their phones, hobby papers began breathlessly reporting new sales records put up by the house. One of its very first sales topped even the Copeland auction, generating $5.4 million in winning bids. The numbers fetched by mint-condition cards led Mastro to predict correctly that all cards of value would start going into slabs —"that we will no longer touch cardboard," as he put it at the time. As his sales grew, one card grading company dubbed Mastro the "Ringmaster of Memorabilia."

"He works with them like an art dealer," a rival dealer said of Mastro and his clients. "He makes it so that they at least temporarily are enjoying the attention, being a part of this, getting swept up in it.

I could never dream of being as charming as him. He has a magic with social skills. He can navigate in a way that other people can't imagine."

The lesson of the T206 Wagner had been obvious. A serious collector needs more than just good condition to make a serious purchase; he also needs a titillating backstory. Mastro affixed rich narratives to cards and artifacts whenever possible, to make collectors feel as if they weren't buying cardboard so much as becoming a part of American sports history. While most dealers would let a Mickey Mantle card speak for itself, Mastro hired writers and researchers to make it so alluring that collectors felt they had to have it. The idea, he said, was to "give them goose bumps. Make them interested in it and get their blood boiling." So if he was selling a bat used by Ted Williams—as he once did—Mastro wouldn't just tell you that Williams hit his four hundredth home run with the bat. He would send a film crew to Minnesota to tape an interview with the onetime Boston Red Sox batboy who came into possession of the lumber. Then he would put the video online to accompany the auction listing.

By 2001 Mastro's baseball card sales had proved so successful that he branched out into auctions of Americana. Soon his then partner, Rob Lifson, would bring in a monumental artifact of the Civil Rights Movement. One day Lifson discovered a quiet auction on eBay that claimed to be selling the bus on which Rosa Parks had made her landmark stand against Jim Crow segregation. Lifson got in touch with the family running the auction. They had circumstantial evidence for their claim but no proof, so Lifson suggested that they pull it from eBay. He set to proving its provenance beyond a shadow of a doubt.

Looking for a cheap storage structure, an Alabama man had purchased the bus years earlier from the Montgomery City Bus Lines Company for next to nothing. Though he was told of the bus's role in American history, he nonetheless proceeded to tear out the seats and fill the vehicle with tools and equipment; it rusted and decayed in the family's yard for years. On his deathbed the man told his daughter that their storage shed was the Rosa Parks bus, and he asked that she watch after it. Lifson spent months investigating the family's story. He had no cooperation from the bus driver, and Parks herself was no help. But Lifson did track down the widow of the longtime manager of the bus company, who had maintained the company archives during the 1950s and '60s. The records in the woman's attic verified the Parks bus by its number. After eliciting interest from a bidder list that included the Smithsonian Institution, Mastro sold the bus to the Henry Ford Museum for nearly half a million dollars. The bus company's records went for about $50,000. To this day, Lifson considers his work authenticating the bus the crowning achievement of his career.

Mastro's auction house developed a reputation for scoring such intriguing consignments. He got his hands on expensive curios that made for great wire story fodder, generating media buzz for his auctions weeks before they took place. In one of his stranger auctions, he sold a baseball-sized clump of Elvis Presley's hair, consigned by the King's longtime hairstylist, for about $115,000. In another, he hawked the wooden leg that belonged to flamboyant Major League Baseball team owner Bill Veeck. And although plenty of established auction houses would have shunned the likes of disgraced figure skater Tonya Harding, Mastro welcomed her as a client and eventually sold the dress she wore during the 1994 Winter Olympics, along with her infamous pair of skates with the broken lace. He declined to sell her notorious X-rated honeymoon tape. "I said, 'Are you nuts? You don't have enough negative publicity?'" he recalled, admitting with a laugh that he would, however, have loved to sell the metal baton that had struck Nancy Kerrigan's right knee, if it could be located.

Like baseball cards, such relics used to be relegated to anonymous attics. Even game-used equipment was considered oddball fare as far as sports collections went. But nowadays, when a slugger like Alex Rodriguez approaches one of the game's most hallowed records, fans view the balls that fly into the stands as something akin to lottery tickets. During the baseball postseason of 2003, Mastro took a call from a Chicago lawyer who'd been at Wrigley Field a few days earlier watching his

Cubs choke in Game 6 of the National League championship series. That was the fateful night Cubs fan Steve Bartman interfered with left fielder Moisés Alou during a foul-ball pop fly that could have ended the inning and helped preserve the home team's three-run advantage over the Florida Marlins. A win would have sent the Cubs to their first World Series since 1945. Instead, they blew their lead and went on to lose Game 7 as well.

Only the game's close observers noticed that Bartman never actually came down with the ball: it rattled around the seats on the third-base side. The fan who emerged with it was the lawyer calling Mastro a few days later. When Mastro told him that the ball's backstory could make it worth a few thousand bucks, the lawyer said that he'd already been offered $70,000. Mastro told him he'd been crazy not to take it. The lawyer insisted on an auction.

Mastro hyped the story and got it into some major daily newspapers, making the "Bartman Ball" the centerpiece of his next auction. The bidding soared to $113,000. The winner was a fellow named Grant DePorter, the manager of Harry Caray's Restaurant, a Chicago eatery founded by the legendary Cubs announcer. (Within hobby circles it was rumored that a more aggressive bidder, Canadian comic-book artist Todd McFarlane, had passed out during the auction's wee hours, handing the lot over to DePorter.) The restaurant insured the ball for $1 million as it fielded suggestions from Chicagoans as to how the memento should be disposed of. In the end, the ball was filled with explosives and ceremoniously detonated in front of television crews and a throng of pitiable Cubs fans. Later, the remains were boiled and the resulting steam condensed and incorporated into Caray's pasta sauce.

It was a lighthearted attempt at exorcism, but Mastro was there to collect his cut. "A hundred and thirteen thousand dollars," he laughed to me. "And you blow up the ball."

After he'd opened his auction house, Mastro competed fiercely with his onetime business partner and estranged friend, Rob Lifson, who had helped him purchase his all-important first T206 Wagner. Although sports-memorabilia auction houses are privately owned companies and therefore don't release sales figures, most hobbyists would agree that the two firms have raked in more money through cardboard sales than any of their competitors. Mastro and Lifson had worked on card auctions together before going their separate ways; now they both have a hard time masking their loathing for each other. Mastro, with a disdain for all things amateurish, described Lifson as a dilettante for, in part, operating his Robert Edward Auctions out of the basement of his home. Countering that slight, Lifson jokes that his commute is still too long.

Surely, Lifson is no amateur. He rivals Mastro not only in his auction figures but also in his encyclopedic knowledge of the material he sells. I met with Lifson one afternoon in his basement office, situated in an upper-middle-class development of contemporary homes in Watchung, New Jersey, where he and his two coworkers were toiling on the catalog for their next auction. They devote the majority of their working hours to catalog production—taking cards and "presenting them to the world in the most flattering light," as Lifson put it. Amid all the research materials and baseball cards scattered around the office, Lifson has a small studio in which to photograph the notable baseball jerseys, equipment, and paraphernalia he sells. Unlike other auctioneers, Lifson doesn't dabble in much outside of baseball.

He'd recently sold an original copy of the first constitution of the Philadelphia Olympic Ball Club. The eighteen-page rule book, dated 1838, was billed as "the single most significant item that could possibly exist relating to the birth of organized baseball." The run-up to the auction typified Lifson's operating style. He put about a hundred hours of work into prepping the document for sale, doing original research and devoting nine catalog pages to its background and description. He even commissioned noted baseball historian John Thorn to write an accompanying essay. "The consigner was so grateful," Lifson said. "This was his prize, and he couldn't imagine that anyone else would care enough to do this. There was one paragraph, I couldn't tell you how many times I rewrote it. That's because it was important to me, the whole concept. I don't think anyone else could've done it the way we did." The booklet nabbed $141,000 at auction—"and it deserved to," said Lifson—the most money ever paid for a piece of baseball text.

The success of the auction reminded Lifson why he devoted himself to auctioneering: to take compelling pieces of baseball history and present them to the public. For all the high-end card dealing he did in the 1970s and '80s, Lifson never cared for the buy low/sell high speculation practiced by Mastro. He disliked the contentious nature of it, and he wanted to be on the side of both the seller and the buyer. "This is what I was meant to do," he told me. "It's almost an obsession, so for me it's not like work. I can't even help myself." Unfortunately for Lifson, he enjoys such a moment only once a year, when REA holds its regular sale. Many more are spent mulling the dishonesty he believes has spread through his industry like a virus.

If Mastro despises Lifson, it's probably for the same reason many other card dealers shun him: Lifson is the hobby's resident whistleblower, crusading against what he sees as widespread conflicts of interest, most notably in card grading and card auctioning, as well as against the practice of card doctoring. Though he won't discuss any role he may or may not be playing in the current investigation involving Mastro Auctions, Lifson has testified for the Department of Justice on memorabilia issues in the past.

In 2006 he posted on his Web site a contentious screed that began, "Practically every day we are seeing fake items."

The altering of cards is so widespread, and "card doctors" so brazen, that REA has actually been receiving cards submitted for auction to us that are the very same cards that have been sold by REA previously—in some cases just months earlier—and which, since purchase, have been significantly altered, reholdered, and now grade higher according to the grading label. . . . Active and sophisticated collectors, dealers, and auction houses know that this is a problem. They just don't talk about it, except among themselves. In the end, the collector loses.

Such outspokenness has earned Lifson angry phone calls and death threats. Once, one of his competitors challenged his zoning status in an attempt to have his business shut down; Lifson had to make his case before his township's zoning board. His wife used to worry he might be car-bombed.

Lifson described such hazards as the price of business in the hobby. "We're a combination of a leader and an outsider," he said of REA. "In a lot of ways we really do alienate ourselves." Lifson is often evasive when talking about alleged fraud—after all, competitors have threatened him with lawsuits in the past. Instead, he suggests what some other auction houses might do by explaining everything his refuses to do. The list includes altering cards or turning a blind eye to altered cards, shill bidding, letting consignors secretly bid on their own lots, entering his own cards or his employees' cards in his auctions without disclosing it, and resubmitting a card for grading, again and again, until it receives the grade a seller wants. He's laid out many of his principles in a code of ethics he likes to preface his catalogs with; he was characteristically disappointed when other auction houses didn't immediately follow suit with their own pledges.

His stubbornness has won him the loyalty of righteous-minded collectors, but he can be scrupulous nearly to a fault. For instance, when Lifson is selling a card he believes doesn't deserve the high grade it received from a third-party grader, he will describe it as overrated in his catalog, possibly devaluing a lot in his own auction. When he plans on doing this, he tells the consignor he'll "have to live with the description" and offers him the option of pulling the card from REA's auction. Usually, the consignor will take it elsewhere, as one significant collector did shortly before I met with Lifson, who described such experiences as "painful."

Yet Lifson seems incapable of operating outside of this code he's established. As he put it, "There's a beauty to being rigid about it." He's particularly rigid when it comes to the common issue of "breakouts." That's when a collector or auction house will break a graded card out of its casing and resubmit it to the grading company, in hopes of landing a notch or two higher on the scale the second—or third, fourth, or fifth—time around. The ethical lines here are unclear. Grading cards is an utterly subjective practice, and only a few seconds or minutes at most go into professionally determining a card's condition. A collector shouldn't have to pay a dear price simply because he pulled a grader who didn't have his morning coffee. Mistakes do happen, and a difference of one digit on a scale of 1 to 10 could mean the difference between a $40,000 auction and a $100,000 auction. So why shouldn't a collector be able to send in a card again, especially when the grading house has no qualms about giving it another look-see?

For Lifson the answer is simple: collectors who resubmit and eventually score higher grades have compromised the system. As a policy, he refuses to resubmit cards on behalf of his clients. "We have never broken out a card to get it regraded," he said. "I'm not saying it's immoral. I just think there's a purity, a simplicity, to us saying we don't care if we send in a mint card and it comes back in a poor-to-fair holder." When that does happen, Lifson tells his consigner he's stuck with the second-rate grade—unless he wants to head to another auction house.

Plenty of collectors suspect that certain dealers can score better grades for their clients' cards than others can. This suspicion is more than reasonable, for the business of card grading itself is built upon a fundamental conflict of interest—grading companies are paid by the very people whose cards they're evaluating. If all collectors submitted the same volume of cards and did so anonymously, the point would be moot. In reality, auction houses and hotshot dealers and collectors submit a disproportionate number of cards for grading, so that folks like Lifson worry that the authenticators may become beholden to a particular batch of clients. One prominent East Coast collector is believed to have spent more than half a million dollars on the grading services of a single company; naturally, any authenticator would want to keep such a client happy. It's a bit like Moody's or Standard & Poor's evaluating the credit of the same firms that pay their bills.

In the world of baseball cards and memorabilia, the potential conflicts run even deeper. Many of the hobby's most respected third-party experts are also would-be sellers in the same marketplace, especially in an arcane niche such as, say, prewar baseball gloves or football autographs, in which the foremost authorities are often noted collectors. Lifson said that it's almost common practice for some collectors-turned-authenticators to grade their own vintage equipment or autographs and put them up for auction without a disclosure.

"Wherever there are people, you have the potential for unethical behavior—and there are a lot of people in this business," Lifson said with a laugh. "It's a much bigger problem than people realize. There are a lot of things that go on that are really questionable. We sit back here and we read the newspapers and see the headlines—we see this accounting scandal, that embezzlement. And we wonder, *Is our field any worse than any other business?* Our answer is yes. And we say yes because it's totally unregulated. People can set up shop as dealers and auctioneers or something in between and operate with impunity.

"It doesn't mean there aren't a lot of honest people and good business," he added. "But it's really unchecked, and there's no way to even bring this out in the open." Lifson told me he was relieved the FBI had taken an interest in the world of baseball cards. "If they didn't do anything," he said of the investigators, "I would've eventually closed up shop."

Collectors have chattered for years about Mastro's connection to the most famous and most controversial baseball card of all: the T206 Wagner that Lifson paid for, Mastro sold to Copeland, and Gidwitz later bought and finally sold for over $1 million. Many experts who've seen the card up close believe that its edges were trimmed at some point, which would explain how it remains in such stellar condition after more than a hundred years on earth. As much good as the card has done for boosting vintage-card values, the intrigue surrounding it has dogged the reputation of many hobbyists, most notably Mastro.

Alan Ray, the card's original owner, claimed to have proof the card was altered shortly after Mastro bought it; Mastro has fervently denied having doctored it in any way. In 2007 Michael O'Keeffe, a New York *Daily News* reporter who's covered the sports-memorabilia industry for years, coauthored a book with Teri Thompson on the T206 Wagner, *The Card: Collectors, Con Men, and the True Story of History's Most Desired Baseball Card*. With convincing detail, it alleges that Mastro played a role in the card's physical transformation. When I ran into Mastro shortly after the book's publication, at the 2007 national card show in Cleveland, he dismissed the book with a wave of the hand, claiming that the authors' probing only further sullied a tarnished hobby.

Surely any high-stakes collectibles market attracts its share of hucksters and con men, but the relatively new field of sports memorabilia, with its apparently limitless auction results and minimal regulation, seems especially vulnerable. When O. J. Simpson, who was convicted of stealing his own game-used footballs at gunpoint, confronted a dealer in Las Vegas in 2007, audiotape recorded at the scene caught him asking, "Motherfucker, you think you can steal my shit and sell it?" It was a reasonable question, given that stolen items turn up in sports auctions with disturbing regularity, as O'Keeffe had detailed in a number of reports in the *Daily News*. In the most notorious case, a group of baseballs signed by former U.S. presidents and stolen from Cooperstown in 1972 turned up in a Pennsylvania sports auction some thirty years later. Some of the balls had also been sold earlier through one of Mastro's auctions.

In 2006 Mastro Auctions president Doug Allen had to pull a Super Bowl ring from auction when it was discovered that the jewelry belonged to former Green Bay Packers offensive lineman Jerry Kramer, who was still smarting from losing it on a United Airlines flight a quarter of a century earlier. The bidding had reached $21,000 when the lot was spiked. During the very same sale, Allen had to pull a 1975 NFC Championship ring that had apparently been stolen from retired Dallas Cowboys guard Bruce Walton a couple of years earlier.

The most elite memorabilia collectors thoroughly research their prospective buys, and often they'll raise red flags about an item's authenticity well before an auction begins. During the summer of 2007 some basketball collectors questioned the legitimacy of a University of North Carolina at Chapel Hill warm-up jersey that had supposedly belonged to Michael Jordan and was being offered by Mastro in a blockbuster auction held at the House of Blues in Cleveland. The auction house had submitted the threads to a reliable jersey authenticator called Memorabilia Evaluation and Research Services, but the company had returned the shirt with a grade of "unable to authenticate." The object in question was indeed a UNC warm-up jersey from the early 1980s, but the name on the back appeared to have been changed. Mastro's auction house didn't disclose the finding; instead, it went to an authenticator who was willing to offer the jersey his blessing, according to O'Keeffe. It sold for $11,000. In an online forum jersey collectors quickly debunked the authentication, and the reputation of Mastro's auction house suffered for it.

Mastro told me that the bile directed at his business had more to do with personal enmity than anything else. "No one likes each other," he said. "The dealers don't like each other, and I understand that. We've all done a lot of things to each other. Lifson and I were best friends at one point and we hate each other now. . . . And I understand why a lot of these guys don't like me. It's not just jealousy. I've extracted my pound of flesh out of them. I handle myself like a businessman most of the time, and my job was to take their legs out. I did that in a very surgical manner."

*　*　*

After years of having their legs taken out, Mastro's enemies found reason to rejoice in March 2009. A new company calling itself Legendary Auctions issued a press release announcing that it had acquired the assets of Mastro Auctions. All of the company's auction lots and bidder accounts were being transferred to Legendary immediately. In the blink of an eye Mastro Auctions was no more.

Legendary Auctions listed its offices as being just a half hour from Mastro's in suburban Chicago, and its head as Doug Allen, erstwhile president of Mastro Auctions. In a statement, Allen stressed the ethical code that would be enforced at the new company: "The principals employed . . . will put their own collecting interests aside and concentrate solely on providing opportunities for our customers." Overall, the development appeared to be little more than a name change, despite the fact that Bill Mastro's name wasn't listed in connection with the new concern.

In his statement on his auction house's shuttering, Mastro sounded a lot like a politician who'd abruptly decided he needed to spend more time with his family. "Circumstances make it clear to me that the business needs to move in a different direction at this time and Legendary Auctions is a positive step that allows everyone to be taken care of, especially our customers who have been so loyal," he said. "I am looking forward to taking some time off for now, and wish Legendary Auctions only the best as they move forward."

It wasn't clear how much, if anything, the brutal recession had had to do with Mastro Auctions' closing. Just two months earlier Mastro had predicted, in an article in the *Chicago Daily Herald*, that his house would net $50 million in sales for the year, explaining that "a Mercedes is a Mercedes, and if you want and have the means, you'll pay for it." There were, however, rumors of serious cash-flow problems at the company, and some recent consignors had griped about late payments.

Many collectors, of course, wondered what role the FBI investigation may have played in the company's demise. Did Mastro Auctions shutter preemptively, before its name could be tarnished more than it already had been? Mastro wasn't explaining anything to reporters.

Even if he is out of the hobby for good, Mastro probably doesn't care all that much. In his thirteen years at the helm, Mastro Auctions racked up sales of more than a quarter of a billion dollars. In 2004 he sold the auction house to SilkRoad Equity, a Winston-Salem, North Carolina–based investment firm that specializes in venture capital, but stayed on as CEO. After forgiving him large debts, the deal netted Mastro about $5 million at the time, he claimed.

When I heard the news of Mastro's retirement, I was reminded of something he'd told me about his legacy and the baseball card business: "I always say to people, 'I'm on my way out, not on my way in.' My life is not over. I like to think I have time to do something else with it than just selling baseball cards. . . . If all I'm ever remembered for is this, then I lived a pretty shallow life."

11

A Visit to the Doctor

The T206 Honus Wagner isn't the rarest baseball card. It isn't even the rarest T206 baseball card. As hard-core collectors know, the T206 "Slow" Joe Doyle error card is in fact about ten times rarer than the Wagner. Due to a printing error that was quickly corrected, two different T206 cards were issued picturing Doyle, an unexceptional right-handed hurler who played five seasons during the dead ball era. The first and vastly scarcer version reads, "Doyle, N.Y. NAT'L." This was an understandable error: Joe Doyle played for the New York Highlanders of the American League, but "Laughing" Larry Doyle played for the New York Giants of the National League. After discovering the mistake, the printer immediately tried to remedy the situation by dropping the "NAT'L" beneath Joe Doyle's image. The resulting card, which simply reads "Doyle, N.Y.," is the far commoner of the two.

Card fetishists owe a heaping debt of gratitude to that diligent, anonymous printer, for what a difference four dropped letters can make. A first-class specimen of the rarer Joe Doyle will fetch hundreds of thousands of dollars at auction, whereas its more prevalent brother will receive a tiny fraction of that. The number of Doyle error cards in existence is probably small enough to count on two hands, yet nobody knows for sure exactly how many are out there. One of the few credible calculations came from card-grading behemoth Professional

Sports Authenticator of Santa Ana, California. On its Web site the company includes a "set registry," a comprehensive list that details which registered collectors own which rare cards. In addition, PSA keeps a running "population report" that tells collectors exactly how many of which cards the company has handled. The report claimed that there were at least nine confirmed samples of the Doyle error card in existence. In the fall of 2008 Rob Lifson publicly challenged that assertion.

The Robert Edward Auctions head had recently received a Doyle error card, one of the most prized consignments ever to come across his desk. He made it the centerpiece of his upcoming annual auction and, because he'd never sold one before, he set to learning everything he could about it. His research revealed that the number nine was probably several too high for the Doyle. The error card, he argued on his blog, was too often confused with the corrected version in collectors' listings. Then Lifson backed up his argument with a tantalizing proposition. He offered a reward of $1 million to anyone who could prove him wrong. The money would be split among any nine collectors who could bring forth authentic copies of the Doyle error card.

In reality, the much-ballyhooed prize served as little more than a low-risk publicity stunt for his upcoming sale of the Doyle card, for Lifson was fairly certain that nine credible examples would never arrive in his mailbox. He was right. After a few months—and even after dropping the million-dollar number to eight—he had received only two submissions. The error, it seemed, was scarcer than anyone had imagined.

Lifson knew of at least one other purportedly authentic Doyle—the one featured in a recent coffee-table book put out by PSA, *Collecting Sports Legends: The Ultimate Hobby Guide*. The Doyle error card in the book had been authenticated by PSA, encased in one of the company's hard plastic slabs, and given an exalted grade of 5 out of 10, or "excellent." With such a stellar rating, the rarity would have to be one of the world's most valuable baseball cards. But upon closer inspection Lifson saw trouble in the book's reproduction of the card—something looked off with the printing of "Doyle, N.Y. NAT'L." As he later posted on his blog, Lifson believed that the "NAT'L" had been tacked onto the end of "Doyle, N.Y." at some point after the original printing process. The last few letters, he argued, appeared to be in a slightly larger typeface than the first several. "This is not the case on other known-to-be-authentic rare Doyle cards," he wrote.

Lifson said there were two possible explanations. Either the original card had been altered or it represented a new and previously undiscovered variation on the Doyle error. But the latter suggestion came off as a bit of postscript diplomacy. Anyone who'd spent any time with Lifson or read his blog pasts could see that he was suggesting the card was an out-and-out fraud—and, by extension, that it had slipped past the reputable graders at PSA.

Normally, such an insinuation would make only small waves. After all, unscrupulous collectors doctor cards all the time. What set this case apart was the fact that the card in question had recently sold for $400,000.

The card-grading facilities of PSA occupy the bowels of a sleek, modish Orange County office park. There, a considerable chunk of the world's baseball cards arrive every year, each in search of an authoritative grade and a permanent, hard-plastic shell. In addition to the card-grading operation, the office houses PSA's autograph- and game-used-equipment-authentication service, PSA/DNA, whose experts put their stamps of approval or disapproval on thousands of high-end sports collectibles annually. The two services fall under a public umbrella company called Collectors Universe, which trades on the NASDAQ exchange. The corporation's employees inspect the condition of collectibles ranging from sports cards and stamps to currency and diamonds.

Collectors Universe got its start in the late 1980s grading upscale coins. Back then, baseball card obsessives were looking anxiously over their shoulders at the coin hobby, wondering if a similar third-party grading service would take root in their field. In 1986 a coin enthusiast named David Hall had founded what would become Collectors Universe on the belief that the buying and selling of coins—like that of baseball cards—suffered from an inherent conflict of interest: the guy vouching for the quality of the item was usually the same guy selling it. For a fee, Hall and his experts would offer a more disinterested eye. A little more than two years after introducing the service, Collectors Universe had graded and slabbed more than a million coins, bringing some newfound structure to a long-standing hobby. As old-school collectors saw it, however, these sheathed specimens signaled an end to their hobby, since they promoted the idea of old coins as investments and not just collectibles. Soon enough, traditional Wall Street investment firms started playing around with coin portfolios. The bottom fell out of the coin market in the early '90s, and dealers saddled with depreciating slabbed coins had to close shop.

This cautionary example notwithstanding, the slabbing of baseball cards was all but inevitable. The explosion of the vintage-card market in the early '90s had helped introduce widespread fraud; proponents of grading argued that third-party professionals could help ferret out the counterfeit or doctored cards hidden among the real things. Perhaps even more important, the transparency introduced by card grading would give collectors more confidence when buying cards sight unseen on new online auction sites such as eBay, which was replacing the card shops that had begun shuttering after the baseball strike. Naturally, what a seller might describe as a "near mint" card was often closer to "fair" in the buyer's eyes. The assignment of a firm, impartial grade would obviate any such disparity.

Card grading had its share of raucous detractors. Collectors would be entrusting graders, who are as predisposed to human error as anyone, with an extraordinary power—in effect, the ability to determine the value of all the cards they handled. Longtime collectors, many of whom were qualified to examine cards professionally themselves, also loathed the idea of forking over money to a faction of self-styled experts as a price of doing business. Old-timers griped that any such obligatory service would exaggerate prices in an already inflationary atmosphere. Nonetheless, PSA launched in 1991.

"Their first year, they were trying to explain the concept of third-party grading at a card show," PSA's current president, Joe Orlando, a former minor-league ballplayer, told me. "A lot of people on the floor were scoffing at the idea. For whatever reason, it just clicked with me. I understood what the problems were. Buyers are spending in some cases enormous amounts of money. You need a third party that has no financial interest in the transaction and who's also a true expert. It almost made too much sense."

Showing a knack for hype, the company's leaders decided that the first card worthy of their grading services would be the famous T206 Wagner recently purchased by Wayne Gretzky. They bestowed upon it the lofty score of 8 out of 10, or "near mint/mint," and confidently slabbed it with the serial number 00000001. It would be the first of many. By 1998 PSA was grading a million cards a year. It has logged as many annually ever since. Other competitors specializing in the grading of sports cards have since sprouted up, with technical-sounding names like Sportscard Guaranty Corporation and Global Authentication Inc. Card grading has become its own subindustry to the baseball card business, and it is now so ingrained in the hobby that it's virtually impossible to sell a card of any value without first having it slabbed by a reputable grader.

The service is costly. PSA, for one, requires that collectors purchase an annual membership, starting at $99, before submitting a single card. The lowest fee for having a card graded is $10, even if it's a five-cent common, and vintage cards worth $10,000 or more won't be looked at for under $250. As with any service, the profits are found in repeat customers. One well-known New Jersey collector, Jim Crandell, who built his fortune as an investment banker and commodities analyst on Wall Street, has had more than twenty-three thousand of his cards graded by PSA, no doubt running a tab into the hundreds of thousands of dollars. Many of the most well-heeled card lovers collect with grades foremost in their minds, and PSA's shrewd use of the set registry has fostered plenty of one-upmanship among them. The competitive Crandell, for instance, has amassed forty-five different vintage sets that meet his minimum standard for condition—a PSA 8 or better.

PSA is the status-seeking collector's service of choice. According to Orlando, it grades more cards than all of its competitors combined, accounting for a considerable portion of Collectors Universe's more than $40 million in annual revenues. "We have an overwhelming market share," Orlando said. "This facility is a well-oiled machine."

Orlando offered me the opportunity to see the machine in action one morning. My guide through PSA's office was Scott Single, a twenty-eight-year-old authenticator who'd been with the company since he got out of high school. Single, a committed sports collector, worked for a while as a card grader in the basement before becoming an autograph authenticator upstairs. He told me that he "can't put into words how awesome it is" to show up to his dream job every day. To give me a taste of the kind of random toys that pour into PSA's mail room, Single popped into an office and pulled an electric guitar from a soft case. An illegible signature had been scrawled on its maroon body. "Robert Smith," Single clarified—the legendary frontman of the Cure. "How great is it to be able to come into work and see stuff like this?" Indeed, PSA can seem as much a repository for the subjects of boyhood daydreams as a workplace. During my visit, one employee walked into the office in a crisp black suit, carrying a briefcase in one hand and a catcher's mitt in the other.

As Single led me downstairs to the card-grading facility, a guard watched us approach on a network of surveillance cameras and buzzed us through a series of secure doors. The latest influx of baseball cards sat in a banklike vault, visible only through steel bars. I told Single, only half-jokingly, that I was expecting nothing more than a couple of guys tearing open manila envelopes and shoe boxes, flipping cards across the table to one another. "That is the farthest from the truth," he said gravely. "It's a thorough, step-by-step process. Everyone down here has their own area of expertise."

After emerging from the vault, a card first heads to the receiving center, where a team of employees enters the specifications for some five thousand new arrivals every day. Then the card is kicked over to what PSA dubs the "investigations department." Here, a team of researchers leafs through a library's worth of hobby books in order to identify odd cards or cards with strange variations. "A lot of the vintage stuff have different backs, like the T206s," explained Single. "All the time we get stuff that we may have never seen before." Once a card has been classified beyond doubt, the researchers send it to the grading room for examination.

As we peered into the grading room, Single whispered to me, "It's always quiet in here." Sixteen men, most of them apparently in their twenties or thirties, were working in silent concentration, each in his own cubicle. As always, the fluorescent lights were turned off, and the room would have been pitch black if not for the small penumbra of light that fell across each grader's desk, into which he held a sports card, gently turning it over in his hands. The tools of the trade: desk lamp, ruler, jeweler's loupe, black light. The graders sat close enough to touch one another, but they all seemed to operate in their own little world, a few of them even wearing headphones to block out any noise. There was no banter, and they took no notice of their visitor. The work looked brutally taxing on the eyes. "We try not to disturb them," Single said.

Different grading companies have different standards, but their examinations all begin with the same task: to determine whether a card has been counterfeited or doctored. A fake card will be rejected by the grading company, while a doctored card will be deemed "authentic" but won't receive a number grade, often rendering it worthless on the open market. Patent fakes are usually easy to spot—few forgers have the printing skills to perfectly replicate a baseball card, whether vintage or modern.

Cards that have been altered from their original state are a trickier business. The graders use their tools to determine whether a card may have been trimmed, sanded, or toned, or undergone a host of other deceptive techniques to make it more aesthetically pleasing and valuable. For instance, a simple ruler can often tell a grader when a card has been trimmed to give it a fresh edge, because the card's dimensions will fall short of an unaltered example from the same set. Also, a card's edge, when viewed through a jeweler's loupe, can tell you that a razor or emery board has been applied to it. A black light can reveal chemicals applied to the surface of the card, perhaps to cover a stain, create a new sheen, or even artificially age the card. The same light can expose worn edges that have been slyly reinforced with new paper stock. The best graders have been poring over cards this way for much of their lives.

"If you want to become a grader, you have to work in every single area here first," Single told me. "You have to work in the investigations department and learn about the cards. You have to work in the sealing department and feel the cards and handle them. That way you know how to touch them. You can't just pick up a card—you have to learn it. Then you can become a grader."

If it seems nothing untoward has been done to a card, then it receives a grade reflecting its condition. At PSA, at least two graders look at each card independently. They evaluate how sharp the corners are, how crisp the colors are, and whether the smallest bit of damage appears anywhere on the card. Creases, holes, or significant stains call for large point deductions. Rounded corners will place a card in the bottom half of the scale. Even elements beyond the collector's or original owner's control, such as the centering of the picture, can knock a card's score down the ladder. Grading is, of course, highly subjective, but PSA strives for consistency, as evidenced by its hyperdetailed definition of a "near mint" card: "Just a slight surface wear visible upon close inspection. There may be slight fraying on some corners. Picture focus may be slightly out-of-register. A minor printing blemish is acceptable. Slight wax staining is acceptable on the back of the card only. Most of the original gloss is retained. Centering must be approximately 70/30 to 75/25 or better on the front and 90/10 or better on the back." "Gem mint" and "excellent mint" may sound awfully close but in fact they are four points apart on the 10-point scale.

After two graders have evaluated the same card, they share their scores. If the scores match up the case is closed. If they differ, the card goes to a tie-breaking grader who makes the final call. Each PSA grader handles anywhere from three hundred to six hundred cards in a day, according to Single. Assuming an eight-hour workday, that leaves anywhere from about forty-five seconds to a minute and a half to appraise a single card. The hobby's skeptics love to point to this harried schedule when questioning the validity of card grading. Orlando brushed these doubts aside. "They take as much time as they need," he said of his graders. "There are experts in the marketplace that evaluate paintings. They can look at a painting and say almost immediately that it's a counterfeit. It's the same thing for cards. This is what people do all day for a living, and they're very good at what they do. A minute may not sound like much, but it's a long time. It's the nature of the beast. If we're doing over a hundred thousand cards, they're not all going to be T206 Ty Cobbs. The graders know exactly what to look for. It's like they're programmed."

After a card's grade has been settled, it moves down the hall to the encapsulation room, where an employee prints out the card's "flip"—the identifying tag that accompanies the card inside the case. It's another employee's job to assemble the case and, using a black light and an air gun, remove any debris before it's enclosed. Then the encased card moves to yet another chamber, where its slabs will be permanently sealed with an ultrasonic welding press.

"You're going to want to cover your ears," Single told me as we entered the sealing room. Once inside, we heard a spine-rattling screech every few seconds, as if one train after another was pulling out of the station. Single handed me a pair of earplugs from a boxful kept for visitors. Vito, the short, wiry, mustachioed welder I was introduced to, forgoes hearing protectors. He and his coworkers, who drop the boom on thousands of cards every day, are used to the unpleasant squeal of the press. There are different-sized welding plates for every piece of sports memorabilia imaginable—vintage cards, modern cards, unopened wax packs, checks signed by players, game ticket stubs. "We try to accommodate everything," Single said. He handed me a sealed but not yet welded slab with an old baseball card inside, then encouraged me to twist it. The slab was flimsy. But then Vito welded it and handed it back to me. The slab was as unbending as a two-by-four, requiring some serious elbow grease to be opened again. It dawned on me that the card inside will probably never again be touched by human hands.

A grader gives that card one last look to make sure everything is right, and then it goes into the mail and back to its rightful owner who, within a few days, will be either thrilled or devastated by the number in the top right corner of the slab. As Orlando promised, his card-slabbing factory was indeed a well-oiled machine. If the other grading companies work with any comparable efficiency, it seems plausible that someday all the cards in the world could be slabbed and graded, never again subject to greasy fingers or debate. The investment-minded collectors who view their hobby as a marketplace can take comfort in that. Those who collect for collecting's sake, or for the love of colorfully printed cardboard, not so much. For them, PSA's operation is more like a Wonka factory running in reverse, a place where the baseball cards of their youth go to lose what made them fun.

Lifson's suspicions about the Joe Doyle card in the PSA book made for heated discussion among vintage card lovers, many of whom gather to chat at an online forum called Network54. Throughout a lengthy, impassioned thread headlined "Wow! PSA! T206 Doyle!

Wow!!!!!" a raft of dealers and collectors evaluated side-by-side photos and concluded that the $400,000 card in question was almost certainly a fake. The lettering, they agreed, was just too damning. "It's one of those cards that on a first glance you say, 'that doesn't look right,'" wrote one respected card auctioneer. "Disturbing," a noted T206 expert said flatly. "My jaw continues to drop in disbelief and, sadly, disgust," another collector summed up. "Even without my glasses, I know better than to let this one pass."

One poster said he knew of at least four fraudulent Doyle errors floating around the hobby, all of them slabbed and graded by respected companies. One grading company, Sportscard Guaranty, encapsulated a fraudulent Doyle error back in the '90s, quickly realized its mistake, and bought the card back to take it off the market. The poster urged his fellow collectors to keep a high-resolution Doyle scan on hand for comparison whenever they came across a purportedly authentic copy of the rarity. He also remarked that the owners of the fraudulent Doyles know that they own forgeries but don't care because they've been graded as genuine articles. Therein lies the irony of authenticating rare baseball cards. Once a card has passed the experts' eyes and been encased, in effect it becomes legitimate, regardless of whether it was ever tampered with.

Hobby ombudsmen like Lifson believe that card doctoring is widespread enough to warrant the term "epidemic." Even less hyperbolic collectors agree that there are dealers out there trading in dubious cardboard, some perhaps making a good living out of it. To see exactly how these men transform unexceptional cards into pristine treasures, I took a drive one afternoon to the town of Harbor City, California, about thirty-five miles up the coast from PSA's offices.

There I met with Kevin Saucier, a forty-four-year-old corporate-risk manager who is arguably the hobby's most eminent and outspoken card doctor. When I pulled up to his yellow rambler, Saucier waved me past the small palm trees and fountain to the detached garage where he keeps his baseball card alteration "lab."

Saucier is far different from your average card doctor—he's never altered a card for profit. To the contrary, he dabbles in alterations only so he can discover which techniques lie on the cutting edge of card doctoring, so to speak, and then show his fellow collectors the telltale signs that they should be looking for. He first became interested in card alteration years ago, when he bought a card that turned out to have been "trimmed" to improve its edges. Since then, he's become an authority on the subject. He invited me to his house to show me some of his most successful alteration techniques, under the agreement that I won't write in so much detail as to help out would-be frauds.

An unabashed skeptic, Saucier is quick to cry fraud when he sees a questionable card. He's been outspoken enough on the subject of card alteration to alienate quite a few dealers and graders, as well as those collectors who believe he's impugning the pedigrees of their cards. Saucier believes that the grading companies are neither diligent nor disinterested parties, because their profits demand high volume, quick turnaround, and happy repeat customers—a situation that has led him to vigilantism. His preferred method is to doctor cards and then submit them to the grading companies; when the illegitimate cards return encased with legitimate grades, he posts the full results on the Web to publicly shame the authenticators. There was a time when collecting baseball cards had grown stale for Saucier, but the technical gamesmanship of doctoring has given him a new lease on his favorite pastime. It's all about experimentation. He's frozen, burned, baked, and boiled cards, all in search of new ways to alter their appearance. Nowadays, he destroys more cards than he buys.

"I think to myself, *I'm a crook and I'm going to get it past you,*" he said. "How am I going do it? First of all, I've got to know what you know. I've got to know how you inspect. And then I've got to take it to the next level."

He brags that so far he's batting nearly 1.000 on his submissions to grading companies, with about three dozen doctored cards successfully slabbed. He's also created an online gallery of his handiwork at AlteredCards.com, along with detailed advice about how to detect various types of doctoring. "Under a halogen light, inspect the card corner and corner surfaces for inconsistencies in color, uneven wear, stray, unattached fibers as well as small high and/or low spots. Using your loupe, examine the suspected corner(s) and look very closely for individual fibers that may have been used as an attachment," begins a discussion of spotting rebuilt corners that runs for seven paragraphs and includes even more photos, including a couple taken under black light.

Saucier's mission is to prove that almost anything can be done to a card—and that almost anything can get past even the experts. A legion of collectors believes that he's doing an invaluable service to the hobby. "Some of these collectors, they'll spend ten thousand dollars on a card without taking a good look at it," he told me, wide-eyed in befuddlement. "Well, if they were buying a ten-thousand-dollar car they would kick the tires, take a look under the hood, bring it to a mechanic. But with a baseball card they'll buy it blind."

Sophisticated card alteration calls for a lot of tinkering with chemicals, which is why Saucier took to it. Before going into insurance he worked for ten years as a firefighter specializing in hazardous materials, a job that required a series of chemistry courses as well as a class in which he learned the processes needed to determine unknown chemicals. Saucier won his department's highest valor award for rescuing a co-worker from a hydrochloric-acid spill at a factory in Torrance, California; scars from the incident still pock his entire neck.

Saucier's lab contains half a dozen chemicals that he uses regularly to remove stains and change colors on cards, each one in a tiny bottle labeled only with a letter. He doesn't want to reveal the chemicals when he gives demonstrations to graders. As he doctors a card, he always makes sure to build in a hidden "identifier," a minuscule stain or nick, so that if the card ever got out on the open market he could identify it as one of his own. And because vintage baseball cards are too valuable to destroy, Saucier does most of his experimentation on common nonsports cards.

The first skill he taught me was how to soak a card. Ever since childhood, when I ruined a boxful of Topps commons trying to wash them in the sink, I've assumed that applying a generous amount of any liquid to a baseball card will foul it. Not so. Fully submersing a card in water will clean its surface, and if it's dried properly it will return to its original shape, showing no signs of its bathing. Safe as it is, soaking requires a hardy leap of faith, especially when trying to clean a card potentially worth thousands of dollars.

"It's all or nothing—you've got to bite the bullet," Saucier said, dropping a circa-1910 American Tobacco card featuring the Prince of Wales into a shallow tray of distilled water. "You haven't lived until you've soaked a Babe Ruth."

He rubbed his thumb gently on the card's grimier spots, and the blemishes began to lift. After a few minutes, he removed the card, swaddled it in a couple of napkins, and placed it between a pair of wooden slats, placing a five-pound weight on top. When fully dry in a couple of days the card will look vastly more appealing. "It removes stains, it removes the dirt, and, frankly, with all the grading companies, it's an acceptable practice," Saucier said. "It's still altering a card in my opinion. But technically it's not." Only when stronger chemicals enter the picture does card cleaning become an undebatable alteration.

What Saucier did next is fraudulent by anyone's standards. He bleached a card. "Keep in mind, we're doing in five minutes what we would normally do in two hours," he said, mixing a bleach solution more concentrated than usual. He dropped another well-aged tobacco card into the mixture and swirled it around for a moment. "Take a look at it—it's cleaned up quite a bit. Of course, it smells like bleach. So you resoak it in water to get the smell out." He gave it a soak and pulled it out. "There, we've got a nice white card." The stains were gone, the white background looked vibrant—clean but not too clean, as

Saucier pointed out—and the card no longer smelled like a swimming pool. Saucier may well have bumped it up a grading notch or two.

"If it's nice and clean and crisp, they're going to bypass everything else and say it's a nice-looking card," he explained. He handed me a card that had been graded a 6 by one of the authenticators, though it should have been rejected as altered. There was a white dot on the player's image—a bleach stain. "If you could smell this card through this holder, it would smell like three of these chemicals," Saucier said, shaking his head. "I sent it in that way on purpose to see if they'd catch it. They graded it. I think they're in a hurry."

Why does Saucier consider that slip unacceptable? Because even the slightest boost in a card's grade can put it in a league apart from its undoctored cousins. With men like Jim Crandell searching for only the most well-preserved examples, a card graded an 8 is exponentially more valuable than a card graded a 3. Saucier has already improved a vintage card from a 3 to an 8 through alteration, driving it halfway up the grading scale. Just a few doctored cards, he argues, can compromise an entire field.

An able card doctor can do worse than artificially improving a card's condition—he can turn it into a different card altogether, like the Doyle error. One of the most nefarious techniques in card alteration is known as "rebacking." The cards in some vintage tobacco sets, like the T206, were printed with a multitude of different backs that plugged different cigarette brands. The rarer backs, like those advertising Uzit or Drum cigarettes, can make a player's card considerably more valuable than the same card with a run-of-the-mill reverse. So a card doctor can shear the unusual back off of a common card or even a nonbaseball card, splice it onto the image of a Hall of Famer, and—*presto*—he has an ultrarare, century-old baseball card. From time to time, collectors come forward announcing the discovery of a new, previously unknown card. Not surprisingly, Saucier is skeptical of many such "finds."

Merging two cards together to create a counterfeit is difficult but not impossible. "Rebacking is an art unto itself," Saucier said. "You've got to take a back off one and put it onto another. You can't have any seams in it, and the joints have to come together perfectly. And you can't have residues."

Done properly, the process can require as many as thirty different stages of soaking, peeling, gluing, bleaching, trimming, and sanding, all carried out over the course of a week. Saucier has the necessary dexterity and patience for it. "I'm obsessive-compulsive," he explained. "Every collector is to some degree." He showed me one method he's devised for rebacking, though he asked that I don't detail how he does it. After just a few minutes he conflated two vintage pieces of cardboard—tobacco cards from the UK issued around 1914—into a one-of-a-kind. Saucier would let the soggy and misshapen result dry and then fine-tune it over the next few days, promising to mail me the final product.

He showed me how he can take the eyesores that decimate a card's value and make them disappear. Creases he quickly flattened out with a spoon. Pinholes he covered with gentle massaging. And frayed edges he turned fresh with a razor blade. After showing me these tricks, he tried to turn me into a card grader. He handed me two doctored cards that have been authenticated and slabbed, along with a 10 X magnifying glass, and told me to look closely at them for a few minutes and pinpoint what's wrong with them. "If you get stuck, use the fifteen X," he said, stepping out of the garage to pull on a cigarette.

One of them was a circa-1910 American Tobacco baseball card featuring the Giants' left-handed pitcher Rube Marquard, graded a 2, or "good"; the other was a 1911 Imperial Tobacco hockey card showing Hall of Fame Quebec Hockey Club goalie Paddy Moran, graded a 3, or "very good." Looking through the glass, I examined the front, back, and perimeter of each card, searching for anything that looked amiss. Saucier walked back into the garage and asked me what I'd found. I told him that one of the edges on the Marquard card looked to have been trimmed. "The edges haven't been touched," he said. Then I had no idea, I told him. He flipped the card over and pointed out a slight discoloration on the tobacco advertisement.

"There's been a stain removed," he said. "The stain was horrid—a big, dark glob of crap right here. Took it off, and the card looked worse.... So I took the whole card, bleached it all, recolored it, retoned it, and kept doing it and doing it and doing it. I toned everything around it, so the color of the stain is the same color of the card."

He then asked what doctoring I found with the Moran card. "I can see some discoloration there," I said, pointing to a spot on the card's back. Wrong again.

"If you flip to the other side," he said, "that corner is rebuilt, that corner is rebuilt, this side is trimmed, and that side is trimmed."

Granted, this was my first day as a card grader, but I missed every alteration Saucier performed on the cards. After just a few minutes of exploring them, I'd come to sympathize with the graders Saucier condemns as insufficient. The task would be difficult even with a trained eye.

When I brought up the subject of the controversial Doyle card, Saucier could barely conceal his glee. "Dude, that was a hell of a catch," he grinned, commending Lifson. He grabbed his copy of *Collecting Sports Legends* and laid out his own case for why he believes it to be a fraud. It's more than just the dubious font that Lifson noticed, he said. He pointed out the suspicious break in tone to each side of the lettering, as if the original print had been bleached at some point. "You see from here to here how white it is, and from here to here it's just a bit more toned," he said. "Nobody's going to give a shit once it's in a holder. Somebody's going to buy it."

Saucier finds comfort in one fact, though—that the possibility of the card's being a fraud is even being discussed. For years, card doctoring had been a taboo subject among collectors. Baseball card owners can get awfully prickly when a guy like Saucier questions the authenticity of their little treasures, as he's done publicly on Network54. In 2007 one user posted a photo of his prized 1910 Standard Caramel–issued Mordecai Brown "ghost" card, in which the player appears almost spectral due to an error in the color printing process. Though many vintage ghost cards are rare, valuable, and wholly legitimate, Saucier insists that they can be easily forged with certain chemicals. (He showed me as much, convincingly.) He had no reservations about calling the Brown card a sham. "I can almost guarantee you that is a doctored card," he posted. "So much so I would bet money (a lot) on it." The owner seethed back, "If Kevin knows for a 'fact' that my Brown was doctored, then either he did it himself and unleashed a fraud on the hobby, or can explain here how he knows with such certainty." Saucier declined, so as not to give an online tutorial in card doctoring.

Some Network54 users send Saucier their slabbed cards to be independently examined. Crandell, for one, has called Saucier "one of the top three card experts in the world," adding that he won't buy a high-priced card without Saucier inspecting it. A few have even asked, controversially, that he maintain an online catalog of the professionally graded cards that he's deemed to be doctored. Of course, a few others have denounced Saucier as a "clown" and a "hobby novice playing with bleach and trying to talk a big game."

"Some people say he's causing problems," Lifson said of the card doctor. "I don't feel that way. It doesn't mean he's right or wrong— I just think he's calling attention to a real problem. The problem is not that Kevin Saucier is out there. The problem is that we don't have more Kevin Sauciers out there. There's a lot of natural political pressure to not talk about these things. All these people have lots of money invested in this stuff."

A couple of weeks after my visit with Saucier, I received an envelope from him. Inside was a British tobacco card, encased in plastic and wrapped in a note: "Here is the rebacked card we made together. The borders are not perfect but that wasn't the result we were looking for.

The card has been toned, glossed and slightly reshaped. I did leave a built-in identifier for you to find."

I slipped the card out of its case and gave it a close inspection. The borders were off just a bit, as Saucier said, but otherwise it looked like a perfectly legitimate hundred-year-old tobacco card. Even looking at the edges I couldn't tell at all that the card had been spliced together from two different specimens. All of the corners matched up and the card lay perfectly flat on the table. No glue was visible. Saucier had toned the card just enough to conceal his meddling. As for the hidden identifier, I was at a complete loss.

If Saucier had done this with an American Tobacco card showing an all-star ballplayer, I would have been holding a one-of-a-kind that just might slip through the gates at a grading house, on its way to fetching a six-figure bid in a card auction. He could make a decent living fabricating cards, and one grader has suggested he do just that if he ever falls on hard times. Shady dealers have offered him money in exchange for learning his tricks, too, but Saucier doesn't see his life ever coming to that.

"It's easier to go on the dark side," he told me. "You can take a twenty-dollar card and turn it into a two-thousand-dollar card and make a shitload of money. But I'd hope that someday, somewhere, you'll be held accountable for it."

12

It's Just a Piece
of Cardboard

Of all the explanations I've heard for why little boys and grown men alike collect baseball cards, none is as convincing as the one proffered by Topps's own card master, Woody Gelman. It's something he said in 1967 to the *New York Times* reporter who ended up embarrassing him. Tellingly, Gelman blurred the line between adult and child: "You start instinctively, as a child. Part of collecting is the desire to complete something, to find everything in one category. Part of it is a recapturing of the past. You discover again how to play. You go back with a vengeance."

The desire to complete something, to discover every card out there —that's what drove kids in the 1880s to beg their fathers to buy Old Judge cigarettes before all other brands, why they mobbed the doors of cigarette factories, vouchers in hand, demanding albums for their baseball cards. The same desire sent a crippled, middle-aged Jefferson Burdick crisscrossing the country for years, to flea markets and attics, in search of picture cards he'd never seen before so that he might paste them into albums and catalog them before they killed him. It also drove Gelman himself to stuff his Long Island basement full of vintage cards, drawing on their designs for his own Topps creations, so that he might transmit to kids the card collector's "disease," as he once put it. He helped infect a generation of boys—my father's, in the 1950s and '60s—some of whom, like Michael Gidwitz and Bill Mastro and Kevin Saucier, never managed to cure themselves. Their generation, in turn, infected my own.

I exhibited my first signs of affliction shortly before the 1987 baseball season, at age eight, when I fell in love with the most unusual offering of the decade. That year, the Topps designers chose to frame player photos with a distinctive wood-grain trim. It didn't resemble anything that sprouted in the natural world, however—it was more like the faux wood siding on your mother's Plymouth station wagon, or the flimsy wood-effect paneling on the walls of your neighbor's basement. Though I didn't know it at the time, the design was something of an homage to the Topps "woody" set from 1962, an era when, as Gelman's protégé Len Brown put it to me, "you could look at a baseball card and say, 'That was a 1962.'" Well, there was no mistaking an '87, either. You knew it as soon as you saw it. And if you suffered from severe cartophilia, as I did, then you simply had to have it.

I spent hours reading the statistics and text on the backs of those '87s, poring over them as if they revealed the mysteries of the universe. Back then, the good folks at Topps gave us the dish on our diamond heroes in the form of trivia fun facts. I marveled at some of the juicier nuggets the researchers managed to unearth, such as the fact that New York Mets ace Sid Fernandez wore number 50 in tribute to his home state of Hawaii, the fiftieth state; that Oakland Athletics third baseman Carney Lansford was a direct descendant of British admiral Sir Francis Drake; and that longtime Milwaukee Brewers hurler Moose Haas held his own as an amateur magician and certified locksmith.

Even better were the nicknames: "Shoes" (the Pittsburgh Pirates' R. J. Reynolds), "The Polish Prince" (the San Francisco Giants' Mike Krukow), and "Cuffs" and "The Inspector" (both handles for Toronto Blue Jay Bill Caudill). How could you not feel endeared to St. Louis Cardinals reliever Jeff Lahti, knowing that he owned an apple orchard in Oregon and that his friends called him "Jam Man"? For those of us fans who would never sit directly behind a big-league dugout, baseball cards made us feel a step closer to our idols.

I was only in the third grade in 1987, not yet polluted with the false promise that my cards would someday make me rich. I simply loved dropping a couple of quarters on the store counter, walking outside with a wax pack, and tearing into it not knowing what I'd find. I didn't mind if the whole pack turned out to be commons, so long as there was a Yankee in there somewhere. Or even a relatively unknown journeyman with a goofy name or a comical photo. And when I got home, the cards went into a shoe box rather than a binder or a plastic case. I still had the attitude that Kevin Saucier clings to whenever some fetishist collector goes off the deep end: "It's just a piece of cardboard."

That's all baseball cards were to me. And so I took the liberty to flip them, to doodle on them, and to stuff them in my back pocket before I hopped on my bike and headed to a friend's house. I spent so much time with those cards that even today I can recall their smallest details. On the rare occasions that I open up an old shoe box and leaf through those '87 woodies, I experience a bit of that recapturing that Gelman spoke of so knowingly.

Even if the baseball card hobby is no longer what it was, I found it hard to believe that some kids out there don't find the same allure in cardboard that I once did. I also figured there must be at least some born-again, nonfetishist collectors out there who scrounge for those elusive few cards that kept them from completing sets as a child. To get a look at the current state of baseball card collecting—and perhaps a glimpse of its future—I headed one morning to the best gauge I know of: the National Sports Collectors Convention or, as the annual four-day midsummer event is known to hobbyists, "the National."

My impressions upon arriving at the International Exposition Center in Cleveland, Ohio, weren't exactly favorable. Near the doors one of the card companies had stationed a pair of striking and toned young women —both around twenty years old, I estimated—to greet collectors as they walked in. The promo girls were wearing skimpy umpire-themed outfits, with snug black-and-white tops and head-turning shorts. I would expect to see these bubbly coeds handing out Coors Light key chains at the local sports bar, but I was more than a little surprised to run into them at a baseball card show. They doled out free packs of sports cards to a procession of forty- and fifty-something men who blushed and fumbled for words. The scene was hard to watch.

Perhaps it was just the cavernous feel of the convention hall, but the event seemed much more subdued than the card expos I attended as a kid in Catholic churches and VFW halls. There were more than enough dealers in attendance—hundreds of them filled the space to capacity, their wares laid out neatly in glass cases, their business cards stacked alongside waiting to be snatched. But there was a shortage on the other side of the tables. Along certain stretches of the hall there appeared to be almost as many sellers trying to unload things as there were customers trying to buy them. One dealer told me that there was a time when collectors at the National lined up three deep at his table. "Not anymore," he said.

Most notably missing from the National were children. At nearly thirty years old, I felt like a spry pup alongside the vast majority of collectors there, most of them appearing to have settled nicely into middle age. There were plenty of goodies for a ten-year-old kid to marvel at but precious few that he could afford to walk out the door with. Most of the major booths traded in blue-chip cards and memorabilia. One enterprising auction house was trying to sell the ball that would break Hank Aaron's all-time home run record—before Barry Bonds even hit it. The company promised a hefty reward to the fan who emerged from the pileup, ball in hand.

Even the more anonymous booths tended to price out kids, showcasing expensive graded cards rather than the affordable stuff. As for the new cards on display, the breadth was staggering. The companies showed off dozens of contemporary baseball card issues, many of them going for several bucks per pack.

One noted collector told me that the market even for vintage cards will eventually go down, asking that I not use his name because his dour assessment of the hobby tends to anger his colleagues. "I don't think that the market in the long term will hold up," he said. "I turn sixty next summer. My generation has had so much discretionary income. You've got some things going for ungodly amounts now because you've got boomers who collected when they were kids. When my generation starts getting near seventy-five or eighty years old, they'll be trying to sell it all off. There will always be people around collecting cards, but there won't be an awful lot of them. When this current generation grows up, they won't care squat about any cards you or I collected, and the market won't be there."

As I looked around the buzzless room at the National, his doom-and-gloom assessment sounded awfully convincing.

Amid all the upmarket sellers of graded vintage cards and game-used equipment, one dealer at the National offered something different. His name is Bill Henderson, and he advertises himself as the "King of Commons." He's attended every single National since the event's inception in 1980, and somehow he's still making adequate money for himself and a few part-time employees by selling the cards that most people don't care for: the commons.

Henderson's business model seems to run against all common sense when it comes to baseball cards. As it became apparent that dealers would have a hard time earning a living selling new product, the shrewdest of them put their money into the oldest of cards, featuring only the most desirable players and only in the finest condition. Many sellers wouldn't invest in any cards manufactured after 1960.

Henderson, however, has continued to sell cards from all decades, even those whose issues are considered relatively worthless. He doesn't discriminate between the All-Stars and the one-season-and-out scrubs, either. And he doesn't make a big deal about a card's condition. In fact, as a general rule, he doesn't deal in graded cards. Sure, condition partly determines Henderson's prices, but whether it's mint, excellent, very good, or poor, a card is a card in his view. In other words, Henderson exists solely to help people complete their sets—the original premise of card collecting, going all the way back to the creations of Buck Duke.

Henderson's operation struck me as so novel that I later paid him a visit at the King of Commons headquarters, just a couple of hours northwest of Chicago in Janesville, a small, tree-laden city that bills itself as Wisconsin's Park Place. Henderson had his house built in 2000 expressly to accommodate his card business, which takes up the entire basement of the 2,200-foot structure. Downstairs, he showed me hundreds of thousands of cards—perhaps millions; he isn't sure—many of them castoffs from other people's collections, now filed neatly in cardboard boxes labeled by year and condition.

Like a lot of other dealers operating today, Henderson started swallowing up the dusty batches of cards that mothers were dragging out of their attics in the mid-1970s. In 1976 he ditched his job as an accountant to handle baseball cards full-time, advertising his service in local penny savers. He had a lot of steals come his way in those days, like the shopping bag filled with Topps cards from the 1950s that an old woman let him have for $1. She put the money toward a new coffeepot.

Henderson took anything and everything that had a baseball or football player on it. "I would always break down collections," said the sixty-three-year-old. "I had a tax service then, and I was [priced] very reasonably, like H&R Block. For me, it was the same thing with cards. I felt like a lot of people wanted to sell stars and the fancy stuff, even back in the beginning, in the seventies. I felt like someone's got to take care of the chaff. And that's why I decided I was going to be the King of Commons."

The moniker fits. As a baseball-history junkie who's also an unexceptional former athlete, Henderson has always gravitated toward the game's footnote players. One of his favorites as a kid was Bob "Hurricane" Hazle, an outfielder who hit .403 in forty-one games for the Milwaukee Braves in 1957, only to slink back soon to the minor leagues on his way to anonymity. "I didn't succeed that well in sports, so I figure I'm pretty common," said Henderson. "The guys who worked hard to make it but didn't succeed all that well—they were kind of my heroes. When I started out, I wanted that to be my mainstay. I got some small notoriety for it."

Henderson traveled all over the country going to card exhibitions. If there was a show at a hotel in Texas or a mall in New Jersey, he headed there in his diesel station wagon, perhaps with his wife or a friend or two in tow, to sell his accumulated commons and pick up a few new ones—"like a treasure hunt, if you had the money to get there," he told me. When other dealers didn't want commons cluttering up their inventories, Henderson took them off their hands for cheap. One connection hooked him up with troves of cards from Woody Gelman's Card Collector's Company on Long Island. If it was a massive quantity of cards, Henderson wanted it, regardless of condition. He hired a married couple in their eighties—"Hall of Fame card sorters"—whose job was to sift through and classify the boxes of cardboard he brought home.

Of course, those early card shows pretty much disappeared with the diesel wagon. Henderson now visits only a handful of events each year besides the National—it simply isn't worth his time and money to travel to make a few paltry sales at, say, the expo center in Fort Washington, Pennsylvania. But his business stays alive thanks to eBay and Beckett.com, as well as the random baseball fans still searching for random players. His cards, going back to the early 1950s, start at a quarter apiece. He's carved out a reputation as the guy to come to when you need a 1950 Bowman Bob Swift, a 1962 Post Cereal Don Blasingame, or a 1983 Topps John Pacella. Henderson calls it "the factory worker's inventory." They're not the finest cards but they'll do.

Even these days business remains brisk enough that Henderson needs three retired buddies—Randy, Bob, and Kenny—to come in two days a week to pull cards, assemble orders, and maintain the Web stores. Henderson starts his day going over orders and ends it sorting cards in front of the television at midnight. "People aren't buying for investment right now in my niche," he said. "They buy because they want it. Maybe somebody's wanting to work on a Cubs set—I had a father and son come in for that. I've got another guy working on football from the early fifties. This is nothing they can retire on. I just enjoy the contact and treating the people good and trying to be fair. It's paid off for me."

When I visited him, Henderson was surprised to have seen a recent spike in orders for '70s baseball cards. He figured that the buyers were men in their forties trying to fill their incomplete sets from childhood, submitting orders for single cards or maybe a batch of a dozen commons. For those who care about baseball cards, that should be encouraging news. Henderson surely appreciates it. But what about the children of those collectors, the boys for whom it has never been a ritual to go down to the corner store or pharmacy to buy a few packs of Topps? I asked him. Does he expect to have those kids for buyers someday?

Henderson, smiling, reminded me of his age. "Fortunately," he said, "that's something I won't have to worry about."

It is, however, something that Topps and Major League Baseball should worry about. Even though the secondary market for baseball cards continues to hum along, regularly shattering sales records, the number of children buying new packs of cards remains relatively minuscule. The card makers still haven't managed to break their poststrike slump. As of this writing, sales of sports cards have tumbled to less than a quarter of their 1991 high. Kids drifted to Pokémon and PlayStation and apparently haven't drifted back.

Like any large industry on the down slope, the card business has consolidated itself in the past few years. Fleer was forced to liquidate its remaining assets in order to pay back its creditors in 2005. The company auctioned its venerable name to the highest bidder, and Upper Deck snatched it up for a cut-rate $6.1 million. Fleer then closed its South Jersey offices and disappeared, along with its 120-year legacy in the world of candy and gum cards.

That same year, Major League Baseball tried to respond to collector complaints of a card glut by licensing more selectively. It abruptly dropped Donruss, which had been making baseball cards for twenty-five years, and decided to deal solely with Upper Deck and Topps. Donruss lives on primarily as a maker of football cards, though the company occasionally rolls out a baseball set featuring Hall of Famers or upcoming prospects from the amateur draft—all of them with their big-league logos airbrushed out or in high school uniforms, per legal requirements.

In March 2007 Topps faced its own crisis. After the publicly traded company's profits had fallen to about a fifth of those in its heyday, Michael Eisner, the erstwhile chief executive of the Walt Disney Company, launched a takeover bid through his private Tornante Company, offering $385 million. In the torturous months that followed, Topps shareholders, feeling lowballed, shopped around for higher bidders, even entertaining a buyout offer from Upper Deck, which would have given the California card maker every venerable name in the business. Eisner's group stuck to its bid of $9.75 a share and Topps shareholders ultimately approved the deal.

Eisner may not have bought a great company, but he certainly bought a great name. "I see it as a cultural, iconic institution not that different from Disney," he explained to the *New York Times*. "It conjures up an emotional response that has a feel good, Proustian kind of uplift." The trick now, of course, is to revive the Topps name. Eisner has already been handed a huge opportunity to do just that. In the summer of 2009, Major League Baseball abruptly announced that it

would be ending its contract with Upper Deck, making Topps the
game's exclusive card maker.

For generations of kids, there was no clear line between baseball and
baseball *cards*. The two industries were always cross-promotional. The
league could do worse than turning over the entire card business to a
company as iconic as Topps. But history shows that the great eras of
baseball cards—the 1880s, the 1930s, the 1950s, even the 1980s—all
benefited from a small pool of rival card makers forced to compete
with one another to put out the best product. The only people who
ever loved the idea of a Topps monopoly were the folks at Topps.
Now, if the hobby continues to sputter, Eisner and gang will have no
one to blame but themselves.

Hopefully, Topps will continue to scale back the confounding number of sets the company has released in recent years. When I was a kid,
there were just three or four major sets on the market, all of them affordable, so my baseball card–obsessed friends and I were all working
from the same relatively small pool of cards, poring over them as we
attempted to fill out our sets. I'll always remember the wood-grain
borders on those 1987 Topps cards. I'll always remember the glorious
handlebar mustache of a smiling Rollie Fingers on his 1985 Donruss
card, just as I'll always remember the horrid 27.0 earned run average
posted by Kansas City Royals hurler José DeJesús in 1988, as noted on
the back of his card the following year. I remember these things because my friends and I spent our summer afternoons laughing over
them together, engaged in daylong trading marathons.

The baseball card industry lost its way because Major League Baseball, the Major League Baseball Players Association, and the manufacturers all apparently forgot that the communal aspect of collecting is
one of the things that makes it enjoyable. How can kids talk about
baseball cards if they don't have any of the same ones? And how can
they collect cards if they can barely afford to buy them?

Topps should accept the fact that baseball card sales will never return
to what they were in the late 1980s and '90s—as well they shouldn't.

The industry then was driven by unsustainable speculation, and though for a while it yielded a bonanza for manufacturers and dealers, the frenzy probably did more harm than good in the long run, by souring the many collectors who got burned. And let's face it, as a cultural force baseball isn't what it once was, certainly not in the eyes of youngsters. If television ratings are any barometer, football can stake a fairly legitimate claim to being the new national pastime. The fallout from baseball's steroid era has done neither the game nor the card hobby any favors, either. And it doesn't help card makers that video games and Web applications get more impressive and pervasive by the week.

Yet all of this isn't to say that baseball cards can't once again be a viable hobby among children, which it will have to be if Topps wants to keep rolling out cards. As that anonymous dealer collector at the National pointed out, today's graying cardboard lovers won't be around forever. Baseball card collecting survived for more than a century because it managed to capture successive generations of young boys. To lure kids today Topps needs to realize that hacked-up pieces of flannel aren't quite as magical as consumer-marketing folks seem to believe. Neither are player autographs. It's the simplest hallmarks of yesteryear's cards —the arresting designs, the biographical tidbits, even the goofy comic strips —that have always gone a long way in the eyes of a child. If Topps wants to make new cards more like vintage cards, that's how they should do it.

Topps, to its credit, has grown wise to its strained relationship with children, now offering a line of baseball card packs priced around $1 apiece. It's even restored the bubble gum. But the company still devotes much of its time and energy targeting money-minded collectors with products such as Topps DNA Relic cards, which include hair samples from dead historical figures including Charles Dickens, Jacqueline Kennedy Onassis, and Ronald Reagan. The creepiness of such prizes aside, kids shouldn't be tearing into packs hoping to find a chase-card lottery ticket. They should be hoping to find their favorite players. Once upon a time, those All-Stars *were* the chase cards.

And once upon a time no one wondered whether his cardboard heroes might "pitch, bat and catch their way around the desktop—digitally," as, in March 2009, Topps announced the players would on its webcam-activated 3D Live cards. "The physical baseball trading card is now just the beginning of the experience," Eisner proclaimed in a Topps press release. But for the true cartophile the physical baseball card has always been just the beginning of the experience. The problem with the industry today isn't what baseball cards have always been; it's what baseball cards have become.

So I have proposal. Instead of trying to reinvent the baseball card, Topps and the league should restore it to what it once was. They should convince everyone—children and adults alike—that baseball cards are exactly what they were before the boom times of the 1980s and '90s: cheap playthings, suitable for tacking to the wall, flicking on the playground, or stuffing into a shoe box. New cards should be sold as offering the buyer nothing beyond themselves—no opportunities to strike it rich or to see players "come to digital life." As the King of Commons' nearly thirty years in business attest, so long as there's baseball there's no reason that there shouldn't be a market for the baseball card, no matter the condition, no matter the value.

After all, it's just a piece of cardboard.

Notes

Introduction

6 *By 1991, sales of baseball cards* . . . : Macinow, Glenn. "Score Board Inc." *Nation's Business.* Vol. 79. (April, 1991): 10

7 *A trade magazine called American Printer* . . . : Mallardi, Vincent. "Stacking the Deck." *American Printer.* Vol. 209, issue 4. (July, 1992): 44.

7 *The 1991 National Sports Collectors Convention* . . . : Williams, Pete. *Card Sharks: How Upper Deck Turned a Child's Hobby into a High-Stakes, Billion-Dollar Business.* New York: Macmillan, 1995: 155–56.

Chapter 1

Telling the story of tobacco cards would have been far more difficult without the scholarship of George Kirsch, Richard Kluger, Robert Durden, Lew Lipset and Dean Sullivan among others. I drew on their works where noted.

11 *Before an estimated 5,000 soldiers died* . . . : "Salisbury Confederate Prison." http://www.salisburync.gov/prison/1.html

11 *The first 120 Union detainees arrived* . . . : Salisbury Confederate Prison Association: Prison History. http://www.salisburyprison.org/PrisonHistory.htm

11 *As several prisoners memoirs bear out* . . . : Kirsch, George B. *Baseball in Blue and Gray: The National Pastime During the Civil War.* Princeton, N.J.: Princeton University Press, 2003: 43.

12 *G.B. Adams, of Massachusetts' Nineteenth Regiment, wrote* . . . : ibid, 39.

12 *As the New York Clipper noted in 1865* . . . : ibid, 116

12 *with new clubs sprouting* . . . : ibid, 117.

12 *The game, he wrote, "had its early evolution when soldiers* . . .": Spalding, A.G. *America's National Game.* New York: American Sports Publishing, 1911: 13.

13 *His parents having died when he was a baby* . . . : "Andrew Peck Dies at 82." *New York Times.* Mar. 22, 1918: 13

13 *One soldier described the camp* . . . : Kirsch, 37.

13 *The company produced* . . . : *Peck & Snyder, New York, 1886, Illustrated Catalog and Historical Introduction.* Princeton, N.J.: Pyne Press, 1971.

14 *Under the guidance of their British-born center fielder* . . . : "Legend of the Cincinnati Red Stockings." http://www.1869reds.com/history/

15 *Before the Civil War, Americans had been* . . . : Kluger, Richard. *Ashes to Ashes: America's Hundred-Year Cigarette War, the Public Health, and the Unabashed Triumph of Philip Morris.* New York: Vintage Books, 1996: 16–19.

15 *"The decadence of Spain began* . . .": "Cigarettes." *New York Times.* Jan. 29, 1884.

15 *His father, Washington Duke, had fought* . . . : Kluger, 20.

16 *The elder Duke sent young Buck* . . . : Durden, Robert F. *Bold Entrepreneur: A Life of James B. Duke.* Durham, N.C.: Carolina Academic Press, 2003: xiii.

16 *"There ain't a thrill in the world* . . .": Durden, xiii.

16 *who is credited with inventing the cigar-store Indian* . . . : Murell, Duncan. "The Duke." *Southern Cultures.* Summer, 2006: 6–29.

16 *The company superimposed* . . . : Roberts, B.W.C. and Richard F. Knapp. "Paving the Way for the Tobacco Trust," *The North Carolina Historical Review.* July, 1992: 264.

17 *To make sure that the country* . . . : Winkler, John. *Tobacco Tycoon: The Story of James Buchanan Duke.* New York: Random House, 1942: 66.

17 *"There were no news reels* . . .": Folwell, Arthur H. "A New York Childhood: Cigarette Pictures," *The New Yorker,* May 4, 1929: 25.

18 *"Who are these beauties* . . .": "The Beauties of Chicago," *Chicago Tribune.* Aug. 12, 1888: 17.

18 *A Methodist minister in Washington* . . . : "Girls Who Like Fast Men." *Washington Post.* Jan. 30, 1888: 3.

18 *when a tobacco maker had the gall* . . . : "Mrs. Cleveland's Pictures in Cigarette Packages," *Washington Post.* Nov. 27, 1887: 3.

18 *Another inflammatory card* . . . : "Not Miss Halford's Picture." *Washington Post.* Aug. 29, 1889: 2.

18 *Cops raided the studios* . . . : "Pictures of Nude Women," *Washington Post.* Sept. 13, 1887: 2.

18 *"What a horrid suggestion* . . .*":* *New Orleans Daily Picayune.* July 29, 1888.

19 *Allen & Ginter packed their cigarettes* . . . : Kluger, 18.

19 *When it came to insert cards* . . . : ibid, 18.

19 *The genteel citizens of Atlanta flooded* . . . : "Female Baseballists." *Atlanta Constitution,* July 16, 1886: 7.

20 *the National Association of Base Ball Players had debated* . . . : Sullivan, Dean A., ed. *Early Innings: A Documentary History of Baseball, 1825–1908.* Lincoln, NE: University of Nebraska Press, 1995: 82.

20 *This practice stopped* . . . : ibid, 128.

21 *By 1885, the minimum annual haul* . . . : ibid, 139.

21 *After a successful run of 12 cards* . . . : Lipset, Lew. *The Encyclopedia of Baseball Cards.* Vols. 1–3.

23 *The final installment of Old Judges* . . . : ibid, 21.

23 *"To many a boy, back in the eighties* . . .*":* Folwell, 25.

24 *In 2008, one particularly scarce Old Judge* . . .: "REA Auction Set Numerous Records." *Sports Collectors Daily.* May 14, 2008. http://www.sportscollectorsdaily.com/latest/rea-auction-set-numerous-records.html

24 *"I told him I wouldn't handle cigarettes* . . .*":* Winkler, 60–61.

24 *In response to collector demand* . . . : Petrone, George S. *Tobacco Advertising: The Great Seduction.* Atglen, PA: Schiffer Publishing, 1996: 58.

24 *"The life of the dude is made a burden* . . .*":* "Gimme the picture please!" *Rocky Mountain News,* June 24, 1888: 4.

25 *"Tell all my friends* . . .*":* Leeds, Josiah W. "Our Anti-Tobacco Crusade." *The Friend: a Religious and Literary Journal,* April 2, 1892.

25 *"Today he swears by the 'Troubadour Straight Cuts' . . ."*: "Cigarette Mysteries." *Chicago Daily Tribune.* June 23, 1889: 29.

25 *Parents and teachers rummaged through . . .*: "Indignant Parents." *San Francisco Daily Bulletin,* Jan. 4, 1888.

26 *One dealer told the Tribune . . .*: "Nobody Obeys the Law," *Chicago Daily Tribune,* Nov. 12, 1889: 6.

26 *"We would give a chromo to the Mayor . . ."*: "The Cigarette Pictures." *Durham News and Observer.* Jun. 25, 1887.

26 *One Manhattan plant alone . . .*: "Cigarette Pictures." *Milwaukee Journal,* Sept. 25, 1894: 7.

26 *tobacco companies wouldn't have shrunk their profit margins . . .*: Durden, 19.

26 *When there were rumblings of a strike . . .*: Roberts and Knapp, 261.

27 *The five highest-producing tobacco firms . . .*: Kluger, 25.

27 *He was coughing up nearly $1 million a year . . .*: ibid, 25.

28 *The heads of the five major tobacco firms . . .*: ibid, 26.

28 *"The great question that agitated them . . ."*: "Cigarette Pictures Must Go." *Daily Picayune.* Jun. 11, 1890: 2.

29 *"They have probably concluded to kill the boys . . ."*: "No More Pictures," *Puck.* June 4, 1890: 237.

Chapter 2

The bulk of this chapter comes from my many interviews with Mike Gidwitz and other hobbyists.

34 *"Right now the greater-fool theory . . ."*: Athineos, Doris. "A $1 million Honus?" *Forbes.* Nov. 4, 1996.

35 *"I realized that if I went to the New York Metropolitan Museum of Art . . ."*: Purdy, Dennis. "Mike Gidwitz Interview." *Vintage & Classic Baseball Collector,* Mar./Apr., 1997: 47.

36 *Between 1890 and 1907, it had devoured . . .*: Armentano, D.T. "Antitrust and Monopoly: Anatomy of a Policy Failure." *Independent Institute,* 1996: 88.

37 *At least 524 professional players are featured* . . . : Reader, Scot A. *Inside T206: A Collector's Guide to the Classic Baseball Card Set.* Self-published, 2006.

38 *His granddaughter, Leslie Blair, has bolstered that version* . . . : "Wagner's granddaughter tells real story behind T-206 card." *Sports Collectors Digest.* Oct. 23, 1992.

38 *Some believe that the American Tobacco Company mailed the strip to Wagner* . . . : Mastro, Bill. "My Mentor Frank Nagy." http://www.t206museum .com/page/periodical_51.html

Chapter 3

The story of the creation of bubble gum relies heavily on the diligent reporting of Robert Hendrickson, while J. Warren Bowman's larger-than-life story couldn't have been told without the contemporary profiles that appeared in *Time* and the *Saturday Evening Post.*

49 *an August day in 1928 when a 23-year-old accountant* . . . : Hendrickson, Robert. *The Great American Chewing Gum Book.* New York: Stein and Day, 1984: 143

50 *The gum that Diemer created* . . . : ibid, 143.

50 *The very same batch failed to produce* . . . : ibid, 143.

50 *In 1897, Frank H. Fleer created* . . . : Taylor, Ted. "Fleer's Roots in Cards Go Back to 1923," *Sports Collector's Digest,* May 2, 1997: 100–01.

50 *Fleer gave pieces a hard sugar coating* . . . : "Gilbert Barclay Mustin." *New York Times.* Aug. 1, 1999.

50 *The day after Christmas 1928 wrapped chunks of Fleer* . . . : Hendrickson, Robert. "Since 1928 It's Been Boom and Bust with Bubble Gum," *Smithsonian Magazine.* July, 1990: 74ff.

51 *"People chew harder when they are sad* . . .*":* Redclift, Michael. "Chewing Gum in the United States and Mexico: The Everyday and the Iconic," *Sociologia Ruralis.* Oct., 2002: 7.

51 *In 1930, Fleer first swaddled a piece of Dubble Bubble* . . .*":* "Fleer Funnies." http://www.bubblegum-comics.com/FleerFunnies.html

52 *Goudey was rolling out gum 24 hours a day* . . . : Letter from Goudey executive George C. Thompson to collector Bruce Dorskind, Nov. 8, 1977. Quoted courtesy of Bruce Dorskind.

52 *a precious $50,000* . . . : ibid.

52 *Rud Rennie wrote, "We came home . . ."*: Alexander, Charles C. *Breaking the Slump: Baseball in the Depression Era*. New York: Columbia University Press, 2002: 65.

53 *That year, player salaries were trimmed* . . . : Alexander, 72–3.

53 *Enos Goudey bought himself a $125,000 mansion* . . . : Fogel, Marshall. "The History of Goudey Gum Company." *Professional Sports Authenticator*. Jul. 8, 2003. http://www.psacard.com/articles/article3886.chtml

53 *He sold Goudey in 1932* . . . : "Enos Gordon Goudey." http://www.goudey .org/Goudey/Enos-Gordon-Goudey.html

53 *William Wrigley came to call Goudey "The Penny Gum King"*: "E. Gordon Goudey." *New York Times*. April 12, 1946: 27.

53 *Goudey's total sales were a modest $335,000* . . . : From the Topps files, Records of the Federal Trade Commission (FTC). National Archives Records Group 122. Docket 8463 (Boxes 1448–65).

53 *When competitor American Chicle filed for bankruptcy in 1937* . . . : Thompson letter to Dorskind.

54 *"Pennies were rare suckers . . ."*: Brauer, Norm. "Ten Year Old Boy." *Vintage and Classic Baseball Collector*. May/Jun., 1998: 46–47.

55 *even the most avid collectors would discover a bounty* . . . : "Enos Gordon Goudey." http://www.goudey.org/Goudey/Enos-Gordon-Goudey.html

55 *under its Canadian imprint, World Wide Gum, Goudey released* . . . : Benjamin, Christopher and Dennis W. Eckes. *Sport Americana Price Guide to the Non-Sports Cards*. Edgewater Books, 1991: 111.

55 *"I believe that someone suggested that we include . . ."*: Thompson letter to Dorskind.

56 *When Goudey was foundering during the winter of 1961 to 1962* . . . : Fogel.

57 Born in Pennsylvania Dutch country . . . : Cullinane, Leo. "He Drives Parents Crazy." *The Saturday Evening Post*. Nov. 1947: 20ff.

57 *Bowman headed south to Tampico, Mexico . . .* : "Bowman's Bubbles." *Time.* Sep. 13, 1937.

57 *Though his coffee gumdrop never came to fruition . . .* : Cullinane, 45.

58 *Bowman opened his own plant in Philly under the name Gum, Inc . . .* : ibid, 45.

58 *He employed beautiful young women as street vendors . . .* : Redclift, Michael. *Chewing Gum: The Fortunes of Taste.* New York: Routledge, 2004: 40–41.

59 *the gum quickly supplanted Fleer's Dubble Bubble . . .* : "Bowman's Bubbles." *Time.*

59 *In 1932 he spread his gum empire overseas . . .* : Cullinane, 45.

60 *But the court found in Bowman's favor . . .* : ibid, 47–48.

60 *One evening in 1937 he dreamed up . . .* : ibid, 47.

61 *"Gum Inc. gets its wars hot off the battlefield . . ."*: "Speaking of Pictures . . ." *Life.* May 9, 1938: 4.

61 *Bowman was said to have sent Horrors of War cards into the sky . . .* : Marks, Jeff and Bob Marks. "Bubble Gum King." *The Wrapper*, No. 208 (Jan. 1– Feb. 15, 2005): 8.

61 *"A few years back I used to collect bubble gum cards . . ."*: "Bubble Gum and War." *Chicago Daily Tribune.* Jul. 31, 1939: 10.

62 *George Moll, Bowman's chief collaborator, was a devout Baptist . . .* : Nelson, Murry R. "An Alternative Medium of Social Education: The Horrors of War Picture Cards." *Social Studies,* May-Jun., 1997: 100ff.

62 *When a shipment of the cards arrived in Japan . . .* : "Japan Seizes Phila. Gum For 'Propaganda Pictures.'" Philadelphia Evening Bulletin, Newspaper clipping collection. May 21, 1938. Philadelphia, Temple University Libraries, Urban Archives, Philadelphia, PA.

62 *The Japanese embassy in Washington complained . . .* : Cullinane, 47.

63 *One of those kids was the noted war historian and Korean War vet Stanley Weintraub . . .* : Author interview with Weintraub, Feb. 1, 2008.

64 *The president urged that baseball continue normal play . . .* : Bazer, Gerald and Steven Culbertson. "Baseball during World War II: The Reaction and

Encouragement of Franklin Delano Roosevelt and Others." *NINE: A Journal of Baseball History and Culture.* Vol. 10, No. 1 (Fall 2001): 11–129.

64 *In 1944, the Yankees opened the season* . . . : Rader, Benjamin G. *Baseball: A History of America's Game.* Champaign, IL: University of Illinois Press, 1992: 173.

64 *Used at least during the 1943 season* . . . : Dickson, Paul. *The New Dickson Baseball Dictionary.* Harvest Books, 1999: 28.

64 *though the women learned the art of femininity* . . . : Rader, 175.

65 *Wrigley couldn't find a home for the women* . . . : "All-American Girls Professional Baseball League History." http://www.aagpbl.org/league/history.cfm

65 *stadium attendance plummeted* . . . : Rader, 173.

65 *He had a Philadelphia mansion* . . . : Cullinane, 48.

66 *Fleer gave its supply of jelutong* . . . : "Do They Chew Gum?" Los Angeles Times. Jun. 22, 1947: E10.

66 *"The wartime chewing-gum shortage has dealt Americans a cruel blow . . ."*: Ephron, Edith. "In Celebration of a Minor Vice," *New York Times.* Dec. 24, 1944.

66 *In one survey, a majority of American soldiers declared gum* . . . : Gott, Philip P. and L.F. Van Houten. *All About Candy and Chocolate.* Chicago: National Confectioners' Association of the United States, 1958: 10–108.

66 *When an Indianapolis café owner told his young customers* . . . : "Gum Pickets Win Victory." New York Times. Aug. 10, 1946.

66 *By the late '40s, there were 2.5 billion pieces* . . . : "21 Billion Sticks." Wall Street Journal, Aug. 17, 1958: 1.

66 *a 1947 outbreak of sore throats and vomiting* . . . : "Bubble Trouble," *Time.* Jul. 7, 1947.

Chapter 4

I'm hardly the first writer to delve into Burdick—George Vrechek, Mark Lamster, and Sean Kirst of the Syracuse *Post-Standard* have all been here before. My thanks to Vrechek, for granting me permission to quote the letters of Lionel Carter that he had published in *Sports Collectors Digest,* and to

Kirst, for referring me to Juengel. The bulk of this chapter draws upon Mayor's account from the Burdick directory at the Met; from Burdick's own writings in *Hobbies* and his *Catalog;* and from my interviews with Carter and others.

69 *As Mayor would recall later* . . . : *Directory of the J. R. Burdick Collection.* Metropolitan Museum of Art, 196?.

69 *Jefferson Burdick had traveled from upstate New York* . . . : Cummings, Paul. "An Interview with A. Hyatt Mayor." *Archives of American Art Journal.* Vol. 18, No. 4 (1978): 14–16.

70 *"I did not know then how large it was* . . .": Cummings, 15.

70 *"Mayor didn't have the curatorial staff to do it himself* . . .": Author interview with Elliot Bostwick Davis, Mar. 12, 2008.

70 *Mayor received the first shipment of Burdick's cards* . . . : Cummings, 15.

72 *a casual friend who'd once worked alongside Burdick* . . . : Kirst, Sean. "Decades Later, a Friendship Has Been Chiseled in Stone," *Syracuse Post-Standard,* Nov. 14, 1997.

72 *"a glorious picture window of the past":* Burdick, J.R. *American Card Catalog.* East Stroudsburg, PA: J.R. Burdick, 1960 edition.

72 *"Practically every small boy saved these* . . .": "Syracuse's 'Mr. Card Collector' is Expert's Expert on Old Hobby." *Syracuse Herald-American.* Dec. 25, 1955: 1.

72 *"Perhaps the cards held in closest affection* . . .": Burdick, J.R. "An Outline of American Cards, Part IV., Insert Types," *Hobbies.* Apr. 1950: 64.

73 *"No one, probably, has ever had a complete collection* . . .": Burdick, J.R. "Cigarette Cards," *Hobbies.* Jan. 1936: 118.

74 *"I feel terrible, just awful* . . .": Author interview with Lionel Carter, July 28, 2007.

75 *"Jeff Burdick lifted card collecting* . . .": Irving W. Lerner, *Who's Who in Card Collecting,* Philadelphia: Irving W. Lerner, 1970.

76 *"A book is just a pound of waste paper* . . .": Burdick letters to Carter.

77 *"He was just a quiet guy* . . .": Author interview with Milton Juengel, Mar. 10, 2008.

78 *"Tuesday I'm going to Lakeland . . .":* Burdick letters to Carter.

78 *"Illness probably prevented him from marrying . . . :":* Mayor, in the directory to the Burdick collection.

78 *"One would think the many beautiful designs . . .":* Burdick, J.R. "Cards for the Ladies." *Hobbies.* May 1939: 8.

79 *"I would like to have an example of every card . . .":* Caygill, Marjorie. "Creating a Great Museum: Early Collectors and the British Museum." http://www.fathom.com/course/21701728/session5.html

79 *"I fully recognise that there are those who think . . .":* Wharton-Tigar, Edward. *Burning Bright: The Autobiography of Edward Wharton-Tigar,* Metal Bulletin, 1987: 254.

79 *Born a year after Burdick . . . : Dictionary of Art Historians.* http://www.dictionaryofarthistorians.org/mayora.htm

80 *"The print department at the Met . . .":* Russell, John. "An Ideal Curator." *New York Times.* Aug. 14, 1983.

80 *"Undertaking," he quipped . . . :* Mayor, A. Hyatt. *Selected Writings and a Bibliography.* New York: Metropolitan Museum of Art, 1983.

80 *"meant to be seen by people . . .":* "Of Posters, Postcards and Photos." *New York Times.* Mar. 14, 1982.

80 *"Hyatt not only went out of his way . . .":* Mayor, *Selected Writings.*

81 *"at once became the American headquarters . . .":* Directory to the Burdick Collection.

81 *"I do think that every collector . . .":* Burdick letters to Carter.

81 *"Never stick cards down with paste":* Burdick, American Card Catalog.

82 *"My health is definitely . . .":* Burdick letters to Carter.

82 "I thought baseball cards were put in bike spokes . . .": Singer, Mark. "The Talk of the Town: Cards," *New Yorker,* Aug. 13, 1990: 26–7.

83 *"The decision to place baseball cards . . .":* Davis, Elliot Bostwick. "The Amazin' Met." *Groton School Quarterly.* May 1994: 7.

84 *"People were saving all these cards . . .":* Burdick, J.R. *The American Card Catalog.* Syracuse, N.Y.: J.R. Burdick, 1953 edition.

85 *Burdick also managed to obtain* . . . : Kirk, Jay. *Collector's Guide to Baseball Cards*. Radnor, PA: Wallace-Homestead, 1990: 37.

85 *"We bought him more and more . . .":* Mayor, in the directory to the Burdick Collection.

86 *"Jeff Burdick is a prince . . .":* Orem letter to Carter.

86 *"The enclosed sugar bag . . .":* Burdick letter to Carter.

87 *Burdick looked tired* . . . : Directory to the Burdick Collection.

Chapter 5

Most of the information in this chapter comes directly from the Topps file of the Federal Trade Commission, stored at the National Archives research facility in College Park, Md.; from interviews I conducted with Sy Berger and others; and from interviews published elsewhere, as noted.

91 *"Don't Talk, Chum—Chew Topps Gum":* Hendrickson, 147.

92 *All this time, all the early days* . . . : Ambrosius, Greg. "Sy Berger." *Sports Collectors Digest*. Oct. 21, 1994: 111ff.

92 *In 1950 alone* . . . : Topps FTC files.

92 *When a Boston-based manufacturer* . . . : ibid.

93 *"You wouldn't dare put that taffy . . .":* Ambrosius, 112.

94 *If the player did appear* . . . : Bailey, Arnold. "Magic Photos." *Card News*. May 11, 1992: 80.

95 *"I spoke to the players . . .":* Topps FTC files.

95 *To make the players more comfortable* . . . : ibid.

96 *Wes Westrum, the longtime catcher* . . . : Kane, Martin. "The Baseball Bubble Trouble." *Sports Illustrated*. Aug. 16, 1954: 44.

96 *"Back in those days . . .":* Topps FTC files.

96 *"You could walk up to one . . .":* Kane, 44.

97 *"from the arrival of Jackie Robinson . . .":* Tygiel, Jules. *Past Time: Baseball as History*. New York: Oxford University Press, 2001.

97 *"The crowds watching television . . ."*: Kahn, Roger. *The Era, 1947–1957: When the Yankees, New York Giants and Brooklyn Dodgers Ruled the World.* Lincoln, NE: University of Nebraska Press, 1993.

97 *By the early '50s . . .* : "Little League Chronology." http://www.littleleague .org/Learn_More/About_Our_Organization/historyandmission/chronology .htm

98 *"I thought when a kid's trying . . ."*: Ambrosius, 113.

99 *The court originally found . . .* : *Haelan Laboratories Inc. v. Topps Chewing Gum, Inc.,* 202 F.2d 866, 868 (2d Cir.), 346 U.S. 816 (1953).

100 *"The most furious trading . . ."*: Kane, 44.

100 *By 1956, Bowman . . .* : Topps FTC file.

101 *"We went down like . . ."*: Ambrosius, 112.

101 *Only Topps had the right . . .* : Topps FTC file.

101 *seven American bubblegum makers . . .* : ibid.

102 *"The youngsters . . ."*: ibid.

102 *In the early '60s . . .* : ibid.

102 *As Fleer officials complained . . .* : ibid.

103 *"Topps has wielded . . ."*: ibid.

105 *"lined up like they were . . ."*: Author interview with Bouton, Apr. 16, 2008.

107 *"The confusion caused . . ."*: Topps FTC file.

108 *As the itemized reports show . . .* : ibid.

108 *By 1960 . . .* : ibid.

108 *"I must frankly state . . ."*: ibid.

109 *"Berger wandered around . . ."*: Miller, *A Whole Different Ball Game: The Inside Story of a Baseball Revolution.* Chicago: Ivan R. Dee, 2004: 146.

109 *"We have it so good . . ."*: Rader, 207.

110 *Fleer managed to secure . . .* : Topps FTC file.

110 *"Let them stick with Williams..."*: ibid.

111 *To skirt the gum clause...*: ibid.

112 *In 1959, he wrote a letter...*: ibid.

Chapter 6

I assembled Gelman's story mostly through interviews with friends and family, as noted below.

116 *"He was a catalyst..."*: Author interview with Art Spiegelman, Dec. 3, 2007.

116 *Before taking his job with Topps...*: Author interview with Len Brown, Mar. 26, 2007 and Nov. 28, 2008.

118 *the man hired by Gelman to draw...*: Author interview with Jay Lynch, Mar. 22, 2007.

120 *"Gelman wasn't just a creative genius..."*: Author interview with Bill Mastro, July 29, 2007.

120 *"The cards wag the gum"*: Eskenazi, Gerald. "Getting the Picture." *New York Times.* April 19, 1964.

121 *Gelman's father-in-law...*: Author interview with Richard Gelman, Mar. 22, 2007.

122 *Appropriately, the mail-order company's...*: ibid.

122 *He once told an interviewer...*: Clark, Steve. *The Complete Book of Baseball Cards.* New York: Grosset and Dunlap, 1982: 56.

123 *"There is one New Yorker..."*: La Fontaine, Barbara. "Today's Trivia, Tomorrow's...?" *New York Times,* Dec. 3, 1967.

123 *"He'd told everyone to look for it..."*: Author interview with Bhob Stewart, Nov. 25, 2007.

125 *So Gelman started an informal Topps archive...*: Spiegelman and Richard Gelman interviews.

126 *He discovered many of McCay's original strips...*: Spiegelman interview.

126 *In 1966, some of McCay's...*: Canaday, John. "Little Nemo at the Met." *New York Times.* Feb. 13, 1966.

126 *"collector, editor and the best friend . . .":* Sendak, Maurice. "Little Nemo." *New York Times.* Nov. 25, 1973.

127 *One of Gelman's grandest schemes . . . :* Spiegelman interview.

127 *grew up in poverty and uncertainty . . . :* Richard Gelman interview.

128 *"That was awful working for them . . .":* Holm, D.K. *R. Crumb: Conversations.* Jackson, MS: University Press of Mississippi, 2004: 44.

129 *"It was just a beat-up old factory . . .":* Author interview with David Saunders, Nov. 22, 2007.

130 *"A little bit of questioning . . .":* Gelman, Woody. "What's Bad?" *New York Times.* Feb. 14, 1962.

132 *But it was probably inspired most . . . :* Brown interview.

132 *In one illustration, entitled "Destroying a Dog" . . . :* Saunders interview.

134 *"In their minor art form . . .":* Edwards, Owen. "Wacky Packs." *New York.* Oct., 1973.

134 *He died of complications due to a stroke . . . :* "Woody Gelman," obituary. *New York Times.* Feb. 11, 1978.

135 *But once the bidding was over . . . :* from the Guernsey auction results, courtesy David Saunders.

135 *"The business and romance of collecting . . .":* Wolff, Craig. "Pieces of Sport Fantasy Fetch High Prices in the Real World." *New York Times.* Aug. 20, 1989.

136 *"Almost everything went beyond expectations . . .":* Author interview with Arlan Ettinger, Jul. 1, 2008.

136 *The write-up in the Guernsey catalog . . . :* "Archive File Copy Binders of Topps Card Sets." http://www.thetoppsvault.com/filebinders/filebinders guernseys.htm

Chapter 7

To tell the story of Marvin Miller's fight with Topps, I relied on my interview with Miller as well as his autobiography. My telling of the card boom in the 80's and 90's draws mostly from interviews I conducted, as well as from clips in hobby publications and the mainstream press at that time.

139 *When Marvin Miller was elected . . .*: Miller, 142 ff.

139 *In the 20 years since World War II . . .*: ibid, 5-6.

140 *"Pro sports has no place . . ."*: ibid, 38.

140 *During his first few weeks on the job . . .*: ibid, 144.

141 *"When you considered . . ."*: Author interview with Marvin Miller, Sept. 11, 2007.

141 *The rule had been introduced . . .*: Sullivan, 113, 139.

141 *When he heard about Fleer's futile attempts . . .*: Miller, 144.

141 *"I'd learned enough about licensing . . ."*: Miller interview.

142 *Most players didn't realize . . .*: Bouton interview.

142 *So Miller urged players . . .*: Miller, 145–49.

143 *the negotiations over a new arrangement . . .*: ibid, 149.

144 *When Miller struck a deal with Kellogg's . . .*: ibid, 149–50.

144 *The company had sold its pool . . .*: Topps FTC file.

145 *"Fleer was very antsy . . ."*: Author interview with Ted Taylor, Sept. 4, 2007.

145 *"Even if the product was merely a casual idea . . ."*: *Fleer Corp. v. Topps Chewing Gum, Inc.* 501 F.Supp. 485 (E.D.Pa.1980).

147 *The same card could turn up . . .*: Stoller, Michael A. "On the Economics of Anti-Trust and Competition in a Collectibles Market: The Strange Case of the Baseball Card Industry." *Business Economics.* 19: 18–26.

147 *Topps had tallied sales . . .*: Ambrosius, Greg. "Fleer's court battle with Topps paved way for hobby growth." *Sports Collectors Digest.* Oct. 2, 1998: 50.

148 *"We'd pick an area of the country . . ."*: Author interview with Kit Young, Feb. 14, 2007.

148 *"I can't describe the enjoyment . . ."*: Author interview with Gar Miller, Feb. 7, 2007.

149 *Beckett had grown up in the '50s . . .*: Pearlman, Donn. *Collecting Baseball Cards: How to Buy Them, Store Them, Trade Them, and Keep Track of Their Value as Investments.* Chicago: Bonus Books, 1990: 27–32.

149 *"bring some order out of the chaos . . ."*: "Beckett helping guide sports card industry." *Sporting News.* Aug. 5, 1991.

149 *he published a rudimentary price list . . .*: Lemke, Bob. *Sports Collectors Digest.* "Bleacher Bum." Feb. 13, 1998.

150 *"Would it be sacrilegious to say . . ."*: Williams, 62.

150 *it was acquired by Apprise Media . . .*: MacFadyen, Kenneth. "Apprise Snatches Near-Mint to Mint Beckett Pubs," *BuyOuts.* Jan. 31, 2005.

151 *When Beckett sued a competitor . . .*: "1983 Year in Review." *Sports Collectors Digest.* May 1, 1998: 52–53.

152 *the Wall Street private equity giant Forstmann Little . . .*: ibid, 52.

154 *"Essentially, the entire rookie card phenomenon began . . ."*: Ambrosius, Greg. "Rookie Cards." *Sports Collectors Digest.* Aug. 14, 1998: 38.

154 *A Los Angeles Police Department detective . . .*: "1982 Year in Review." *Sports Collectors Digest.* April 17, 1998: 53.

154 *Although the men were convicted . . .*: Williams, 50.

155 *"Turning Cardboard Into Cash . . ."*: Sheinin, Dave. "Turning Cardboard Into Cash: These Are Boom Days for Baseball Cards" *Washington Post.* Aug. 22, 1990.

155 *"A Grand Slam Profit . . ."*: Lynch, Jack. "A Grand Slam Profit May Be in the Cards." *New York Times.* Nov. 13, 1988.

155 *"Cards Put Gold, Stocks to Shame . . ."*: Rippel, Joel. "Cards Put Gold, Stocks to Shame as Investment." *Orange County Register.* July 5, 1989: C8.

156 *"the key player isn't really Rose . . ."*: Helyar, John. "The Fine Art of Buying Baseball Cards, Or, Why a Pete Rose is Due for a Crash." *Wall Street Journal.* Oct. 23, 1985: 1.

156 *81 billion baseball cards . . .*: Mallardi, 44.

157 *"baseball is supposed to be the all-American game . . ."*: Wartzman, Rick. "I Will Swap You a '52 Mantle for Your '85 Buick." *Wall Street Journal.* May 11, 1990: A1.

157 *A respected veteran umpire . . .*: "Sports People: Baseball; New Charge for Umpire." New York Times. May 3, 1990.

157 *As outspoken hobbyist Lew Lipset wrote . . .*: Wartzman.

Chapter 8

The bulk of the Upper Deck story comes from my interviews with Paul Sumner and Jay McCracken, though much of this story I couldn't have told without Pete Williams's earlier reportage. The Ripken story comes mostly from press clippings at the time, as well as from the stories Darren Rovell has published over the years.

160 *"I can print a card that looks . . ."*: Ambrosius, Greg. "The Beginning of Upper Deck." *Sports Cards*. April 1994: 40–48.

161 *"One, do you want a better baseball card . . ."*: ibid, 42.

163 *Buice later said . . .*: Rovell, Darren. "'Hungry' Journeyman Buice Enjoys His Millions." ESPN.com. Aug. 7, 2003.

164 *From 1986 to 1989, the players' union . . .*: Sandomir, Richard. "Revenues Put Baseball Union in League by Itself." *Los Angeles Times,* Sept. 15, 1989.

164 *When Upper Deck came knocking . . .*: Williams, 72.

164 *"When your product comes into Price Club . . ."*: Author interview with Jay McCracken, Aug. 14, 2009.

165 *"baseball never looked so sweet . . ."*: Verducci, Tom. "V.J. Lovero, 1959–2004." *Sports Illustrated*. Jan. 19, 2004.

166 *Geideman knew the company's founders . . .*: Williams, 112.

167 *Geideman put some serious thought . . .*: Rovell, Darren. "Junior Mint." Slate.com. May 29, 2008.

167 *The mounting buzz and pressure . . .*: "Griffey Jr. Recalls Attempted Suicide." *New York Times*. March 16, 1992.

167 *But the hype proved warranted . . .*: "Ken Griffey Timeline." http://sportsillustrated.cnn.com/baseball/mlb/features/2000/griffey/timeline1/

168 *Geideman had hammered out the set's lineup . . .*: Williams, 113 ff.

168 *the Upper Deck Griffey rookie would become . . .*: Rovell, Slate.com.

169 *Fleer execs had no idea . . .*: Kurkjian, Tim. "1989 Bil Ripken baseball card fouls out." *Baltimore Sun*. Jan. 19, 1989: 1D.

170 *Unopened cases that guaranteed . . .*: Antonen, Mel. "Curse a Blessing to Ripken Card." *USA Today*. Jan. 24, 1989: 2C.

170 *If people are crazy enough* . . . : "Baseball Card Confidential." *Baseball Cards.* May 1989: 26.

171 *Fleer's seemingly endless variations* . . . : "Billripken.com Card Versions." http://billripken.com/versions/index.html

171 *Ripken was happy to let a dealer* . . . : Barning, Vivian. "The hobby's buzzing about Ripken's bat." *Baseball Hobby News,* March 1989: 12.

171 *The photo was taken* . . . : Green, Paul M. "Hysteria." *Baseball Cards.* May, 1989: 42.

171 *When the company sent blueline proofs* . . . : "Baseball Card Confidential." *Baseball Cards.* May 1989: 26.

172 *"I had no idea that word* . . .*"*: Kurkijan, 1D.

172 *Ripken had actually penned the phrase himself* . . . : Rovell, Darren. "Billy Ripken Obscenity Bat: He Finally Talks 20 Years Later." Dec. 9, 2008: http://www.cnbc.com/id/28116692

172 *Three years later, at the height* . . . : Shapiro, Evan. "A Deal of Real Heroes." *New York Times.* July 25, 1992.

173 *A card columnist for New York's* Newsday . . . : Cohen, Norm. "The Curse Heard 'Round the Card World." *Newsday.* Dec. 16, 1989.

175 *the company logged sales of a quarter of a billion* . . . : Williams, 171.

175 *Bill Hemrick filed a $10 million lawsuit* . . . : ibid, 174.

175 *But it was quite another for Upper Deck* . . . : ibid, 188.

Chapter 9

177 *During one particularly impassioned broadcast* . . . : Author interview with Chevalier, Sept. 5, 2007.

178 *By 1994, the average salary was just south* . . . : Halpert, Michael J. "The Economic History of Major League Baseball." http://eh.net/encyclopedia/article/haupert.mlb

178 *revenue from national television broadcasts had fallen off* . . . : Bernstein, Aaron and David Greising. "Baseball Strike Talk Turns Serious." *Business Week.* June 27, 1994.

180 *"If there was one thing that spelled . . .":* Author interview with Taylor.

182 *By the time they walked off the field . . .* : "Players Union Swings a Heavy Bat." *Kansas City Star.* Aug. 28, 1994.

182 *Topps' director of new-product development . . .* : Rothenberg, Randall. "Topps Makes a Move Into Magazines." *New York Times.* Dec. 22, 1989.

183 *In its 1990 annual report . . .* : Topps Corporation. 1990. Annual Report to the Securities and Exchange Commission for the Fiscal Year Ending March 3, 0–15817: 9.

184 *In 1996, Topps went so far as to abandon . . .* : Hultman, Tom. "Lifeblood of the Hobby Not As Strong Today." *Sports Collectors Digest.* Jan. 3, 1997: 120–122.

184 *"In the late 80's and early 90's . . .":* Garrity, John. "A House of Cards." *Sports Illustrated.* July 29, 1996: 104ff.

184 *Topps put up a loss . . .* : "Company Shuts Down Gruen Plant." Scranton *Times.* Jan. 3, 1997: A1.

184 *In 1999, a Houston-area neurologist . . .* : Zuckerman, Gregory. "Baseball Cards See Sales Slump in Pokemon Era." *Wall Street Journal.* Oct. 28, 1999: B1

185 *At the end of his stint with Shop at Home . . .* : Nation, Ryan. "The Evolution of Don West," SLAM! Sports: http://slam.canoe.ca/Slam/Wrestling/2006/01/31/1420308.html

185 *"There are too many baseball cards . . .":* Burdick letters to Carter.

186 *In 1994, more than 350 sets . . .* : Lemke, Bob, ed. *2007 Standard Catalog of Baseball Cards.* Iola, WI: Krause, 2006.

186 *a Fleer survey of children . . .* : Hultman, 120.

186 *"When a pack of cards went from $1.45 . . .":* Zuckerman.

187 *"Dealers who sponsor 'trading nights' . . .":* Hultman, 120.

187 *The diabolical idea of the high-end insert . . .* : Williams, 140–41.

187 *By 1996, the sports-card manufacturers were putting . . .* : Isaacson, Kevin. "Rebuilding the House of Cards." *Sports Collectors Digest.* Jan. 17, 1997: 46–48.

188 *"I can tell you that the people making these decisions..."*: Barning, Frank. "Barnstorming." *Sports Collectors Digest.* Aug. 28, 1998: 60.

189 *In New York, the city's consumer-affairs department...*: O'Shaughnessy, Patrick. "Lawsuit is in the Cards." *New York Daily News.* Dec. 8, 1996

189 *"He'd open the packs right here..."*: ibid.

190 *In 2003 Donruss dropped more than...*: "Stitch and Catch." *Boys Life.* Volume 94, Issue 3.

190 *Donruss would give one piece...*: Rovell, Darren. "Donruss will add swatches to cards." ESPN.com: http://espn.go.com/sportsbusiness/news/2003/1020/1642358.html

Chapter 10

Most of Bill Mastro's profile here is drawn from my interviews with Mastro and others. Many of the controversial stories surrounding him, however, were first reported by Michael O'Keeffe and Teri Thompson, writing in the *Daily News* as well as their fine book, *The Card*.

193 *In early 2007...*: Author interview with Carter.

193 *It contained some 50,000 cards...*: "Lionel Carter Collection." http://press.mastroauctions.com/images/press/2007/Premier/April/Lionel Carter.pdf

194 *"These cards are in a class..."*: "70-Year Baseball Card Collection Set for Auction." http://www.sportscollectorsdaily.com/vintage-card-news/70-year-baseball-card-collection-set-for-auction.html

194 *Carter had known Mastro in the '60s...*: Author interview with Mastro.

196 *on the very day he sold a Honus Wagner...*: Thompson, Teri and Michael O'keeffe, "Feds Crash National Sports Collectors Convention, Hand Out Subpoenas." *New York Daily News.* Aug. 1, 2008.

198 *"I don't know if it's an appropriate credit..."*: Mastro, Bill. "My Mentor Frank Nagy."

199 *Mastro paid Lifson back...*: O'Keeffe, Michael and Teri Thompson, *The Card: Collectors, Con Men, and the True Story of History's Most Desired Baseball Card.* New York: Milliam Morrow, 2007: 9-15.

199 *He sold the card to Copeland for $110,000 . . .* : ibid, 103.

200 *"Are these the big bidders?"*: Reif, Rita. "Auctions: The Baseball Juggernaut." *New York Times.* Mar. 22, 1991.

200 *the lots raked in $4.6 million . . .* : Peers, Alexandra. "Sotheby's Rare Baseball Card Is a Hit as Childhood Pastime Joins Big Leagues," *Wall Street Journal.* Mar. 25, 1991: C1.

201 *"If you buy something that is absolutely . . ."*: O'Keeffe and Thompson 72.

202 *after Mickey Mantle's 1995 liver transplant . . .* : "Barry Halper, noted memorabilia collector, dies at 66." Associated Press. Dec. 19, 2005. http:// sports.espn.go.com/mlb/news/story?id=2265127

203 *"that we will no longer touch cardboard . . ."*: "Mastro's auction tops record." *Sports Collectors Digest.* Dec. 18, 1998.

205 *In one of his stranger auctions . . .* : "Elvis' Hair Brings Big Bucks," *St. Petersburg Times.* Nov. 17, 2002.

205 *he hawked the wooden leg . . .* : Grange, Michael. "Veeck's wooden leg goes from bar to auction block." *Globe and Mail.* Oct. 8, 1999: S1.

206 *Within hobby circles it was rumored . . .* : Firfer, Rick. "Up in Smoke: The Unique Story of a $113,000 Baseball and the Curse." *Sports Collectors Digest.*

206 *Later, the remains were boiled . . .* : Greenberg, Jon. "'Cursed' Ball Simmers in Chicago." MLB.com.

212 *a group of baseballs signed by former presidents . . .* : O'Keeffe, Michael. "Hall of a Caper Has Happy End." *New York Daily News.* April 1, 2001.

212 *Doug Allen had to pull a Super Bowl ring . . .* : O,Keeffe, Michael. "Super Bowl Ring is Lost, Then Found," *New York Daily News.* April 30, 2006.

213 *some basketball collectors questioned the legitimacy . . .* : O'Keeffe, Michael. "Auction Jersey Revealed as Fraud." *New York Daily News.* Aug. 19, 2007.

214 *"Circumstances make it clear to me . . ."*: "Legendary Auctions Acquires Assets of Mastro Auctions." *Auction Report.* Mar. 10, 2009: http://www .auctionreport.com/?p=1298

214 *Just two months earlier Mastro had predicted . . .* : O'Keeffe, Michael. "Bill Mastro folds sports memorabilia's largest auction house amid FBI probe." *New York Daily News.* Mar. 23, 2009.

Chapter 11

This chapter relies mostly on my visits and interviews with Kevin Saucier and the PSA team.

217 *As hard-core collectors know* . . . : Author interview with Lifson.

218 *Lifson backed up his argument* . . . : Lifson, Rob. "REA Offers One Million Dollar T206 Joe Doyle Reward!" http://blog.robertedwardauctions.com/?p=109

220 *Collectors Universe had graded and slabbed more than a million coins* . . . : Ambrosius, Greg. "Q and A with PSA President David Hall." *Sports Collectors Digest.* Oct. 20, 1995: 161–164.

221 *"Their first year, they were trying to explain* . . . *"*: Author interview with Joe Orlando, Sept. 4, 2007.

221 *One well-known New Jersey collector, Jim Crandell* . . . : "The Massive Breadth of the Jim Crandell Collection." Professional Sports Authenticator: http://www.psacard.com/smrweb/backissues/smr1106/crandell.chtml

226 *Throughout a lengthy, impassioned thread* . . . : "Wow! PSA! T206 Doyle! Wow!!!!!" Net 54 Vintage Baseball Card Forum.

227 *Sportscard Guaranty encapsulated a fraudulent Doyle* . . . : Lifson interview.

229 *Under a halogen light* . . . : Saucier, Kevin. "How to Detect Rebuilt Corners." Alteredcards.com: http://www.alteredcards.com/rebuilt.htm

Chapter 12

237 *"You start instinctively* . . . *"*: La Fontaine.

245 *Fleer was forced to liquidate* . . . : Spanberg, Erik. "An industry reshuffles to capture its youth." *Christian Science Monitor.* Aug. 1, 2005.

245 *Topps faced its own crisis* . . . : Lauria, Peter. "Eisner Topps Web of Digital Content," *New York Post,* March 13, 2007.

245 *"I see it as a cultural, iconic institution* . . . *"*: Taub, Eric. Webcam Brings 3d to Topps Sports Cards." *New York Times.* March 8, 2009.

248 *"The physical baseball trading card* . . . *"*: "Topps Launches Game-Changer for Baseball Cards." http://www.prwebdirect.com/releases/2009/3/prweb2215814.htm

Acknowledgments

Of all the people who made this book possible, there are two I should thank here first: Jamison Stoltz, my editor at Grove/Atlantic, and Leonard Roberge, my editor in all other ways. It was Jamison's wonderful idea—not mine—to do a popular history of baseball cards. I'm forever thankful that he saw the writing I'd done on the industry, thought me capable of pulling off a book, and shepherded me through the entire process with patience and skill. Every writer should have such an ally, especially one he can share a name with, even if it's just in the phonetic sense.

Without Leonard's guidance, encouragement, and inexhaustible red pen, I might never have delivered a manuscript. He helped me outline the book in full and parsed its every line. He spent hours upon hours reading and rereading these chapters, cleaning up my messes and shaping the story as best he could. In short, he was my collaborator, and he put as much care into the project as I did. I'm indebted to him for his hard work and grateful for his friendship.

My good buddy Josh Levin, sports editor at *Slate*, commissioned the piece that ultimately led to this book. He was gracious enough to take the time to read much of the manuscript and provide invaluable feedback. I'm also grateful to my mentor, Erik Wemple, editor of the *Washington City Paper*, who taught me whatever it is I know about reporting and writing. And I'm not sure this book would have happened without the help of my agent, Daniel Greenberg of Levine Greenberg; my cousin, Susanna Tully; and the Mollie Parnis Livingston Foundation.

I greatly appreciate the hard work of everyone at Grove, especially president Morgan Entrekin, who took a chance on this first-timer; Deb Seager and Martin Wilson, for their publicity efforts; Don Kennison, who copy edited the manuscript; Michael Hornburg and Sue Cole, who turned the manuscript into a book; and Charles Woods and Gretchen Mergenthaler, for their design work.

I'd also like to thank the cardboard lovers in these pages who let an outsider into their lives at their own peril. I had everything to learn from them, and they had precious little to gain from me. Notable among them are Rob Lifson, Mike Gidwitz, Kevin Saucier, Bill Henderson, Bill Mastro, Lionel Carter, Bruce Dorskind, and Sy Berger. Rob, in particular, was always happy to take my calls and shed light on some farflung corner of the baseball card world. I deeply admire his work ethic and his scholarship. Many other collectors and dealers, too numerous to list here, were gracious enough to answer this lapsed collector's questions when he called or showed up out of the blue.

There were a number of other writers whose work I necessarily leaned on at times, and they should be acknowledged beyond the end notes. They include Michael O'Keeffe of the *Daily News*, who's given the strange world of sports memorabilia the coverage it deserves; Pete Williams, who literally wrote the book on Upper Deck; George Vrechek, the Burdick scholar; Robert Hendrickson, the authority on bubble gum; Bob Lemke, editor of the *Standard Catalog;* Lew Lipset, all-around card savant; and the staff of hobby chronicler *Sports Collectors Digest*, the back issues of which made for indispensable reading.

The staffs at a number of research institutions were generous with their time and resources. Among them are the National Baseball Hall of Fame Research Library in Cooperstown, N.Y.; the Library of Congress; the Metropolitan Museum of Art; the National Archives at College Park, Md.; and the Wisconsin Historical Society.

Lastly, I want to acknowledge the love and support of my parents, Meg and Bill, who gave me a childhood filled with wax packs, rookie cards, and other wonderful things; my brother, Eddie; my sister, Jill; and my girl, Jess.

Dave Jamieson has written for *Slate*, *The New Republic*, *The Washington Post*, and *Washington City Paper*, among others. A winner of the prestigious Sidney Award and the Livingston Award for Young Journalists, he lives in Washington, D.C., with a closetful of worthless baseball cards, all of them in excellent condition.